CASE STUDIES IN LEISURE MANAGEMENT PRACTICE

Edited by John Buswell

PITMAN PUBLISHING
128 Long Acre, London WC2E 9AN

A Division of Pearson Professional Limited

First published 1993

A CIP catalogue record for this book can be obtained from the British Library.

ISBN 0 273 61942 X

Printed and bound in Great Britain by Ipswich Book Company

The Publishers' policy is to use paper manufactured from sustainable forests.

Contents

Contributors

John Buswell is currently Field Chair in Leisure Management and Head of the Leisure and Tourism Management Division at Cheltenham and Gloucester College of Higher Education. He worked previously in teaching and leisure centre management. He has also been an External Examiner for the Institute of Leisure and Amenity Management (ILAM); a member of the ILAM Examinations Board; Chairman of the Leisure Management Education Consortium; and Leader of the Sports Council National Demonstration Project 'From School To Community'. He is currently a member of the ILAM Leisure Education Panel and a member of Editorial Board for the ILAM/Longman Guide to Good Practice in Leisure Management. He has research interests in quality management, service delivery and occupational experiences.

Kit Campbell is the principal of Kit Campbell Associates (KCA), a specialist leisure recreation and tourism consultancy based in Edinburgh. He is the author of *Provision for Swimming*, the national strategy for swimming and swimming provision published by the Sports Council in March 1993 and endorsed by the Institute of Baths and Recreation Management, the Amateur Swimming Association and the Royal Life Saving Society UK. KCA work in all parts of the UK and have been involved in many pool projects as well as most other types of sport and recreation facilities.

Dave Courteen is the founder and director of Fitness Express. Having studied at Carnegie College of Physical Education and gained a BTEC HND Business and Leisure Studies, he was Sports Manager at a Suffolk Holiday and Country Club complex for five years before forming Fitness Express with college colleague Steve Taylor in April 1987. The company provides a facility and management consultancy service for the health and fitness industry. Beginning with three employees and one management contract, Fitness Express now employs 60 leisure professionals and has six management contracts. His role within Fitness Express is the acquisition of new business and clients include Allied Dunbar, Thomas Cook, Legal and General, Arthur Andersen & Co.

Siân Johnson is a managing consultant with Greene Belfield Smith, the leisure and tourism consultancy division of Touche Ross. Before joining Touche Ross, she worked in consumer marketing. In 1981 she set up her own consultancy, Applied Leisure Marketing Ltd, where she designed and developed the Leisure Attractions Database. In 1991 she joined Touche Ross, bringing with her the database, which now holds records of over 1,000 visitor attractions, covering pricing and performance information over the period 1984–93. As well as continuing to work on leisure attractions, she has become involved with a range of consultancy projects across the tourism industry.

Martin Kinna has been in the conference and exhibition industry since 1968. He has worked both as an exhibition and conference manager as well as the Conference and Exhibition Director at London's Barbican Centre. In 1990 he set up his own consultancy business, Martin Kinna Associates, specialising in project work from design concepts for conference and exhibition centres, staff development and training and marketing and research. He has been on the faculty of the International Association of Professional Conference Organisers (IAPCO) for nearly 10 years and teaches regularly for many conference and related organisations including the International Congress and Convention Association (ICCA).

Terry Stevens is Professor and Dean of the Faculty of Leisure, Tourism and Health Care at the Swansea Institute. He spent 12 years between 1974 and 1986 in senior positions in the public and private sectors developing and managing visitor attractions. He is a specialist in attraction management. He is retained consultant with three national tourist boards and is also a registered specialist with the World Tourism Organisation and the International Labour Organisation. He has undertaken a wide range of consultancy work at home and overseas. A regular contributor to *Leisure Management* magazine, he has published two books and has over 30 publications.

Irene Waters was previously Senior Lecturer in Arts in Society at Newcastle-upon-Tyne Polytechnic. She is now a freelance researcher and writer.

1 Introduction

John Buswell

The rationale for the book

Leisure management is entering a new phase of its development as an emerging 'profession' with a body of core knowledge and skills. An established career structure is now in place and not confined to the public sector. Its scope has been considerably widened in recent years to include large complexes requiring skilled and sensitive management in addition to specialist facilities embracing heritage, arts and cultural activities, entertainment and sport and recreation.

Leisure management practice is now the focus of study and review as both the literature and qualifications proliferate. Professional bodies like ILAM and IBRM have developed their own qualifications to meet the requirements of a growing industry and there are now over 100 graduate and post-graduate programmes in Leisure and Tourism related studies and over 200 BTEC courses at Diploma, Certificate and Continuing Education Levels.

However, within the literature there is a paucity of case study material for illustrative and analytical purposes. There are, currently, moves to establish a pool of typically problem posing and problem solving case studies for academic use. The needs of the leisure manager striving to keep abreast of change, and to learn from other contexts, have, hitherto, been largely neglected.

The case studies in this book are more concerned with the day-to-day management and operations of leisure facilities than they are with strategic or philosophic issues; although some of the studies do adopt a contextual viewpoint in parts.

The book also has a European perspective with a third of the facilities studied coming from countries like France, Denmark, Norway, The Netherlands and Germany. The book is published in the year in which the Single European Market was created but it reflects much wider trends in the leisure business. As we shall observe in later chapters, there has been movement by organisations in both directions; the effects of EuroDisney upon European leisure provision will be quite profound; many leisure operators will adopt a more European outlook, not least in the employment and development of staff; there will be more pressure on the competitive edge and cost-effectiveness of both public sector and commercial sector organisations. Indeed, Dixon-Kloosterman (1991), of the Henley Centre, pointed out that:

> 'No leisure service provider can ignore the European dimension any longer. Rising incomes, the vast investments in transport infrastructures, and the huge trans-frontier summer migrations mean that definitions of the domestic market must be reviewed continuously. There are forces at work in today's Europe which could be setting a whole new leisure scene.'

The structure of the book

The book is divided into a number of sections which represent particular categories of leisure facilities across Europe although the list is, of course, nothing like an exhaustive one. The studies reflect a diverse range of interests and activities and they also cut across boundaries between leisure and tourism; they highlight particular features in each category as well as identifying some common issues.

The case studies are mainly commercial and public sector facilities whose foci, range of interests and service concept fall into three broad categories – sport and exercise; visitor attraction sites; and arts and entertainment. They represent either purpose-built indoor facilities or resources or facilities which have been adapted and greatly enhanced for their current usage. The remit, therefore, does not embrace urban parks and open space management nor countryside recreation although many of the issues and management practices would apply equally to their contexts.

The selected categories

The three specialisms of swimming pools, leisure centres and health and fitness clubs reflect the large network of facility provision and the increased recognition of the role of sport and exercise in modern, pluralistic society. They also embrace the functions of the early traditional public baths to the contemporary, glossy image of the health and fitness club.

The *swimming pools* highlighted by Kit Campbell are fairly normal, conventional ones in terms of facilities and image but demonstrate what can be achieved by sound management and good service delivery. They reflect the shift to more enterprising and sophisticated management and the greater emphasis on financial management skills (Dutch pools are also being contracted out), closeness to customers, customer care and 'on-the-job' staff training.

The *leisure centres* studied are an interesting mix of public and commercial facilities. It was decided to focus on CCT in the British cases because of the current impact of the contracting culture on their operations; one has a client perspective and, inevitably focuses on aspects of monitoring as well as drawing out many of the issues in the client/contractor relationship; the other represents the contractor's view and highlights the centre's commitment to quality service within a corporate approach and the scope afforded by the contract.

The three *health and fitness facilities* are located within the commercial/private sector although all have quite different philosophies and missions; each has clearly identified its target audience and what it is offering to them. One is a UK corporate facility highlighting the growing concern that organisations have in their employees' well-being; another has an American influence and approach in developing its club atmosphere and its range of equipment and activities; the third case study, a small concern in Norway, developed by an enterprising individual, offers a combination of exercise with physiotherapy and rehabilitation. All three have different facilities and rationales but are equally concerned with the quality of life of their customers and have given much thought to value for money through marketing, staffing, customer care and, ultimately, meeting customer requirements.

Chapters 5 and 6 in the book have visitor attraction sites as their focus. Theme parks and heritage centres, as the case studies demonstrate, are at the leading edge of innovation and commodification in the leisure business and appear to encapsulate the very essence of the multidimensional leisure experience. Terry Stevens' expose of theme parks adopts a slightly different approach to the other contributions; his chapter represents an authoritative 'state of the art' review of theme parks and he uses a number of short illustrative case studies to substantiate and draw out a number of facets of, and substantive issues in, their operations. In so doing he points to trends in theme parks provision and the European legacy of parks like Tivoli Gardens in Denmark and De Efteling in The Netherlands.

Siân Johnson's chapter demonstrates the rapid developments we have witnessed, in recent years, in the heritage market. Her case studies are an interesting mix: Tullie House, a municipal museum turned into a popular visitor attraction; and 'industrial' attraction, which became the most successful of its type within a year of opening in 1991 – Cadbury World; and, finally, a fascinating analysis of Nausicaa in Boulogne which is set to capitalise from the opening of the Channel Tunnel.

Chapters 7 and 8 concentrate on a core specialism whose roots go back some way in the history of the leisure industry but which, again, has experienced structural and functional change. Arts and Entertainment for our purposes embraces conventional facilities for high culture such as opera and for mass entertainment as the modern cinema but also purpose-built facilities for special events and for the conferences/exhibitions market. Their role as purveyors of culture and as meeting places for events is more widely defined in the 1990s and is inextricably linked with the notion of a wider leisure experience.

Martin Kinna's case studies are from three countries (Denmark, France and Britain) and adopt a slightly more developmental perspective. He looks at the rationale for the provision of conference centres and some of the wider benefits since their operations are tangentially concerned with the social and economic structure of the areas in which they are located. He describes the characteristics of the conference and exhibitions market and the requirements of organisers and promoters. The relationship between technology and factors like staffing, programming and service design is revealed to be a symbiotic one, particularly in 'state-of-the-art' facilities like the International Convention Centre in Birmingham.

Irene Waters' chapter provides an interesting mix of case studies. The

European example focuses on an ambitious project inextricably linked with national policy and status; its operation has been affected by the tensions between professionals and politicians and there are a number of lessons to be drawn from its study.

Hexham Arts Centre is also a public sector funded facility but with more local connections and origins. It serves the most rural district in England (Tyndale) and is trying to build up its visual arts presentation. It is an adapted facility incorporating a library and theatre as well as a studio and workshops. Apart from a wide programme of productions it is also concerned with amateur activities and outreach work.

The MetroCentre Cinema is the busiest 10 screen cinema in the world and is one of a chain of commercial cinemas across Europe owned by UCI. It displays a closeness with its customers and a sensitivity in its marketing and customer service.

The contributors have demonstrated great insight into the operation of the specialist establishments as well as awareness of trends in the wider industry. It was not easy to find good authors with the access to appropriate facilities, particularly in mainland Europe. They have all approached their topics slightly differently and have enriched the book as a result. Collectively they highlighted many examples of good management practice and not merely in state-of-the-art facilities with excellent specifications or where problems have never existed. The case studies, therefore, complement other recent texts including the *ILAM/Longman Guide to Good Practice in Leisure Management*, and are designed to inform and compare. They are aimed at the needs of practitioners, although acknowledge the developing pattern of education and training for leisure management.

The focus of the book

The book recognises the pressures on leisure managers and organisations to respond to change and has, as its thrust, operations and service delivery in a number of different contexts. The book is not so much concerned with the development of service/operations strategies as with their interpretation and implementation (see Figure 1.1). Strategy is designed to harness the essence of the organisation's operation – its uniqueness with its mission and its customers. It also involves balancing what is possible in the service delivery against what is realistic not forgetting that the leisure industry (like all services) has the potential for producing dissatisfied customers because of the *intangibility* and *heterogeneity* of the service package being offered.

Much of what is consumed in the leisure industry is not a tangible or physical product and is subject to the perceptions and changing sentiments of the customer. The more intangible the service the greater the importance of tangible reference points, eg physical appearance; price; risk perceived (Horovitz 1990). Consumption or usage, of course, also takes place at the point of delivery and, therefore, has so many factors at play. One of these is staffing, with the possibilities of variable approaches by the same individual at different times, or different approaches by different people; *heterogeneity* can mean lack of standardisation and consistency in what customers receive.

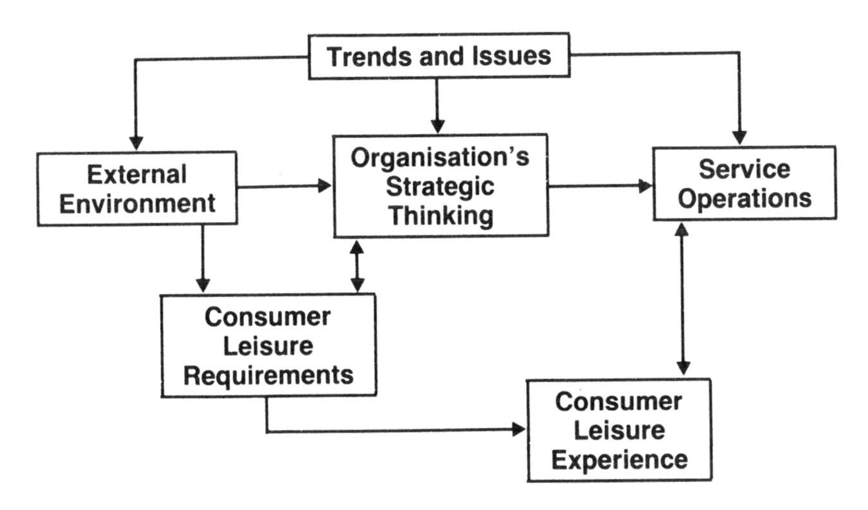

Figure 1.1
A macro model of leisure service delivery

Service operations in leisure management

Harris (1989) defines operations management as:

> 'the management of a system which provides goods or services to or for a customer and involves the design, planning and control of the system'.

The case studies emphasise such a systems approach although each highlights particular components such as staffing, procedures, information, use of plant and equipment or marketing.

Operations management is the central function of the leisure organisation and is principally concerned with the efficacy of the service and, perhaps, the quality of the leisure experience. Operations management problems revolve around the conflict between customer satisfaction and resource productivity:

1. Capacity measurement – the balance between resources. How many staff? How many customers? The physical and perceptual capacity of the facility or health and safety matters.
2. Utilisation of resources – the optimum deployment, eg has CCT had any effect on local authority sport and leisure facilities in the UK?
3. Problems with aims and objectives – again local authority leisure facilities have either suffered from indeterminate aims and objectives or have had to reconcile conflicting ones (social and commercial).
4. Systems design – concerned with established methods of working, the environment, atmosphere or the lay-out of facilities. It is a continuous process of change and modification related to how people circulate, use a facility and move from phase to phase. Facilities like theme parks have demonstrated considerable skill in systems design and in understanding

consumer behaviour as they retain customers for a whole day and longer.

The service package

Any organisation should be in business to meet its customers' requirements and it achieves it through its service concept or package. This is the combination of core and peripheral activities to produce the activities/product mix and the way in which they are delivered. The key to the success of the facilities studied is the way in which the service strategy, the service package, the promises are communicated to the customer.

Communication is the way to establish the edge over the competition and to send the appropriate message to the customer. A pattern across the case studies demonstrates this quite clearly – effective marketing strategies to help attract customers and to create realistic expectations. The intangibility of the service concept management of each facility and the product/activity mix is appropriate to the context. The 'moments of truth' (Carlzon 1987) or personal encounters which take place in leisure facilities transcend all phases of the operation. Marketing is clearly significant in attracting customers to each facility in the first instance, but it is also necessary to reinforce the message and to reassure customers.

However, once customers have been attracted or retained then the effectiveness of day-to-day operations becomes crucial to the quality and success of the service delivery. Indeed, marketing and operations are inextricably linked in the leisure business because of the inseparability of production and consumption, ie the customer experiences the activity or pursuit as it is being delivered to them – there is not the opportunity to put it right later!

Therefore, a feature of leisure organisations in varying degrees is the *involvement of the customer* in the process. There is always some direct interaction between staff and customers although technology, interpretation and procedures are playing an increasingly important part (for example, heritage centres or theme parks).

Integral to the service package, therefore, is the interface between the customer and the operation (see Table 1.1). It will include the physical environment, the activity purchased, the nature of the service, contact through procedures and interpersonal skills. However, it is difficult to establish precisely what is being purchased since the outputs or personal outcomes are often different for the same package.

Service characteristics

Nevertheless, we can make some generalisations with the case studies highlighted and each type has its own service characteristics determined by the underlying technology of that service and linked to the service map or service 'blueprint' that underpins its operation (ie the various stages that make up the package and the relationship between the resources and procedures in each). For example:

Leisure centres are not just functional activity centres but should have con-

Table 1.1 Relationship between the consumer and the facility.

Broad category	Activity	Involvement of customer	Key features
Sport and Exercise	• swimming • multi-sports • health/fitness	Active	Facilities are enabling and local
Visitor Attraction Sites	• themes • heritage • education • entertainment	Interactive	Site/facility inherent to the experience. Many national and foreign visitors
Arts and Events	• community arts • films • opera • conferences • exhibitions • entertainment	More passive	Quality of facility increasing in its importance. Local and regional orientation

venient parking, welcoming receptionist, telephones answered promptly and clean, pleasant changing rooms.

Swimming pools have similar requirements and may extend beyond swimming *per se* with wave machines, flumes, geysers, tropical plants, and spectator comfort.

Conference centres may not just have comfortable seating and air conditioning but need proximity to hotels, responsive staff and flexible systems and configurations.

Heritage centres offer a combination of knowledge, information, interpretation with entertainment, education and enjoyment. The interactive approach in many such enterprises fully supports Carlzon's view of the 'prosumer' (the customer as both a producer and consumer) in the process.

Health and fitness centres reflect peoples' lifestyles and may not be perceived so much as contexts for exercise as sanctuaries for relaxation, catharsis and self-esteem.

Theme parks offer thrills, spills, fun and excitement but also, perhaps, escapism, fantasy (or virtual reality!), landscaped gardens and a day out.

Arts and entertainments facilities do not simply entertain, amuse and provide passive consumption but provide exhibitions, insights and the very transmission of culture (high or popular).

Current issues and trends

The leisure industry is now very big business in the UK employing some 1.6 million people and accounting for £25.6 billion or 4 per cent of Gross Domestic Product. In Europe, leisure and tourism is the fastest growing industry employing 35 million people, nearly 8.5 per cent of the total working population of Western and Eastern Europe and earns over 5.7 per cent of Gross European Product (Battersby 1992). The European leisure industry is therefore, an important part of a massive European economy and is influenced by a number of facets of an increasingly complex mix of big business, polity and social change which make up the wider environment.

Factors effecting such change include technology, environmental factors, methods of working, demography, Government and EC legislation and Japanese competition and management principles. They impact upon strategic thinking in leisure organisations and, in turn, the way in which services are operated. The main strategic issue facing leisure organisations, apart from the internal challenges which make up corporate strategic plans, is quality *vis-à-vis* increasing competition and consumer expectations. Leisure management is undergoing considerable change at the moment (more so, perhaps, than in some industries) and the manager and the organisation which can react with purpose and alacrity to the changes is more likely to survive and, indeed, succeed.

There are a number of issues and trends in leisure, affecting operations management, which the book attempts to address:

- Increasingly expectant consumers
- Standards and targets
- The growing interest in quality
- Investment in people
- The internationalisation of leisure
- Trends in facility design and the use of technology.

Increasingly expectant consumers

Consumers are becoming more discerning and sophisticated with constantly rising expectations. The general rise in living standards, impact of technology, the influence of the media and the greater emphasis placed on leisure have all helped to create a much more demanding and knowledgeable market. In addition, as those people in work find themselves in jobs which have been enriched by more enlightened management, it is inevitable that they expect greater satisfaction from leisure activities provided by others. It is clear that competition for customers will increase (partly intensified by the single European Market and will be fought over those factors which can bring about customer satisfaction. As you read the various contributions, you will see that many of the organisations highlighted realise this and have been careful to develop a service package which is realistic yet meets customer expectations.

Standards

In order to determine whether customer requirements are being met organisations need to develop service quality standards. They help to verify performance and provide the means for measuring performance and customer satisfaction. In the public sector customer charters (following the Citizen Charter Unit initiative of the Prime Minister) are being developed in a range of organisations. Many are floundering because of the implications for compensation should standards not be met and because the Audit Commission is still to report on the set of performance indicators for local authority leisure services.

An integral part of quality customer service is the identification of standards or targets. Some may be procedural and, for example, determine the time staff take to respond to customers' queries; others are more personal and embrace standards of dress, appearance and communication and empathy (Martin 1989). Others distinguish between technical quality (cleanliness, effective programmes, high specifications) and functional quality – how the service is delivered.

Quality

Leisure organisations, as a result, have begun to analyse their service delivery and to measure customer satisfaction as a means of moving towards a quality service. If we regard quality service as the match between customer expectations and customer perceptions received then we must acknowledge the need to guarantee standards and to nurture a quality culture and ethos in the organisation.

The Japanese philosophy of management and the Disney organisation's approach to customer care have highlighted the importance of developing customer-driven strategies. They also demonstrate the values of employing and developing staff who understand consumer behaviour and customer requirements as well as the operational means to achieving success.

Listening to customers and responding to changing needs is crucial to the success of many organisations. The case studies reinforce this message and illustrate the need to carry out constant market research to encourage customer comment and to have appropriate complaints procedures in place.

Monitoring service delivery in a scientific way also distinguishes the successful organisation, as Mattsson (1992) reminds us:

> 'Because past research has demonstrated the customer's reluctance to complain when a negative service encounter occurs . . . it seems to be important for managers to take a proactive approach in monitoring service quality'.

However, it is not enough to merely keep abreast with customer requirements. The second aspect of service delivery is to ensure quality by meeting customer expectations every time. Comprehensive procedures, relevant work methods, necessary documentation and effective development and utilisation of staff are increasingly recognised as the means of achieving true quality service – particularly in organisations which have adopted a quality assurance approach (perhaps BS 5750/ISO 9000 or especially total quality).

The most recent studies of quality service have identified a multi-attribute approach which integrates the technical and functional qualities or procedures and interpersonal standards (Zeithaml et al 1990).

The five main dimensions were:

tangibles – facilities, equipment, appearance of staff, atmosphere etc.

reliability – the ability to perform the promised service at the standards specified, every time (the contract specification in CCT and customer charters have added a discernible sharpness to them).

responsiveness is the willingness and promptness with which customers are dealt with, particularly from front-line staff like receptionists and instructors.

assurance is the manner in which the organisations can convey trust and confidence through their staff, procedures, equipment and corporate image whether in the swimming pool, fitness room, flume or roller coaster; knowledge, expertise and credibility are key attributes.

Finally, *empathy* is, perhaps the most abstract dimension and can be the determining factor as to whether customers return or renew membership or spread encouraging news to others. It is the very core of sound customer care and goes beyond the 'have a nice day' syndrome of purely mechanistic customer care programmes. The successful leisure organisations today transcend such banalities and through appropriate recruitment, selection, training, staff development and corporate philosophy are able to empower their staff to achieve this vital dimension.

In conclusion the consequences of the quality revolution for leisure management are seen in a number of different guises:

- implementation (or planning) of a quality system like BS 5750
- greater consultation with employees and even empowerment in some instances
- increasing acknowledgement of customer requirements
- more attention to non-users
- the greater significance of marketing processes and marketing techniques
- customer feedback – the commercial sector and facilities like hotels have listened intently to their customers for years but it is a relatively new practice in many public sector leisure centres
- more analysis of the consumer process – parking, circulation, participation, the interface with staff, the response to levels of cleanliness, hygiene, decor and service
- more sophisticated service design – the mix of core business and peripheral activities
- sampling techniques linked to quality assessment
- training – particularly in aspects like customer care and customer service.

Investment in people

Another strategic issue which impacts upon operations management is the way in which the human resource is deployed. Training and staff development are gradually assuming more significance in leisure organisations as the case studies suggest. As Barber (1993) recently pointed out, when considering the challenges facing local authorities, '*This will mean greater investment in training, better communications and more contact with the customer*'.

Apart from more considered recruitment and selection, training needs analyses carried out within a framework of clear strategic thinking and commitment to quality will identify the priorities in staff development and the resources required. Neal and Tilley (1993) recently pointed to four axioms of enlightened human resource management in the leisure industry:

> 'People need to know where the organisation is headed and for what purpose'

> 'Empowerment is a vital factor'.

Empowerment is a key element in total quality management and even, perhaps, in quality assurance. The ethos and structure of the organisation are crucial to its development and leisure provision, because of its many personal encounters and close contact between staff and customers, must surely attach great priority to its application.

> 'Go out of your way to build relationships with people'

> 'The final factor is communication'.

As we shall see later, and as the Japanese and Disney have demonstrated, closeness to staff is just as vital as closeness to customers. 'Management by walking about' (Peters and Waterman 1982), and Transformational leadership (Covey 1992) are not simply skills but, perhaps, more of a competence or ability to apply certain skills. What I am alluding to, of course, is the topical subject of national vocational qualifications and their likely impact on the industry.

Much, of course, has been written about developments in NVQs, GNVQs (and SVQs/GSVOs in Scotland) and the identification of occupational standards and competences through various industry lead bodies (Sport and Recreation – facility management sub-group – the Management Charter Initiative and, now, the new Leisure and Tourism ILB). They have raised questions about what leisure professionals do, how they perform tasks and the skills they require.

The internationalisation of leisure

It was felt that a book of this nature should also adopt a European perspective, not simply because of the recently created Single European Market, but because we can learn much from different philosophies and cultures; we may also gain assurance from identified aspects of commonality. Indeed, Roberts (1992) has pointed to the potential for rapid erosion in the differences in leisure activities and lifestyles as other unifying influences take time to evolve:

> 'Within modern industrial societies, and within their citizens' lives, leisure is typically compartmentalized to an extent which allows common patterns to coexist alongside deep educational, occupational and political schism, and parallel divisions of national and ethnic identity'.

The impetus to break down barriers and cultural differences has been under way for some time with organisations like Centre Parcs, Novotel and Accor making inroads into the UK market and British organisations like Mecca and Forte developing their European outlets. The recent development of EuroDisney poses the interesting question about the imposition of

American style on a resistant French culture and the lessons to be learnt from this massive project.

The Single Market will, of course, bring much change to the leisure industry in terms of consumer trends, markets and service operations. Many leisure facilities in European countries will need to become more multi-cultural in outlook and staffing. As the *Leisure Management Journal* editorial in November 1991 suggested:

'The key to success in Europe will be effective marketing'

as exemplified by Parc Asterisk which has run a special promotion with Next BG, the children's retailer, and De Efteling which has a British public relations company.

The European 'Mutual Recognition Directive' will help to make it easier for leisure professionals to move between European countries particularly where they hold qualifications which have equivalence (National/Scottish Vocational Qualifications?). There will, clearly, be opportunities for the organisation/facility geared up for the Single Market to modify its operations towards a more 'European' approach. It is also important for managers to accept that they can learn from the principles and practices adopted in other cultures even though there may be some aspects of commonality.

Theme parks like De Efteling (The Netherlands), Phantasialand (Germany), Futuroscope and, of course, EuroDisney (both in France) are amongst the World's best and the design of a number of British leisure centres and swimming pools has been influenced by facilities in The Netherlands and Germany (the corollary applies to some extent). British museums and heritage attractions have also set good standards for the rest of Europe.

Technology

Technology is becoming more prominent in many leisure operations whether in terms of booking systems, information systems, crowd control or as a part of the product/activities mix. We see how the interactive approach is such a feature of heritage centres; or how the £185 million International Convention Centre contains state-of-the-art technology in its design and operation; or how some theme parks have a policy to introduce at least one new ride or attraction each year (eg Alton Towers); or how Disney, in their obsession with cleanliness and neatness, support their litter-pickers with a network of pneumatic tubes to instantly carry away the litter; or how the health and fitness sector is enhanced by constant development in computerised fitness equipment and fitness testing; or how the modern leisure centre has great flexibility of use through multi-function areas and choice of configurations.

Indeed, the computer, through virtual reality is now set to create an entirely new leisure experience based on the paradox of substitutability and originality (ie normal needs and motives being met by new contexts and technologies) – an opportunity for the leisure manager to construct and implement a much more controlled service operation.

Furthermore, the use of specialist software packages for ticket operations and for booking systems gives managers more immediate management information for monitoring purposes and for decision-making. Indeed, the monitoring carried out by client units in the new contracting culture in local authority sport and leisure facilities is made more objective through software packages like AXIS featured in the chapter on leisure centres.

Finally, technology can also be harnessed in order to make the service more positive and effective. For example, the involvement of the customer in the process can be enhanced by computerised graphics providing modified challenges and visual contexts for the health club member; or by scientific experiments or critical enquiry initiated by the customer providing the interactive approach in heritage centres.

The commodification of leisure

There appeared to be a case for devoting some words to the effects of Compulsory Competitive Tendering and the more commercial outlook for the public sector in countries like the UK although it must be appreciated that CCT is really only part of a wider trend towards a more market-led approach and a condensing of local authorities into a narrower, enabling role. The likes of Naisbitt (1984) and Pinchot (1986) have pointed to such trends for years and to concepts such as intrapreneuring as well as the more established notion of enterprise. Indeed, the rather proactive West Midlands Chief Leisure Officers' Association (White 1992) has recently promoted the message of enterprising leisure management in local government. In the cultural sector we have seen the introduction of the Museums and Galleries Improvement Fund based on the principle of 'challenge funding' or fund matching.

It is a matter, rather, of highlighting the transition of much leisure provision, particularly in the public sector, from the 'rational recreation movement' we have observed since the 19th century, to a commercial, economically significant and commodified industry sector. Many leisure activities and contexts have moved beyond the social welfare rationale of early baths, sports, parks and other provision or even the public sector provision role promoted by the Cobham Report of 1973 (2nd Select Committee of the House of Lords' Report on Sport and Recreation) and the 1975 White Paper on Sport and Recreation. The commodification of leisure examined by, amongst others, Kelly (1991), Veal (1987) and the Wearings (1992) permeates much of the industry and demonstrates how leisure as an activity is really the consumption of market-provided goods and services. Indeed, the Wearings point out how

> 'the simple act of running has been transformed by fashion, the organisation of commerce, scientific analysis, the media and leisure industry, into a billion-dollar industry'

The challenge is to establish a balance between demand-led and supply-led influences and to reconcile the commercial significance of spare-time activities with their cultural, humanising and civilising role; societal values with individual choice and autonomy; economic with social objectives; enterprise with collective responsibility; and, at the micro level sheer efficiency and expertise in service design, service delivery and operations management with sensitive and effective cultural leadership.

The leisure process (inputs/process/outputs model)

There is, consequently, increasing recognition that leisure management is concerned with not just the selling of a product or a service, but the creation of a leisure experience. It is based on the premise that the consumer goes through a managed process where the customer outcomes are determined by the quality of the inputs (see Figure 1.2). Leisure professionals need to understand the business they are in and to be able to define what they are offering to their customers.

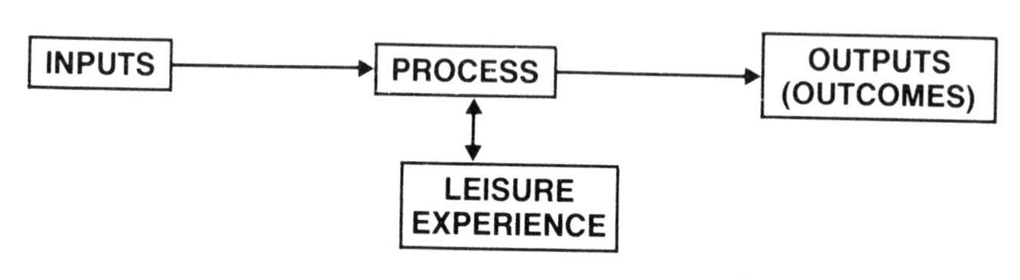

Figure 1.2
A micro model of leisure service delivery

The inputs include:

- The quality, design and appropriateness of the context – facilities resources etc
- The atmosphere, ambience and environment of the context
- The product/service mix, ie core and peripheral activities
- Systems and procedures. Procedures for bookings, membership, complaints, health and safety and customer circulation all impact on customers' perceptions. Likewise, written work procedures and work methods influence the way in which staff work and the organisation functions as well as determining its ability to guarantee consistency of delivery
- Staff both specialist and generalist. They represent one of the most significant inputs, particularly at the interface with customers. Their recruitment, selection, training and development and therefore their skills and competences will develop customer satisfaction.
- Formal communications. Information, publicity, notices, announcements and signage also influence the level of customer expectation and satisfaction.
- Technological developments. Technology (both hard and soft) is becoming increasingly important whether in the guise of flumes and rides, virtual reality or interpretation.

The process

Process management recognises the connections between inputs and outputs. The consumer process involves the total leisure experience with, possibly, a number of stages, personal encounters or 'moments of truth' (Carlzon

1987) which are affected by the various inputs and planned outcomes. Process management in the leisure industry has gained considerable credence through the example of organisations like Disney who have applied great skill and creativity to service design and to anticipating the customer's every need and desire.

Outputs

The outputs, or outcomes, will, of course, vary according to the context. They will depend upon individual customer's motives and aspirations for the chosen activity and will range from specifics linked to the product or activity to more generic ones like enjoyment, satisfaction, fun and socialisation. However, the aspects of commonality that permeate these contexts are all found in the experiential domain. The need for all managers to identify relevant inputs and desirable outcomes is acute. Furthermore, the ability to connect them through a well managed process requires sensitive and perceptive management and will only then result in the enhanced leisure experience the customer is seeking.

The case studies focus on both inputs and outputs and each highlights particular ones. In the leisure centres profiled, programming policy and the programme mix have a considerable bearing on customer satisfaction, which will have a multiplicity of outcomes or outputs. The health and fitness clubs in Dave Courteen's chapter links technology, personal attention and ambience with feelings of well-being and self-esteem and the enhancement of the quality of life. Theme parks also embrace the use of hard technology and softer customer care skills within vibrant, exciting and landscaped environments to generate and stimulate sentiments of fun, enjoyment, escapism and sheer hedonism. Heritage centres also take people away from reality and provide sensory stimuli but in a more subtle and refined manner; their use of interpretive techniques and their sense of history and culture appeal more to outcomes such as education and personal development as well as enjoyment and curiosity. The arts and entertainment facilities highlighted are also involved in the transmission of culture but within a contextual framework of enjoyment, relaxation and appreciation; the product and its presentation are crucial to the outcomes. Finally, facilities such as the venues for special events in the final chapter emphasise the importance of comfort, acoustics, access, sightlines and atmosphere for consumers seeking entertainment, relaxation, social interaction, hospitality and information.

References

Barber, A. (1993) *Leisure and the New Authorities*. Institute of Leisure and Amenity Management.

Battersby, D. (1992) in *UK Tourism. Competing for Growth*. National Economics Development Office. June.

Carlzon, J. (1987) *Moments of Truth*. Ballinger Publications.

Covey, S.R. (1992) *Principle-Centred Leadership*. Simon and Schuster.

Dixon-Kloosterman, K. (1991) 'Become European'. *Leisure Management*. November.

Harris, N.D. (1989) *Service Operations Management*. Cassell.
Horovitz, J. (1990) *How To Win Customers*. Longman (translation).
Kelly, J. (1991) 'Commodification and conscientiousness: an initial study'. *Leisure Studies* **10** (1991).
Mattsson, J. (1992) 'A Service Quality Model Based on an Ideal Value Standard'. *International Journal of Service Industries Management* **3**.
Martin, W.B. (1989) *Managing Quality Customer Service*. Kogan Page.
Naisbitt, J (1984) *Megatrends*. Macdonald.
Neal L., & Tilley, C. (1993) 'Agency support'. *Leisure Opportunities*. April.
Peters, T. & Waterman, R. (1982) *In Search of Excellence*. Fontana.
Pinchott, G. (1986) *Intrapreneuring*. Harper and Row.
Roberts, K. (1992) 'Young People's Leisure in Britain and Germany: a test of European Integration'. *World Leisure and Recreation* **34** 4.
Veal, A.J. (1987) *Leisure and the Future*. Allen and Unwin.
White, J. (1992) *Leisure, the cornerstone of Local Government*. West Midlands Chief Leisure Officers' Association.
Wearing, B. & Wearing, S. (1992) 'Identity and the commodification of leisure'. *Leisure Studies* **11**.
Zeithaml, V., Parasuraman, A. & Berry, L. (1990) Delivering Quality Service. The Free Press.

2 Swimming pools

Kit Campbell and John Bastijn

Introduction

For many years a substantial number of pools in the UK were operated more or less on a 'take it or leave it basis': in other words they were open for long hours on most days and if local people wished to use them all well and good. In fairness to pool managers, however, by and large they were largely left alone to get on with their job with very little direction from other parts of the local authority apart, perhaps, than the Treasurer's Department. As such many operated more or less in a policy vacuum so that managers did not know what wider roles they and their pools should be seeking to perform. It is not surprising, therefore, that many managers were concerned primarily with having the building open and ready for use during specified hours and ensuring adequate water quality.

The setting of clear objectives for managers related to such matters as customer care and attracting certain user groups is a relatively recent innovation. Indeed, it is noteworthy that some of the local authorities submitting entries for the Sports Councils' Recreation Management Award as recently as 1987 stated quite explicitly that they did not set objectives for their pool managers.

In most areas during the middle and late 1980s and early 1990s, however, there was something of a quiet revolution in pool management. Various pressures created this revolution. In part it was a response to increased customer expectations arising from the provision of high quality leisure pools coupled with the need to find ways of minimising net costs and increasing income within the political constraint of not raising charges by significantly more than the rate of inflation. It can also be attributed, much more positively, to the fact that pool managers became increasingly aware of the needs of different pool market segments and augmented their traditional skills in water treatment with new ones in marketing, programming and customer care. In doing so they learnt and adapted some of the management techniques which had been developed mainly for indoor dry sports facilities. More recently the government's equation of value for money with minimum cost as embodied in the Compulsory Competitive Tendering (CCT) legislation has forced all local authorities to set clear objectives and performance targets.

In order to provide a framework within which to describe the case studies it is desirable first to describe briefly four key aspects of pool management:

- The programming of pools
- Increasing pressures on budgets
- Pricing policies
- Staff training.

The programming of pools

A crucial change in the management of pools in the past decade or so has been the development of pool programming. More recently managers have become increasingly aware of the different needs of different market segments and are attempting to plan particular sessions to meet their needs. This programming of pools has almost certainly contributed to the growth of adult participation which has occurred in the past decade.

Effective programming brings a number of benefits for both users and management. For users, the most obvious is that swimming becomes a regular, planned activity rather than a spur of the moment one – just like most other sport and leisure activities and this can lead to higher levels or frequencies of participation. At the same time particular programmes should not be regarded as unchangeable; operators should always be willing to make changes in response to customer demand.

The second major benefit for users is that some people who may not wish to swim in unprogrammed activities can be attracted to pools for sessions tailored to their needs. Asian women are an obvious example; so too are disabled people, 50+ groups and pregnant women. There is a tendency, however, to programme some of these groups mainly into off-peak times. This ignores the fact that there is every bit as much a need to programme peak periods as off-peak ones. Many pools programme women-only sessions for off-peak times but this makes it impossible for working women to attend; others have programmed them around 2000–2100 hours on mid-week evenings and they have proved to be extremely popular. The same principle holds good with other groups.

For operators, careful programming can generate quite specific benefits. The first, and possibly the most important, is that it can widen the range of potential pool users and therefore lead to increased throughput and income. The varying level of lifeguarding needed for different sessions means that careful programming is essential in order to make the most cost-effective use of poolside staff. Wherever possible successive sessions should have similar lifeguarding requirements because this should help minimise staff costs. Long periods of casual use – except perhaps in school summer holidays – can lead to poor economic performance with high staff costs but low usage and therefore low income.

Increasing pressures on budgets

For many years there has been increasing pressure on local authorities to reduce the revenue deficits of their sport and recreation facilities in real terms. Most local authorities responded in two main ways: by attempting to cut costs, and by seeking to increase income. Public sector budgeting and charging policies tended initially to result in the former being given priority although some costs have risen faster than the rate of inflation.

Cost cutting

While many local authorities have been successful at reducing expenditure, the stage has now been reached at many pools where cutting costs is easier said than done – particularly when customer expectations are rising. Some costs – for example capital servicing costs, the cost of a unit of energy, rates and insurances – cannot be reduced even by excellent management. Where pool operators are forced to cut operating costs, therefore, increasingly it will be necessary for them either to defer necessary maintenance; to seek to reduce energy costs; or to reduce staff costs.

Reduced maintenance

For financial reasons, many local authorities had to reduce or defer the maintenance of pools through the 1980s. In some instances they have been forced by budgetary constraints to adopt a make do and mend approach. It is highly likely that the consequence will be a need for increased maintenance and repairs expenditure in the 1990s.

Energy costs

For much of the 1980s it was government policy to raise energy charges in real terms in order to reduce energy consumption. If there were no changes in operational practice and no plant improvements by the end of the decade the energy costs of all pools would have increased significantly in real terms. Fortunately many authorities were able to take advantage of energy conservation technology in order to reduce energy consumption, particularly through those methods with a fairly short pay-back period of up to about three years – pool covers, variable speed ventilation systems and simple heat exchangers, for example. While further investment would decrease energy costs even further at many pools, the more energy efficient a pool is the more costly it becomes to make further improvements and the more likely those improvements are to be of only marginal benefit. The potential for significant further reductions in energy costs is therefore becoming less and less.

Staff costs

As for staff costs, systems of pay enhancement for long and irregular hours may be desirable for 'normal' local authority jobs, but they are wholly inappropriate for those who work in the leisure industry. It follows that individual local authorities and their pool managers and other management staff have not had full control of staff costs other than through determining the level of staffing which they regard as appropriate. Even this limited freedom for manoeuvre is now restricted even further by the recommendations on appropriate levels of lifeguarding from the Health and Safety Commission/Sports Council[1].

It is not surprising, therefore, that many local authorities, faced with the need to be more efficient in order to be able to compete effectively, are seeking to negotiate local wage agreements or reduce opening hours. A number of authorities have introduced part-time contracts with no arrangements for enhanced payments for unsocial hours for all poolside staff. Others have introduced systems of annual hours for staff and in a few instances swimming teachers, formerly on the pool establishment, have become self-employed.

The main potential for savings in staff costs, however, comes from careful programming or a reduction in opening hours. If a pool is 'programmed' constantly for casual use it may be necessary to keep an uneconomic number of poolside staff on duty in case there is a sudden influx of users. The management of a large centre in the west of Scotland which was operated in this way monitored the number of swimmers actually in its pool over a period. It found that for 75 per cent of the time there were under 30 users in a pool with a capacity of 250 people – and three lifeguards on duty[2]. Clearly such staffing levels are uneconomic and it should be possible to determine a more sensible level of staffing to suit particular circumstances which will also accord with the guidelines set out in *Safety in Swimming Pools*[1].

Opening hours are a key factor in operating costs and in the future managers and their parent authorities can be expected to examine critically the need for pools to be open long hours. Changes in opening hours can allow staff shifts to be adjusted to make more cost-effective use of staff.

Increasing income

Some pool operators seem to have found it easier to increase income than to reduce expenditure. Many local authorities and their pool managers have sought to increase income in one or more of three main ways:

- By boosting throughput, for example by programming time for particular user groups or by advertising and promotion
- By raising user charges by slightly more than the rate of inflation
- By attempting to boost users' secondary spend – that is, increasing their expenditure on items not directly related to participation such as food and drinks. This is not easy to achieve; it may be better to concentrate instead on offering at realistic prices additional facilities which have a high perceived value – for example, fitness facilities or saunas.

Some pool operators have been successful at generating increased income by a combination of all three methods: Caribbean parties are a particularly good example. They can attract users at what might otherwise be a slack time (for example Saturday nights); relatively high charges can be levied; and substantial food and beverage spend can be generated.

There is little evidence, however, to suggest that managers have attempted to monitor the impact of particular policies and, therefore, to discover which marketing and promotional techniques are most effective.

Pricing policies

Most local authority leisure services committees have tended to operate with the social objective of wanting to ensure that all members of their local communities are able to use pool facilities. As a result nearly all have set low user charges. On average in 1989–90 only 36 per cent of gross expenditure on indoor swimming pools was recovered from income by local authorities in England and 30 per cent in Wales[3] while in Scotland local authorities on average recovered 24 per cent of the operating costs of sports facilities in 1990–91[4].

In many authorities there has also been no objective evaluation of whether low charges are an effective method of achieving social objectives. As the Audit Commission has commented:

> 'Most authorities implicitly assume that low prices encourage use and are essential to meet social objectives but the real relationship between price and use is not often examined'[5].

It is difficult to avoid the conclusion that often charges are low simply because they always have been. Other facilities such as saunas and sunbeds are significantly cheaper both to provide and operate than swimming pools but user charges for them are normally at least two to three times higher than for pools. Perhaps partly as a result they are regarded as 'luxuries' and may be more highly valued by users. If local authorities and their pool operators can develop more effective and non-discriminatory ways of targeting subsidies at those people who need them, and where possible their families as well, the case for high levels of indiscriminate subsidy to all pool users will be an increasingly poor one. This does not necessarily mean that most subsidies should be abolished. If the result of increased charges and reduced levels of subsidy is to reduce levels of use this will conflict with social objectives. If overall levels of income are reduced it will also conflict with financial ones.

Staff training

Until comparatively recently staff training at many pools was also fairly rudimentary. In part this relates to the fact that traditionally pools were stand-alone facilities with a fairly simple staff structure. Essentially staff were trained in plant operation and lifesaving, with those who wished to do so taking one or more of the training courses available through the former Institute of Baths Management, now the Institute of Baths and Recreation Management. These courses offered a much wider grounding in subjects in which managers required knowledge such as employment legislation and financial control.

One result of the increasing size and complexity of pools, the resultant higher numbers of staff and the increasing emphasis on customer care is that it is now vitally important for all members of staff to receive appropriate training. Those pool managers seeking BS5750 (ISO 9000) accreditation for their management practices are perhaps leading the way but they are by no means exceptional. The range of subjects in which pool staff receive training has extended considerably; in the case of the Perth pool described below, for example, it has even extended to receptionists receiving training in simple French and deaf and dumb sign language.

Introduction to the case studies

The remainder of this chapter describes three case studies. The first two describe pools in Scotland. They are similar in four respects: they provide high quality facilities and were designed by the same architects, Faulkner-Browns of Newcastle; they are owned and operated by charitable companies set up and very largely controlled by the local authority; they are extremely well managed by a committed and enthusiastic staff which work as a team; and they are unusually successful.

The third case study describes generally the approach of Dutch pool managers to their job with particular reference to technical standards.

Case study 2.1: Perth Leisure Pool

Key features

- ▲ *Local authority contractor run leisure pool with many attractions*
- ▲ *High usage and repeat business*
- ▲ *Large catchment area*
- ▲ *Customer care*
- ▲ *Training*

The City of Perth is the main town in the Perth and Kinross District in the northern part of central Scotland and has a population of some 45,000. It has a key location in Scottish tourism terms because almost all visitors to the Highlands pass through the District on their way north or south. This said, many tourists bypass the city rather than visit it.

Perth is also well placed to attract day visitors and does so. It is the main shopping centre for people from a wide area – the District itself is over 2,000 square miles – and because of excellent road communications Edinburgh, which is approximately 40 miles south, can be reached in under an hour.

Perth Leisure Pool opened in 1988 and replaced an outmoded complex which had outlived its useful – and safe – life. From the start the bold decision was taken to plan it as a 'flagship' for the District; indeed, the original brief identified the pool should seek to enhance the attraction of the District as a place in which to live.

The design was the result of a limited architectural competition in which the UK's leading leisure design architectural practices were invited to compete. The initially controversial triangular building designed by FaulknerBrowns contains a total water area of approximately 900 sq m – the equivalent of no less than four 25 m/4 lane pools.

This water area is split into two main pools: the leisure pool of around 650 sq m water area – part of which leads through a swim channel to a small outdoor lagoon; a 25 m/5 lane training pool; and a small rectangular learner pool. The leisure waters are packed with water features ranging from a twin flume (both of which go outside the building) to jacuzzis, a wild water channel, fountains, bubble beds and water cannon. There is also a well equipped health suite with sauna, steam room, spa bath and sun beds; a fitness room; and three catering outlets – an ice cream and cold drinks bar; a pattisserie selling extremely attractive (and extremely fattening!) cakes; and a more traditional 'chips with everything' cafe. While attempts have been made to introduce a more health conscious range of food Scottish customers – particularly children – are very keen on chips. Interesting market research undertaken at the pool has indicated that some parents do not serve chips to their children at home and see them as forming an important part of a 'special treat' visit to complexes like Perth.

All the catering outlets are let out to a specialist catering company. The whole of the building is built with high quality, durable and therefore low maintenance but attractive and colourful finishes and furniture.

The pool is owned and operated by Perth and Kinross Recreational Facilities Ltd (PKRF) which is an 'arm's length' company set up by the former Perth Town Council before the re-organisation of Scottish local government in 1975. The company owns all of the major publicly funded facilities in the District and was set up to attract and invest funds from a local trust, plus additional funds provided by the local authority, in sport and recreation. It has been so successful in generating financial support that each of the company's major facilities has been paid for in full before it opened; clearly this has had a major impact in terms of total revenue costs. Operating deficits are met by the local authority.

In the first four years of its existence Perth Leisure Pool generated over 700,000 visits per year or around 800 visits/sq m of water. This puts it in the top 20 per cent of British pools and is far more than might be expected for the size of the local population. A large part of the reason for this is that it has been remarkably successful in attracting users from outside the District: so much so, in fact, that user surveys undertaken by the management have found that around 45 per cent of all visits are made by non-residents. Clearly, the management has managed successfully to position a visit to the pool as a 'special treat' for children from an unusually wide area but it has not done so at the expense of local users.

Mission and long-term aims

The pool management's mission statement is that 'Perth Leisure Pool operates to provide a quality, cost effective leisure service for the population of Perth and Kinross District as well as day and longer-term visitors'. Within this overall context, the management's long-term aims are:

- To maximise throughput
- To increase income

- To cater for specific target groups, as defined from time to time
- To providing swimming learning opportunities for all ages and abilities
- To adopt a positive approach to sports development by instigating coaching programmes and allocating times for exclusive use of certain facilities by sports clubs and the education authority
- To provide opportunities for the enhancement of fitness and wellbeing of the community
- To provide a training programme for staff that assures the highest possible level of service delivery
- To identify and achieve cost savings without a reduction in the quality of service.

The key thing about these aims is that they are largely customer-centred. Many pool managers have adopted aims which relate more to operational matters – ensuring high standards of hygiene, for example. In Perth operational matters are not taken for granted – far from it – but the emphasis and focus are firmly on the users and the delivery of a high quality service to them.

Management structure

The management team for the pool consists of the manager and three assistant managers each with a specific responsibility for operations, maintenance of marketing. The three assistant managers also act as duty managers. All members of the management team either have or are pursuing qualifications in business studies in addition to pool and recreation management. The management team is concerned primarily with the 'big issues' such as determining policy, financial management, marketing and promotion and setting standards for all aspects of the operation of the pool. PKRF Ltd has delegated considerable autonomy to the manager (within specified limits) with the result that the management team is able to take many key decisions itself and subsequently implement them without delay.

At the next level, three supervisors are responsible for day-to-day middle management duties such as the maintenance of time sheets, ordering stocks and much of the training of attendant staff. At any time there is one supervisor on duty and they also perform a 'roving' role in order to keep an eye on the whole building; they are first in line to deal with any complaints from users. There is also a maintenance supervisor who works to the Assistant Manager (Maintenance).

The pool is open from 0700–2230 seven days a week and operates with three basic daily staff shifts: 0700–1530; 1000–1900; and 1500–2300. The 36 leisure assistants are however split into four shifts of nine people each supervised by a Senior Leisure Assistant. Individual members of staff do not remain permanently in the same 'shift' of people but are rotated in order to foster the cross-fertilisation of ideas together with good working relationships and practices and avoid staff slipping into set routines. When the pool is in full public operation there are normally around 13–14 staff on poolside duties with others responsible for cleaning or taking rest breaks. Finally the pool employs two part-time swimming teachers.

Programming

With both a leisure and 25 m pool in the same building, Perth is well able to accommodate most forms of aquatic activity. It is also able to accommodate users who change their leisure habits, for example from wanting simply to splash around in a leisure pool to taking part in regular keep fit swimming as they become older. The leisure pool is programmed for casual swimming from 1000–2200 on most days although there are a number of special promotions and fund raising events, mainly at weekends. These include a Saturday morning club for juniors and a children's entertainment programme; 'theme nights' and private parties on Saturday evenings are also a growing market.

The 25 m training pool is programmed most of the time for specific activities ranging from lane swimming (three times a day – early morning, lunchtimes and late afternoon) to schools' use, children or adult lessons, casual use, swim club training, canoe club, water polo club and disabled club. There are also special sessions for mothers and babies, mothers and toddlers, pre-school lessons, asthmatics, antenatal groups, a 50+ club and aquarobics. There is also a creche provided at certain times of the day in order to allow parents to swim or use the Health Club.

Customer care

Every pool manager claims to promote high standards of customer care, sometimes without too much justification. In Perth the claim is certainly valid. The high quality building was designed by specialist architects and this high quality is fully reflected in all aspects of its management. To give one simple but telling example, in very few other British pools do receptionists receive training in both simple French conversation (French people being the most frequent foreign visitors) and deaf and dumb sign language. Other front-line staff such as leisure attendants are given regular training in customer care and the staff manual – which every member of staff receives – places considerable emphasis on its importance. The core of Perth's customer care is making users feel welcome and that they enjoy themselves in safety. All poolside staff wear brightly coloured green and yellow uniforms to make them stand out and they are encouraged to be firm but friendly. The attitude of all staff is perhaps best summed up by a quotation from the staff induction manual:

> 'Smile! A centre is remembered by the friendliness and courtesy of the staff in it. A happy environment is important.'

The proof of Perth's success in customer care is that it has succeeded in attracting high levels of repeat business from users from considerable distances even after the opening of competing attractions such as the Time Capsule in Coatbridge (a leisure pool plus leisure ice rink) or Leith Waterworld in Edinburgh, a major leisure pool. User interviews relating to changing facilities undertaken for the Sports Council at the pool – the management has a policy of assisting in suitable research projects because of the feedback which results – also highlighted customer loyalty with many users by-passing several often significantly cheaper pools in order to visit Perth. They did so for a variety of reasons including cleanliness, the friendliness of staff and the high quality of the building and its facilities.

Two key elements in customer care are management information and actually taking the trouble to speak to customers. The pool has a till-based computer system which gives detailed user information on an hourly or daily basis. It is monitored on a continuous basis by the Assistant Manager (Operations). In addition all three assistant managers, in particular, see speaking to customers as an important part of their job and one which should, and does have, a direct influence on how the pool is run. The 'middle tier' of supervisors allows this system to work by taking some of the day-to-day administrative pressures off duty managers. As the supervisors are also in daily contact with users, however, they also have a key role in feeding customer views back to the management team.

Finance

Thanks to the method by which the pool was funded there are no loan charges. As such the pool is inherently cheaper in overall cost terms than most local authority facilities. Its operating deficit per user is approximately half the Scottish average. This does not mean, however, that improvements cannot be made. Instead of cutting costs, with all which that might entail for the level of service provided to the customer, however, PKRF is seeking actively to boost income. It is also hoping to promote a second phase of the building which will both enhance its regional reputation and generate an operating surplus with which to subsidise the leisure pool.

While finance is vitally important, to Perth and Kinross District Council it is not everything. The Council views Perth Leisure Pool as a key factor in making the District the area with the highest quality of life in Britain (it was identified as such in 1992 by a research team from Strathclyde University). This helps attract new businesses and residents to the District and as such expenditure on the pool is not so much a subsidy as an investment which pays high dividends. Economic research has shown that the large number of leisure day trip visitors attracted to Perth by the pool also contribute significantly to the economy of the District through expenditure on petrol and in local shops and restaurants.

Pricing policy

In Scottish terms Perth is expensive with the adult admission charge roughly twice the average and the child/senior citizen entry comparable with the adult charge at most other pools. There are however generous concessions for family groups or those wishing to purchase books of admission tickets in advance and early morning lane swimming sessions – for which pre-purchased visit cards are essential in order that reception staff do not have to collect cash in the early morning – are effectively half price.

Users can purchase 1- or 2-hour sessions, although at off-peak times users may stay as long as they wish for the price of a 1-hour session. The number of users purchasing 2-hour tickets has declined steadily since the pool opened; this may be because the novelty of the pool has worn off but it is more likely that most users realise that for much of the time buying a nominal 1-hour ticket actually allows significantly longer use of the pool. Where session times have to be limited they are controlled using coloured bands for locker keys.

At most pools there is little correlation between price and use, almost certainly because of the very low charges which are normal. The most recent price increase at Perth of roughly one third appears to have generated some customer resistance although the extent to which the reduction in use which has occurred was a result of the more general recession and reduction in leisure day trips is at present unclear. Whatever the cause, PKRF is keeping prices at the same level for at least two years. Nevertheless it appears fairly successfully to be walking the tightrope between low charges, and hence lack of funds for training, promotion and improving the quality of service, and charges which are too high and therefore deter a significant number of users. It will succeed in charging comparatively high prices only if it continues to provide an adequate quality of service.

In order to be able to discriminate in favour of local residents PKRF has recently introduced a Leisure Pass which allows residents admission to the pool at a discount rate. This also has the advantage that users with the pass are recorded automatically on the Centre's computerised management information system (using a bar code reader), thereby allowing the management to identify those postcode areas from which regular users come most frequently. Conversely this will allow them also to target promotional efforts at those areas from which the pool attracts comparatively few users.

Staff training

High priority is given to three basic forms of staff training:

- Training to help individuals do their present job better
- Training to help individuals develop skills which will enable them to earn promotion
- Training to help individuals remain up to date with their particular discipline or skills.

Training is highly structured for all staff. 'You only get one chance to make a first impression' may be a management cliché but it is also true. New leisure attendants receive comprehensive induction training when joining the staff and this is logged against a standard checklist. Thereafter full-time leisure attendants receive further formal training once a week and part-time staff are encouraged to attend by being paid if they do. Part-time staff also receive specific training twice a year. Much of the training is organised and provided by the supervisors (for example life saving) or assistant managers (for example customer care) but there is also considerable use made of 'bought-in' expertise, for example from the local Colleges and Fire or Ambulance Service. Every individual member of staff keeps a personal training log which is reviewed by a supervisor at regular intervals. In addition, regular appraisal interviews are held with all staff and these procedures enable any gaps in a particular individual's training (which may have arisen, for example, as a result of illness) to be spotted and rectified.

As part of general training, the management team take time to explain their own jobs to poolside staff. This allows all staff to make suggestions for changes to working practices and helps to avoid any feeling of 'them and us'; instead it is a key aspect of team building and emphasises the complementary nature of all the jobs in the building.

As well as general on-the-job training, individual members of staff are also encouraged to identify their own needs for wider training in order to obtain qualifications which will improve their prospects in the employment market. While the pool management has a policy of promoting from within wherever possible, it also wishes to make it possible for staff to move on to more responsible jobs elsewhere. Wherever possible financial assistance is given to enable staff to pursue courses of study. Not only does this help to raise the standard of experience and knowledge amongst the staff but it also enhances staff morale and therefore benefits the operation of the pool.

Key points

- *The Pool was deliberately planned as the District's 'flagship' and is a key factor in creating a high quality of life for local residents and attracting new businesses and residents to the District.*
- *Perth's good communication links coupled to the high quality, high profile building have enabled the pool management to position the pool as a key 'special treat' day trip destination for children from a wide area.*
- *High standards of customer care attract repeat visits from leisure day trip visitors and generate considerable expenditure and, therefore, significant benefits to the District's economy.*
- *The existence of both a leisure and 25 m training pool in one complex allows the management flexibility to satisfy most aquatic needs.*
- *Customer-centred approach.*
- *Management team concentrates on 'big issues' and is able to make and implement decisions quickly.*
- *Deliberate attempts to avoid 'us and them' feelings between management and manual staff.*
- *Strong emphasis on team working but without allowing teams to become fixed groups in order to maximise the cross-fertilisation of ideas.*

- ▲ *High priority given to all forms of staff training both for their present job and to enable them to gain promotion.*

Case study 2.2: North Mainland Pool, Brae, Shetland

Key features

- ▲ *Small trust run pool*
- ▲ *Wide programme*
- ▲ *Community involvement*
- ▲ *Minimum staffing*

Shetland could hardly be more different from Perth. It consists of a string of dozens of islands stretching some 100 km from north to south. The largest, Mainland, also contains most of Shetland's 20,000 population. The main town, Lerwick, has a population of about 8,000 and the main populated islands of Yell, Unst and Whalsay have scattered populations of around 1,000. In general the inhabited islands are linked by ferry; but as ferries operate only during the day, at other times the islands have largely to be self-contained. This is particularly the case with regard to recreation; it simply is not possible to travel to sports facilities on another island at night, never mind the expense. Over the past few years, therefore, purpose-built leisure centres – usually with a 3-badminton court sports hall, a small pool and other facilities – have been provided to serve the main population centres by the Shetland Recreational Trust (SRT).

SRT was created in the early 1980s as a vehicle to use oil revenue to build and operate sport and recreation facilities. Like PKRF it is an 'arm's length' company although serviced largely by the Islands Council; it is chaired by the Council's Director of Leisure and Recreation and other Trustees include the chairs of the Leisure and Recreation and Education committees; the Director of Education; the Depute Director of Leisure and Recreation; and a representative of each community in which a facility is operated by the Trust.

The Trust's first project was a major dry sports centre at Clickimin on the edge of Lerwick. It opened in March 1985 and attracts over 150,000 visits per year. The huge success of the Clickimin Centre encouraged the Trust to provide secondary centres in various parts of the islands. By the end of 1993 there will be eight pool complexes in Shetland: at Clickimin (25 m pool plus leisure waters); on the islands of Unst (12.5 m × 3 lane), Yell (also 12.5 m × 3 lane) and Whalsay (15 m × 3 lane); in North Mainland at Brae (16.67 m × 4 lane); South Mainland at Sandwick (16.67 m × 4 lane); and in Scalloway, the main town of West Mainland (also 16.67 m × 4 lane). All have been far more successful than expected and the Trust believes three special 'island factors' explain a large part of the success of Shetland's indoor facilities:

- The climatic conditions in Shetland
- The absence of any major commercial involvement in leisure and recreation
- The lack of social divisions in the local community.

Like Perth, all the Trust's facilities have been built to a very high standard of specification and with sophisticated energy saving plant in order to minimise maintenance costs.

Mission and aims

The Trust's mission is to improve the quality of life of the people of Shetland. More specifically it aims:

- To serve and give substantial sporting opportunities to all people in each community with particular emphasis on disadvantaged groups
- To balance the interests of the greatest number and the greatest need, meeting the requirements of both majority and minority sports
- To provide and encourage opportunity for communities to discover new recreational interests by the imaginative use of resources
- To stimulate community initiatives and support community organisations within each centre
- To meet these objectives in a cost-effective manner and within set financial targets.

The North Mainland Pool opened in November 1988 and contains a total of approximately 130 sq m of water, a solarium and a small social area at the poolside. The catchment area is wholly rural with a total population of only around 3,000 within 20 miles. In spite of this it caters for around 40,000 community users each year plus an additional 6,000 school visits.

While the Trust and management have a number of financial and staff training objectives, the key aim is to increase the percentage of competent swimmers in Unst through the provision of adult and junior teaching classes and the creation of a personal survival club working towards distance badges and awards.

Management structure

With a small pool in a rural area it is not possible to have a full range of management and staff skills on the pool staff. Fortunately the existence of the other facilities operated by the Trust makes it possible for a central services unit to provide these skills from the Clickimin Centre. The central services available from the Trust at Clickimin include all personnel and wages functions, invoicing and accounts, some administrative support and the analysis of management information. This allows the on-site staff to be few in number and concentrate totally on reception and lifeguard duties and attracting users.

The pool runs with one full time member of staff – the manager – and six part-time staff who act as both receptionists and lifeguards. At busy times there are two poolside attendants and a receptionist; at off-peak times two poolside staff are adequate. The reception desk has a full view of the pool and pool hall which makes this arrangement possible. There are also two relief attendants who are called on to cover for sickness and staff holidays. As well as being in day-to-day control of the pool, the manager is responsible for promoting it within the local community.

All plant is operated by automatic controls with specialist staff back-up available from a travelling maintenance team of three engineers who service and maintain all the plant in the Trust's buildings.

A particular area of interest in all the Shetland facilities is management information. All the various centres have computer-based till systems to record income and user categories. All the tills are connected by telephone line and modem to a master computer in the Clickimin Centre which automatically downloads management information from each local till overnight. The Trust's manager, based at Clickimin, is then able to review the use and performance of each of the facilities in Shetland on a daily basis. Weekly and monthly reports are produced automatically.

As initially set up, this system provided an excellent management information for the Trust's general manager but comparatively little for on-site managers who did not have access to the daily information other than getting it from Clickimin. In order to remedy this defect computer terminals are being installed at each centre to allow managers to download their own till information and receive analysed data automatically from the central computer in Clickimin.

Programming

On Mondays, Wednesdays and Fridays the pool is open from 0800–0900 for early morning swimming and from 1230–1330 for public swimming. During the remainder of the day until 1530 it is reserved for school groups although on Fridays there is a parent and toddler session from 1030–1230. Each weekday from 1530 to 1900 or 2000 the pool is available for public use and after this it is bookable by local organisations until 2200. On Saturdays the pool is open from 1330–1930 and on Sundays from 1000–1700.

The 'public' sessions are in fact highly programmed; encouraging regular programmed use has proved to be critical to attracting and maintaining high levels of use in a small, scattered community. During the year, sessions are programmed for:

- Parents and toddlers
- Children's lessons (under 5s)
- Children's lessons (over 5s)
- Under 6s swimming club
- Aquarobics
- Olympic games (organised fun games for children aged 8–14)

- Adult games (eg volleyball, water polo and underwater hockey)
- Junior lifesaving
- Adult technique courses
- Adult badge nights
- Private lessons
- Men's aquarobics (sponsored event with local men dressed as women!)
- Easter egg dive

A popular swimming club has been formed – the Delting Dolphins – and trains for up to six hours each week. It competes against clubs from other parts of Shetland but in order to promote competitions within the club it is split into three parts known as the Sharks, the Porpoises and the Piranhas.

Customer care

Customer care in an environment where pool staff are on first name terms with most users is quite different from larger complexes. One of the great strengths of Shetland is the very strong community spirit and lack of social tension; the number of community organisations is very high and typically they involve everyone from young children to great grandparents. There are nearly 60 village halls in Shetland used for everything from wedding parties to concerts and meetings and it is almost the case that anywhere with more than about 10 houses within a one kilometre radius but without a village hall there will be a committee planning one. Community-based committees are a fundamental part of life in Shetland. SRT takes advantage of this by having a Joint Consultative Committee at each of its centres to advise the manager and Trust on the needs of the local community. They generally meet quarterly and consist of anything up to about 15 people who are representative of local communities or community organisations. Because members of the committee are well known in their local area – on average there is a member of the committee for every 70 or 80 households in the area served by the pool – the management is kept well in touch with its local market and this has helped to determine both opening hours and programming.

Finance

The subsidy per user is very close to the Scottish average and the Brae pool recovers approximately 30 per cent of its operating costs from income. It is funded by a direct grant from the Shetland Recreational Trust. Each year the Trust publishes a detailed annual report giving full details of income, expenditure and usage. This open approach builds good relations with local communities and helps to explain to them why Shetland facilities are run as they are. Ultimately the Trust receives its income from revenues received from oil companies active in the North Sea. Shetland is the closest land to many of the main oil fields and the terminal at Sullom Voe in the northern part of Mainland receives a high proportion of all North Sea production. In turn Shetland benefits from a barrelage charge for all oil which crosses its foreshore.

Inevitably this income will not last for ever and the majority of it is invested in ways which will ensure the long-term future prosperity of Shetland, for example in the creation of jobs and investment in infrastructure. Other sums are invested for income and produce the funds needed to subsidise the various leisure centres.

Pricing policy

The Trust operates a deliberate policy of low prices in order to maximise levels of use and aims to increase prices each year in line with inflation. They are generally slightly below the Scottish average with concessions for junior swimmers, senior citizens and those who are disadvantaged.

Staff training

All pool staff are required to have a Pool Lifeguarding Bronze Medallion from the Royal Life Saving Society and in addition the pool manager at Brae is the designated trainer and assessor for all pools under the control of the Trust. As well as providing training for her own staff at Brae she also organises a monthly training and assessment session at each of the pools under the Trust's control.

In addition to basic lifeguard training, at each pool operated by the Trust at least two members of staff have been assisted to obtain the Amateur Swimming Association's Preliminary Swim Teaching Award.

Key points

- ▲ *High quality pools are a source of local pride and have a high local profile in communities which traditionally had no indoor leisure facilities other than village halls.*
- ▲ *Well run small pools can generate high levels of throughput in small communities and are flexible enough to be used for a wide variety of aquatic activities.*
- ▲ *Innovative programming to encourage frequent and regular use is essential in attracting and maintaining high levels of use in a small community.*
- ▲ *Several small local pools use central resources in order to minimise site-specific costs but have all the necessary management and technical skills available within the overall SRT team.*
- ▲ *Sophisticated use of information technology to provide essential management information on a daily basis.*
- ▲ *Joint Consultative Committee keeps the manager in close touch with the needs of local communities.*
- ▲ *Pool staff are on first name terms with most users.*

Pool management in the Netherlands

In the Netherlands a manager of a pool or leisure centre has to take the following laws into account:

- The Constitution
- ARBO law: the approximate equivalent of the UK's Factories Act. The law sets out what employers and employees must do. The latter have the obligation to report dangerous situations and the employer must solve the reported problems
- WHVZ law: Hygiene and safety in swimming pools
- Catering Act
- Nuisance Act
- Public Health Act
- Dangerous Substances Act
- Remedies Act (disinfectants etc)
- Police regulations, which may be very local.

The ARBO and WHVZ Acts are both recent and influence the work of pool managers enormously. As most of the pools in the Netherlands are the property of the local government (there are about a thousand pools from which approximately 500 are indoor pools; the rest open air) managers have also to comply with local acts. Only about 100 pools are run on a private basis and even then the deficit is largely carried by the local councils.

The context within which Dutch pool managers operate

Under the Dutch Constitution the Town Council is the Head of the Municipality. Members are elected from the population by voters of 18 years or older by a system of proportional representation. A small town may have a council of seven members and a large city may have 45 members. The Burgomaster, who is appointed by the Queen, is chairman of the Council and of the executive committee and aided by one to four Aldermen chosen from the Council.

The city administration is usually divided into three main groups:

- A service department (education, secretary, deaths and births register, marriages etc)
- A technical department (city engineer, roads, bridges etc)
- A finance department (everything to do with finance).

Apart from these there is a Police Force (the Burgomaster is also Head of Police) and a personnel department.

One of the tasks of local government is to provide sports facilities such as swimming pools and football fields. Once these facilities are provided a manager is appointed; he or she may be a civil servant or, as is now more and more the case, employed by private enterprise. The job of the manager is normally to provide the best possible, safe service for the lowest possible cost.

As in the UK, the programme is likely to include:

- Private tuition
- Tuition for schools (primary schools)
- Swimming for the disabled
- Swimming for the elderly (senior citizens)
- Swimming for mother and child (babies)
- Swimming for pregnant women
- Swimming galas
- Water-polo
- Trim sessions (the use of a wet belt is becoming popular)
- Aquarobics
- Free swimming (times the public can come in to swim at their own leisure)
- Exams for the private tuition and schools pupils to obtain a diploma
- Facilities for clubs
- Sub-aqua clubs

This is a very short list of the popular activities in Dutch pools. Each activity requires qualified trained staff and it is compulsory for the attendants to have first aid qualifications, life saving abilities (in mouth to mouth resuscitation and heart massage). The staff works in shifts of 38 hours over a 5 day week. The working roster has to be approved by an independent organisation in the form of an Employment Medical Advisory Service.

On top of this the manager will also need staff for the ticket office, the catering, the technical systems, water treatment plant, cleaners and office workers. Quite often there is a combination of functions, ie swimming instructor/cleaner; boiler and maintenance man; ticket clerk/administrator; ticket clerk/receptionist. In order to run his establishment the manager recommends charges to the politicians.

The ticket office

The ticket office not only sells tickets but acts also as an information point for the public and in several cases oversees catering (filling vending machines, selling coffee, sweets etc).

The ticket clerk is an important person in case of accidents and emergencies because he or she can use the telephone and the public address system to order people out of the pool and the attendants to their stations all according to a prepared scheme to evacuate the building.

The pool side

According to Dutch laws there must be sufficient qualified staff on the pool side to supervise the swimmers. At least one attendant to one pool. They must have a first aid qualification and an equivalent to the UK's Pool Bronze Medallion.

Water treatment and heating plant

This plant must be capable of maintaining the high standards given in the WHVZ law. This means that there must be a technical person familiar with the water treatment procedures. There are also rules and regulations concerning the use and storage of chemicals.

Cleaning

The establishment must be kept clean and rules are given how many times a week or how many times a day some areas must be cleaned and disinfected. Disinfectants must be of a type approved by the State: other types are not allowed on the premises.

Maintenance

By law, the building must be kept in a good state of maintenance. This means daily inspection of the whole building to see that everything is in working order. If something is unsafe (for example following damage by vandals) and a member of the public or staff gets an electric shock or is injured the manager may be held responsible unless he or she can prove that the building has been checked regularly. In addition, Dutch pool managers have to draw up a schedule for both short- and long-term maintenance.

Environment

With growing concern for the future of the environment managers have to take great care over the dumping of chemicals and disposing of heavy metals into the sewer system is forbidden. TL lamps when renewed must be regarded as chemical debris and treated accordingly and so are used filters from ventilation systems.

Swimming instruction

The swimming ability of children is assessed through a diploma system with the exams supervised by an inspector. The easiest exam is the 'A' diploma for which pupils have to swim 25 metres fully clothed; 75 metres breast stroke; and 50 metres backstroke. In addition they have to tread water for one minute with their hands above the surface.

Estimates

The manager has to prepare annual estimates for approval by the Council each year irrespective of whether the pool is run by the municipality itself or through a private contractor.

Catering

The main question is whether to operate a catering service or seek a specialist contractor on a concession basis. In most publicly run pools the catering is hired out but in privately run pools it is often overseen by the manager.

Marketing

If a manager wishes to start a service such as trim swimming he or she will first undertake research to see if it is what the public wants. If the decision is to proceed the programme must be publicised and leaflets printed. In local government it is always possible to make use of the municipal information service but this means many meetings and consequently a lot of time. The biggest snag with being a local government pool is the time it takes to get things done. If additional funding over and above the approved estimate is required it is necessary to make a request to the Council and if this is agreed, the Council's approval then has to be approved by the Province. This whole process can take three months.

Case study 2.3: Municipal Pool, Deurne

Key features

- ▲ *Municipal complex of pools serving a relatively small Dutch community*
- ▲ *Re-appraisal of programming policy*
- ▲ *Contracting out under consideration*
- ▲ *Marketing within a national promotion*

Deurne is a village about 20 miles from Eindhoven in the south of the Netherlands. The municipality comprises eight villages with a total of 30,100 inhabitants and Deurne is the main village with approximately 21,000 inhabitants. It contains the Town Hall, Police and Fire Brigade headquarters.

Amongst the sports facilities in Deurne is an indoor and open air pool, the indoor part of which was built in 1970. It is 25 × 8 m with depths ranging from 1.1 to 1.6 m with the deepest water in the middle of the pool. The water temperature is maintained at 30 degrees Celsius.

The open air pools were added in 1972 in the form of a 25 × 17 m pool with an overall depth of 1.90 metres; a 40 × 20 m pool with a depth of 0.4–1.2 m; and a children's pool 6 × 6 m with a depth of 0.3 m. For the first three years of operation the water in these outdoor pools was heated to only 24 degrees Celsius and so when the weather was poor the bathers used the indoor pool instead. The number of attendances grew so much that the indoor pool became too small and the municipality decided to cover the deeper outdoor pool with a removable air supported structure from September to May of each year. This was also a success but resulted in high energy consumption. In 1982 it was replaced by a 25 × 15 m indoor pool with a depth from 1.80–3.80 metres. This pool also has 3 and 1 m diving boards and the water is kept at a temperature of 27 degrees Celsius. In the same hall there is also a 15 × 8 m learner pool with a depth from 0.4–1.1 m. The whole complex has a combined ticket office, combined dressing and pre-cleansing facilities. There is also a canteen where snacks such as chips and sandwiches are sold. There is also a fitness centre and in total the throughput of the complex is about 200,000 visits per year or roughly 10 visits per head of population per year.

The swimming pool offers a wide variety of services such as casual swimming, sessions for pregnant women, mothers and children, swimming tuition, sessions for senior citizens, clubs and sub-aqua. Initially this resulted in an extremely complicated timetable which confused many local people with the result that many started to telephone before setting out for a swim to find out if the pool would be available. After long discussions a 'horizontal' timetable was introduced, much to the disgust of the swimming clubs, with each activity at the same time every day and this has proved much more successful. The swimming clubs are now programmed on Saturdays which had previously been a slack day for casual swimming; now every Saturday the throughput is around 1,000 visits although the pool is open only for club members. Sundays were also slack and so the public opening hours were reduced to 0900–1200 with the afternoons reserved for galas and special events.

Pricing policy

For years the policy of the municipality was to keep the prices low with the result that the recovery rate was only 31 per cent – very similar to many pools in the UK. More recently a swimming passport scheme has been introduced in order to promote swimming. The customer pays the equivalent of about £16 per year plus about 35p for each visit.

Management

The municipality has recently concluded that the pool is too expensive to retain in local authority management and is planning to let a contract to a private sector management company with effect from about September 1993. It accepts that a significant subsidy will still be required but is working on the basis that this will be lower than with public sector management and that this will mean higher admission charges.

In the meantime, in order to run the pool as cheaply as possible clubs are allowed to use it without staff present. Clubs using the pool in this way must clean it after their let and the system works well provided there is a competent and committed club committee.

The staff establishment is equivalent to 7.3 full-time employees (including the manager) each working 36 hours per week. This is possible only by making substantial use of part-time staff; so, for example, swimming for pregnant women is supervised by a midwife. Other specialists are also available and the pool is adequately staffed with lifeguards at times of tuition, casual swimming and so on. The cleaning is undertaken partly by a cleaning firm which does the heavy work.

Customer care

The management is obliged by law to keep the pool in a good state of maintenance and clean with water which complies with high quality standards. The staff are dressed in marine blue shorts with a white shirt so that they are readily recognisable to the public. They are trained on the job in first-aid and heart resuscitation and receive regular refresher training in swimming tuition as well as an annual appraisal interview which helps to determine training needs. The salary of a swimming instructor is the equivalent of approximately £15,000 per annum.

Marketing

As the manager has a very small marketing budget equivalent to only about £500 per year very little promotion is possible; even a fairly basic campaign would require several times this amount. Not surprisingly, other pool managers in the Netherlands face the same problem. Accordingly the National Bureau for Swimming Diplomas, which is in touch with all the managers, took the initiative and started a major campaign to promote swimming. Following a market research programme to find out what the public wanted and their image of swimming pools, all pools in the Netherlands were approached to take part in the campaign. Three hundred and fifty did so and each contributed a certain amount of money. This made it possible to get a weekly 30 minute television programme and to provide articles for newspapers and magazines. Now every first Saturday in June is 'Swim Fun Day'.

Each participating pool organises something special on this day and these activities are widely advertised. Furthermore, each pool is able to deliver a magazine with general information about swimming and its facilities to local residents. Depending on the funds available to each manager this can take up one, two or four pages. Each participating pool is promoted using a common house style and flags, stickers and other 'personalised' promotional items are available. There are also gift coupons which are valid at all participating pools.

It was soon found out that the staff in each pool lacked adequate knowledge of other pools in the area so a training programme was introduced for everyone from manager to cleaner. Any pool taking part in the campaign agrees to do so for a period of three years. The campaign is now in its last year and proved to be very successful once it overcame the problem of persuading pool owners to participate.

Key points

- ▲ *The legislative context within which Dutch pool managers work is even more tightly constrained than in the UK.*
- ▲ *The 'A' Diploma swimming ability test is far more demanding than the Key Stage 2 attainment target of 25 m in the National Curriculum for Physical Education for England and Wales or the Northern Ireland Curriculum.*
- ▲ *Dutch managers generally face the same problems as UK managers, particularly the pressure to reduce deficits, and are also having to compete with private sector managers.*
- ▲ *Dutch managers are more willing than UK ones to allow clubs to book exclusive use of their pools without lifeguards being present, or to make use of*

part-time staff for particular sessions, in order to minimise staff costs. In some instances they also entrust clubs with duties such as cleaning.

▲ *Joint promotion of swimming and pools by a large number of managers and pool owners has helped to generate additional use of pools.*

References

1 Health and Safety Commission/Sports Council (1988) *Safety in Swimming Pools*. London: The Sports Council.
2 Kit Campbell Associates (1989) Bishopbriggs Sports Centre (unpublished).
3 Chartered Institute of Public Finance and Accountancy (1989) *Leisure and Recreation Statistics 1989–90 Estimates*. London: The Institute.
4 Chartered Institute of Public Finance and Accountancy Scottish Branch (1992) *Rating Review: Actual Income and Expenditure 1990–91*. Edinburgh: The Institute.
5 Audit Inspectorate, Department of the Environment (1983) *Development and Operation of Leisure Centres (Selected Case Studies)*. London: HMSO.

Acknowledgements

The authors wish to acknowledge the help and assistance received in preparing this chapter from the managements of the case study pools but particularly Sonia Davies (Perth) and Andy Mayers (Shetland).

John Bastijn Manager, Deurne Swimming Pool, The Netherlands.

3 Leisure centres
John Buswell

Leisure centres have slightly different images across Europe. Many indoor purpose-built facilities are sports focused and operate through the aegis of sports clubs even though they are owned by municipal authorities. They are not always managed in quite the same way as British leisure centres where there is much greater emphasis on the casual user.

The first leisure centre was opened in the UK in Harlow in Essex in 1964 (initially run by a Trust). There are now over 1,600 such leisure centres with a number of ambitious schemes leaving the drawing board in recent years – Ponds Forge International Sports Centre, The Dome in Doncaster and The Spectrum in Guildford.

The centres have emerged either as a response to growing demand or in order to set new trends and to influence demand. Squash is a clear example of an activity boosted by the rapid proliferation of facilities. The concept of the leisure centre has also embraced specifics like the leisure pool, ice-rinks, bowls-rinks, health and fitness suites, snooker rooms and even mixed developments including libraries and health clinics.

In the UK leisure centres are the domain of local authorities for the following reasons:

- the Wolfenden Report of 1960
- the Report of the Second Select Committee of the House of Lords (Cobham) on Sport and Recreation 1973
- the Government White Paper on Sport and Recreation 1975
- local government reorganisation 1974

The Wolfenden Report marked a watershed in the provision of sport and recreation facilities in the UK. It identified the problems of poor participation rates, particularly in the young, the lack of appropriate facilities and recommended the setting up of an Advisory Sports Council to promote both facility provision and greater participation. The two parliamentary reports embraced much of the philosophy contained in the Wolfenden Report and identified local authorities as the main provider of the new facilities and services

The Sports Council, subsequently, carried the message forward and began, as part of its remit, the necessary pump-priming role and encouragement of providers. Its first block was £3.5 million in 1972, and through its various campaigns and strategies it has promoted the leisure centre in a number of different ways:

- the concept of the multi-purpose sports hall
- the wet and dry complex
- low cost standardised sports centres (SASH)
- dual-use/joint-provision centres
- converted or adapted buildings (for example, the Old Gaol Leisure Centre in Abingdon in Oxfordshire).

These centres, in the early years of provision, had a number of characteristics. They were novel and were seen as dynamic, vibrant places which encapsulated the growing diffusion of lifestyles in modern Europe. They were relatively cheap to use as demonstrated by the massive subsidies per user visit each attracted. There appeared to be an appropriate supply of staff from physical education teaching and other related occupations who helped to devise early policies and operational procedures (some of them very good, others less so).

The pattern of provision has evolved somewhat since the early days and attitudes have changed considerably towards facility design, programming, service delivery and operations management. The late 1960s and early 1970s were characterised by an obsession with facility provision and a fairly prescriptive, paternalistic and normative approach to identifying the facilities required. There were few guidelines for provision or management. Any legislation had given authorities permissive powers to provide and, in some cases, centres were developed and built to match a similar facility in a neighbouring authority. A number of authorities were guilty of building large, prestigious centres before a network of smaller community-oriented centres, as part of a planned hierarchy of facilities, could be provided. Management was seen as a social caretaking, directly providing, tracksuit-clad role. Many of the early centres were not governed by strict financial targets and, very often, failed to attract the wide cross-section of the public they had been designed and provided for. Many had social objectives linked to the commonly held notion that leisure centres were almost part of the welfare state and should be greatly subsidised to appeal to all groups in the community, including the poor and disadvantaged.

However, early research began to demonstrate that usage was skewed towards the young middle-class, car-owning male who was probably reasonably active in the first place.

Questions began to be asked about the cost-effectiveness of the centres and their overall efficacy in meeting objectives This was coupled with the ideological change in attitude towards the public sector that Margaret Thatcher brought to her new government in 1979 and the gradual tightening of the public purse that had already begun in 1975.

The 1980s, consequently, saw the early signs of commercialisation and the development of targeted, reactive approaches based on programming and some limited marketing. Managers were becoming more competent in certain management functions although their actions were generally confined to normal day-to-day decisions and to operating within budgets.

Many leisure centres in the 1970s and 1980s, therefore, were provided without:

- any real acknowledgement of local people's needs and requirements
- sound operations management
- strict financial targets
- attracting a wide cross-section of the population

Gradually, through the 1980s there was an inexorable move towards the commercialisation of local authority leisure services and the application of the '3 E's' – effectiveness, efficiency and economy. The movement was enshrined in the Local Government Act of 1988, the bringer of Compulsory Competitive Tendering (CCT) which rapidly began to alter the ethos and operation of leisure centres. Indeed, Peter Brooke, the current Secretary of State for National Heritage, reminded us recently that 'CCT had been designed to promote more efficient, effective and accountable management' (*The Leisure Manager Journal*. December 1992).

Leisure centre operations

In recent years leisure centre operations have become more focused and coherent as the body of core skills and knowledge has developed and training and continuing professional development have helped to enhance standards of management. There are a number of facets, pertinent to leisure centre operations such as programming, pricing policy, staffing and service delivery, which will be considered by the case studies.

Programming

Programming can be regarded as one of the few specialist leisure management skills and the multi-purpose sports area, perhaps, provides the ultimate challenge to the leisure centre programmer. The programme determines the product and the activity mix and provides the manager with the opportunity to combine marketing with procedural expertise, an understanding of consumer behaviour and resource allocation. The programme links demand with supply through booking systems, membership systems and a programming policy which reflects the philosophy of use of the centre. The art of programming can range from the straightforward programming of club/group activities (mainly badminton and 5-a-side in dual-use/joint-provision centres) to the subtle mix of activities, groups and events in a large multi-purpose centre.

Despite the growing sophistication of programming techniques we can now observe, in many UK leisure centres, the collaborative efforts of Contractor/DSOs who implement the programming policy which has been determined by the client. Programming agreements appear to range from very prescriptive to more flexible arrangements where the contractor should, perhaps, merely provide a balanced programme. Overall, CCT appears to have tempered the move towards more creative and autonomous programming – even in centres run by commercial contractors.

Pricing policy

Leisure centres, historically, have lacked the managerial autonomy or flair to alter prices quickly and to respond to rapidly changing public needs and wants. Again, CCT provides for full client control over pricing and the general approach appears to confirm that this is the norm. However, the strict financial targets facing many leisure centre contractors have resulted in much greater consideration of the impact of opening hours, programming decisions and differential pricing policies. There is, normally, freedom for the contractor to offer lower prices than those set by the client.

Service delivery

The quality revolution is beginning to permeate leisure centre operations with more reference to service delivery. CCT and its financial targets, together with an increasingly demanding public, have caused many managers to review their operations and to look more critically at the requirements of their customers. The consequences are seen in a number of guises:

1. Implementation (or planning) of a quality system like BS 5750. The Oasis Leisure Centre in Swindon was the first leisure centre to achieve registration to BS 5750.
2. The development of customer service audits (Leisure Futures and the Institute of Leisure and Amenity Management).
3. The growing significance of targets and published standards – Customer Charters and Charter Marks.
4. Client inspections (both announced and unannounced).
5. More market research. It is often written into a contract specification that a certain amount of market research should be carried out apart from the gradual acceptance of the critical importance of marketing and marketing management to any leisure organisations.
6. More extensive customer care training. Customer care training has been the most popular subject for in-house training in the last couple of years and, with the provision of more applied resources and training packs, is becoming more pertinent to the needs of leisure managers.

Staffing

Leisure centres in the 1990s are more discerning towards the deployment and development of human resources. CCT resulted in many contractor/DSOs being pruned although there has been some take-up within client functions (the real financial savings from CCT may not be that substantial).

Although many contract specifications refer to training (and it is one of the more important of the 18 elements of BS 5750 1987: Part 2) it is questionable whether sufficient funds are being directed into training and staff development. The case study of Port Zelande highlights the relationship between the customer, the product and the quality of staff. Llanishen Leisure Centre also regard training as an important component in service delivery and are prepared to fund it.

The three case studies

Leisure centres, particularly in the UK, are undergoing considerable change in a dynamic market and a contracting culture. As Walsh pointed out:

> 'The first question that is raised by the introduction of competition for leisure services is "which business is the leisure service in?" '

Two of the facilities studied are UK local authority operated and represent two very typical, unpretentious community leisure centres, albeit in quite contrasting catchment areas, attempting to deliver a service in difficult times. One of the studies views the operation from the client perspective, the other from the contractor (DSO) side. Service operations in UK leisure centres are manifestly influenced by the contract specification and the relationship between client and contractor. Both are relatively new facilities; Newham Leisure Centre operates in a challenging environment and within a climate of considerable change and cutbacks. Llanishen Leisure Centre, perhaps, has enjoyed more stability and continuity in recent times but has a most impressive record of usage and service delivery.

Port Zelande in The Netherlands provides a contrasting view and is representative of the developments, in parts of mainland Europe, towards commercial leisure complexes. It demonstrates a more focused activity/product mix and a sharper definition of its business sector as you would expect from a commercial establishment. It emphasises, in particular, service delivery and the meeting of customer requirements

Case study 3.1: Llanishen Leisure Centre

Key features

- ▲ *Local authority leisure centre.*
- ▲ *1989 winner of the UK Sports Council Award for Management.*
- ▲ *Influence of corporate approach – Cardiff City.*
- ▲ *Very high usage.*
- ▲ *Good cost recovery rate.*
- ▲ *CCT: the contractor's perspective.*
- ▲ *Closeness to its customers.*
- ▲ *BS 6001: quality monitoring.*

Background

Llanishen Leisure Centre is situated in a pleasant suburb to the north of Cardiff with a mix of light industry and housing. It serves a population of approximately 12,700, including Llanishen and Lisvane, although draws upon a much wider area as we shall see. The centre was officially opened in 27 April 1987, and was the fifth district leisure centre to be provided by the City of Cardiff, although the first to contain a free form leisure pool with wave-making machine and beach area.

Philosophy

The philosophy and ethos of the centre is based on a customer-led service. Responsiveness to changing customer requirements is seen as the key to the centre's success, demonstrated in the centre's 'Value for £' experience (now £1.25!). The importance of offering customers choice was identified early on, particularly with the competition provided by other nearby centres.

The Llanishen mission is based upon the corporate philosophy as espoused by the City Council (see Figure 3.1). The Leisure and Amenities Department has made good progress in recent years to provide a network of leisure centres and other facilities after a rather slow start in the 1970s when the only centre of any type was The National Sports Centre in Sofia Gardens. Indeed, in the last eight years £13 million has been spent on new facilities including four district leisure centres, four community halls and an international (8 lane) athletics stadium. It is also significant that the Leisure and Amenities Department's revenue budget of £10.464 million in 1992/93 represented 25 per cent of the net expenditure of Cardiff City Council. Such is the commitment of the City to the provision of leisure opportunities for its inhabitants. The Department's policies and structure of provision are now quite comprehensive and provide a contextual focus for individual facilities like Llanishen.

Aims and objectives

Apart from the formal objective for general leisure provision in the City, outlined in Figure 3.1, there are more specific objectives for the leisure centres:

1. a variety of facilities should be provided for the general public at a satisfactory standard and minimum cost to the ratepayer;
2. the centres should keep within their annual budget;
3. club usage should not be greater than 50 per cent of usage at peak times;
4. the centres should not have a membership scheme;
5. the bars and vending activities should not make a loss but are considered as an essential part of the service to the public.

Marketing

The marketing strategy of the centre is based upon keeping in touch with its customers and producing glossy but realistic leaflets, posters and regular advertisements and media coverage. It is clearly enhanced by the corporate philosophy as demonstrated by the successful Passport to Leisure Scheme (see Figure 3.2).

1.2 GENERAL DESCRIPTION OF SERVICE

1.2.1 City Council's general philosophy on leisure

1. The City' Council's general philosophy on leisure follows, very broadly, two main principles.
2. The first, and arguably the most important, is to provide facilities so that residents of, and visitors to, Cardiff are able to participate in a wide range of sporting and cultural activities at modest cost.
3. The second principle has, itself, two main aims. One is to give everyone, including those unable actively to participate in leisure activities, the opportunity to see sporting and cultural events of the highest calibre. The other is to boost the local economy by enhancing the image of Cardiff in the eyes of investors and tourists alike by facilitating top quality international sporting and cultural events.

1.2.2 City Council aim

1. To promote and enhance the fitness, health, quality of life and well being of all sections of the City of Cardiff Community, by providing and extending the choice of opportunities for regular participation in sport, recreation and leisure, and enhance the quality of the environment throughout the range of Cardiff's Open Space including its valuable natural resources.

1.2.3 City Council Objectives

(a) Provide a consistent standard of leisure service in accordance with the City Council's aims and objectives ensuring that the service is both efficient and cost effective.

(b) Provide a clean, warm, safe and friendly facility environment to encourage general participation and frequent repeat visits.

(c) Respond to the needs and expectations of all sections of the Community by completing regular quality of service market surveys and provide a mechanism for regular customer and community feedback.

(d) Promote and market the leisure services of the City Council, incorporating all the aims and objectives, increasing public awareness and enhancing leisure opportunities.

(e) Provide a balanced programme of leisure opportunities and specifically promote activities for recognised target groups such as 50+, women, unemployed, unwaged, teenagers, mentally and physically handicapped at both peak and off peak times.

(Continued)

Figure 3.1
Cardiff City Council leisure philosophy

(f) Maximise the use of existing facilities, generating new initiatives, particularly at off peak times, encouraging existing non-participants to take up sport and leisure activities by carrying out off-site and outreach work projects.

(g) Provide a well motivated, well trained, efficient, appropriately qualified and friendly team of staff to provide a high standard of instruction and customer service.

(h) Establish and maintain a sports development strategy that will assist the general development of sporting skills and provide support for individual gifted performers, consulting appropriate organisations such as the Sports Council, Governing Bodies of Sports, etc., as appropriate.

(i) Encourage and develop Community arts initiatives to enhance public awareness and public participation.

(j) Continue to host major sporting events to highlight the City's image and identity, encouraging Tourism and Economic Development through high profile sport and leisure media events.

(k) Promote direct contact with commercial organisations to attract sponsorship initiatives that assist the general development of leisure opportunities in the City.

(l) Regularly review the need to improve existing facilities as well as identify new and specialist leisure facilities.

(m) Maintain the standard of the internal and external appearance of facilities with particular regard to the general decoration and the general fabric of the building.

1.2.4 Special events

1. As a guide to the Contractor the following list has been compiled as examples of the type of activities and events that have been staged previously. It is not an exhaustive list but clearly demonstrates the wide variety of what are both, sporting and leisure orientated pursuits. It is expected that the Contractor, in compliance of all other sections of the Specification documentation, will ensure that events of a similar nature are accommodated during the Contract period.

   Fun Festivals
   Antiques Fairs
   Senior Citizens Spectaculars
   Dog Shows

(Continued)

Figure 3.1 (continued)
Cardiff City Council leisure philosophy

Put Your Health First Days
Disabled Days
Fashion Shows
Choirs and Orchestral Concerts
Squash, badminton and other sporting championships
Carol Concerts
Exhibitions
Circuit Challenge Tournaments
Community Festivals
Women's Days
Open/Come and Try It Days
Brass and other bands Competitions
Wedding Receptions
Swimming Galas
Community and Charity Events

Figure 3.1 (continued)
Cardiff City Council leisure philosophy

Your Passport To Leisure

This entitles the holder to hours of fun and enjoyment

'Where Quality Counts'

is our formula for success at Llanishen Leisure Centre and we are certain that you will agree once you have experienced the Centre's very high standard of service. We also believe that there is something for everyone and we are confident that you will find an activity to suit your taste in our extensive Autumn programme.

Figure 3.2
Passport to Leisure Scheme. Llanishen Leisure Centre

Market research/customer feedback

The centre carries out one survey a month and each will have a different focus – for example, squash usage or the soft play area or the bar (with, perhaps, a prize from a sponsor for people who respond). One such survey of the 'Body Suite' highlighted the debate between those who wanted music while they exercised and those who did not. The surveys also help to maintain the centre's knowledge and understanding of the profile of its users.

Customer comment cards

Llanishen, like a number of centres, relies heavily on comment cards as a means of keeping in touch with customers' experiences and sentiments which are not necessarily complaints (see Figure 3.3). They received 33,000 of these in 1992, placed in a box in the centre or posted back to the centre or the Leisure and Amenities Department. Common comments related to aspects such as:

- pool temperature
- cleanliness/hygiene
- catering and vending

When the comments are complaints, and reveal a problem, there is a procedure for responding to them. There is an acknowledgement within 48 hours and a written response within 7 days of the complaint being received (see Figure 3.4).

The marketing methods employed are, perhaps, one of the key factors in the centre's success. The centre certainly enjoys the corporate benefits of the Department's 'Dragon' Logo and its marketing strategy. There is a requirement in the specification for CCT for the centre to print three brochures a year outlining the programme of activities and other information. There are also requirements for distribution of 12,000 leaflets, for example, dropped every October. The design of the brochure is left to the centre although must be approved by the Client Unit.

Advertising is also part of a corporate policy. The 50+ scheme, for example, was a feature of all the centre's advertising. The centre spends 2 per cent of operational expenditure on its promotions budget together with a separate budget for stationery. It also makes provision for responsive advertising costs, with a certain percentage set aside and reviewed on a monthly basis, when there might be, for example, special deals with the local press.

The centre, significantly, has set itself the target of at least one article or story per month in the local press. If there is no coverage then the contingency is to have targeted advertising. It certainly appears to pay dividends to centres who establish good working relations with the local press/radio and know instinctively when the photographer's quiet times are!

Usage

Advertising and promotion are inextricably linked with monitoring of usage of the centre. Scrutiny of target groups takes place with a review of attendance figures; the review is at least on a monthly basis and feeds into the termly and annual review.

Usage is particularly impressive, and, for the size of centre, is quite remarkable. 1992 saw 684,000 user visits; 115,000 people went through the Body Suite alone which represented a 17 per cent increase on the previous year. Health and fitness as concepts and as activities have been targeted by the centre (like many) and the promotion, underpinned by an excellent facility, has been successful. The centre's popmobility classes saw 50,000 attendances for the year; health and fitness packages for ladies attracted a further 25,000. The Body Suite and aerobics classes between them grossed £200,000 in income during 1992.

CUSTOMER

COMMENTS

We are committed to offering a friendly, helpful and caring service to all our customers. This form enables you the customer, (details overleaf) to provide positive feedback on the service and facilities available to you.

NAME: ....*DATE:* ....
ADDRESS: ....
....
....*TEL:*...
(Completion of your Name and Address is optional)

AGE GROUP	**<10**	**10-20**	**21-30**	**31-40**	**41-50**	**50+**
	1 ☐	**2** ☐	**3** ☐	**4** ☐	**5** ☐	**6** ☐

WE AIM TO PROVIDE:

A CLEAN ENVIRONMENT
SAFE & COMFORTABLE CONDITIONS
FRIENDLY & HELPFUL STAFF

WE TRUST YOU HAVE ENJOYED YOUR VISIT. HOWEVER SHOULD YOU HAVE ANY SUGGESTIONS, COMMENTS OR COMPLAINTS, PLEASE SPEAK TO THE DUTY MANAGER OR ALTERNATIVELY YOU MAY WRITE TO:

MR. I.L DAVIES,
DIRECTOR OF LEISURE AND AMENITIES,
HEATH PARK OFFICES,
KING GEORGE V DRIVE,
HEATH,
CARDIFF.

THANK YOU FOR COMPLETING THIS FORM, YOUR COMMENTS ARE APPRECIATED.

Figure 3.3
Customer comment cards

NAME OF FACILITY:......................................TIME OF VISIT..
WHAT ACTIVITY/SPORT HAVE YOU BEEN PARTICIPATING IN...

HOW OFTEN DO YOU USE THIS FACILITY (PLEASE TICK APPROPRIATE BOX)	*DAILY*	*WEEKLY*	*MONTHLY*	*OCCASIONALLY*
	☐	☐	☐	☐

COMMENTS REGARDING THE FACILITY:	***POOR***	***AVERAGE***	***GOOD***
1. CLEANLINESS & HYGIENE	☐	☐	☐
2. SWIMMING POOL TEMPERATURE	☐	☐	☐
3. PUBLIC SAFETY	☐	☐	☐
4. QUALITY OF COACHING	☐	☐	☐
5. CATERING & VENDING SERVICES	☐	☐	☐
6. STAFF APPEARANCE & ATTITUDE	☐	☐	☐
7. CHANGING ROOMS & LOCKERS	☐	☐	☐
8. BUILDING APPEARANCE & MAINTENANCE	☐	☐	☐
9.STANDARD OF EQUIPMENT	☐	☐	☐

OTHER COMMENTS:

....

....

....

....

....

....

THANK YOU FOR COMPLETING THIS FORM

Figure 3.3 (continued)

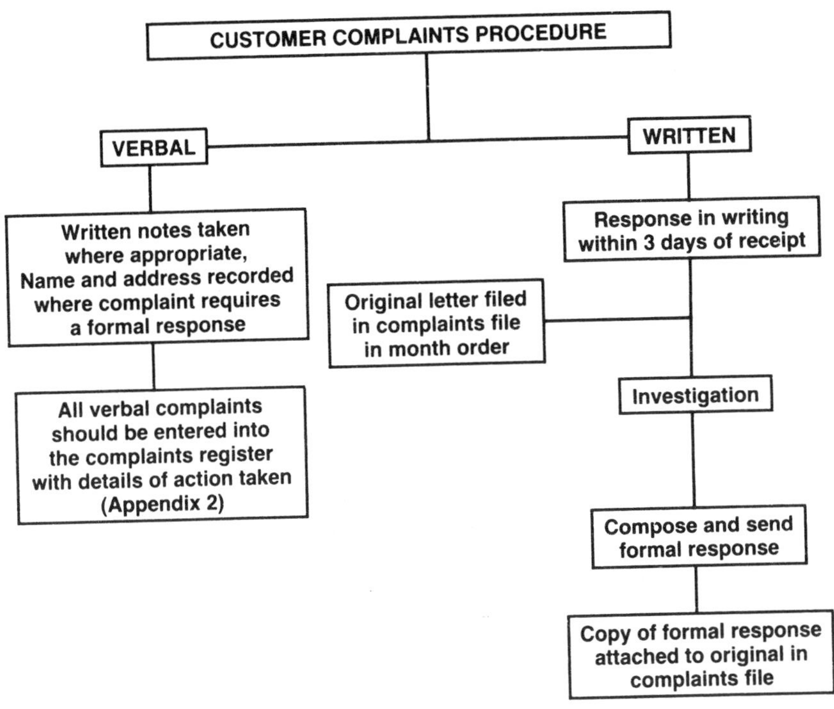

Figure 3.4
Customer complaints procedure

Both wet and dry sides represent very high usage for the facilities available and reflect the quality of the programme, building and service delivery, in addition to the return from the centre's constantly high profile.

Finance

The centre also has regular financial reviews at 3 months, 6 months and 9 months; it works to set budgets. It has strict monthly targets and on its contract performance target measures the growth rate against the previous month's figures. Its recovery rate is 85.2 per cent on current expenditure – a most impressive statistic.

The pricing structure (since April 1992) has been set by the client. It is normally altered once a year. There are two sets of charges:

- standard activities – reviewed once a year by the client through committee
- specific activities – reviewed twice a year by the centre.

Programming

Programming is, again, quite tightly defined in the contract specification and, once planned, should normally be adhered to. Variations to the programme may be allowed by the client; monitoring of the programme is through management information systems, feedback and costs. The programme itself has three phases:

- Winter – January to March
- Spring/Summer – April to August
- Autumn – September to December.

The aim of the Centre is to be innovative within each phase of the cycle, eg step aerobics (with the purchase of 80 steps). Other programmes have focused on the leisure pool or the soft play area or special events. The programme, once planned, is promoted and disseminated through posters and the leaflets referred to earlier.

Programme objectives

The original aim was to develop a wide, diverse programme with the encouragement of minority activities, eg the corporate policy on basketball. The emphasis is on badminton, 5-a-side, keep-fit (circuits and aerobics) and a number of other activities like volleyball, trampolining, party packages and special events.

The booking system allows up to 6 days' advanced booking with a high percentage of casual usage at peak times (Monday to Friday, 4.00–9.30 and Sundays):

- 70% – casual
- 20% – courses
- 10% – clubs

This philosophy is typical of many UK local authority leisure centres where the needs of the casual participant are respected.

Customer care through staff development

The operational staff are mainly salaried with support staff weekly waged. The standard of education of the staff is particularly impressive (70 per cent of the original operational staff had a first degree). Current numbers are 16 full time, 27 part time and up to 54 casual staff. Training and continuing professional development are regarded very highly and, more significantly, are given status in terms of both time and funding as indicated by the Centre's training policy (see Figure 3.5).

The centre's customers are clearly achieving high levels of satisfaction as we observed in the usage figures which include many repeat visits. A new customer care package is in the process of being written by the DSO Manager but the centre's successful strategy is based very firmly on the premise that *good customer care can only occur through good staff care*. The linkage between customer care and training can be seen in Figure 3.6. Approximately, 1.5 per cent of employee costs are spent on training and staff development; staff training is reviewed on a monthly

The DSO Recreation regards training as a high priority in order to maximise the effectiveness of staff and ensure a high standard of service delivery to the customer.

This commitment to training is reflected in the time devoted to monthly in-house training sessions averaging 3 hours per month for all members of staff and approximately 2 per cent of the annual time employed or 5 days per year.

In addition, all posts have a designated level of essential and desirable training to ensure the roles and tasks of the individual member of staff can be undertaken and a consistency of standard achieved.

Where possible, training will be conducted in-house to common syllabuses based on the centre's operational and safety manuals. If external training is required where the necessary expertise does not exist and where a member of staff is undertaking professional examinations, the quality and validity of the course content will be examined to ensure the required information and standards are covered and upheld. The Department has also made the decision to move towards incorporating National Vocational Qualifications where appropriate, as well as acknowledging 'investment in people' programmes.

Figure 3.5
Llanishen Leisure Centre training policy

basis and much of it is done in-house as a result of a training needs analysis.

Service delivery and quality assurance

Llanishen Leisure Centre is particularly successful because it appears to meet customer requirements and expectations and closely monitors changes in those requirements. Indeed, the centre operates within the new Departmental philosophy of '*Total business-total service*' (1993) which is built on the relationship between vision, values, and principles.

The *vision* is to give clients and customers total service through

- striving for the best possible relationship
- complete harmony of ideas
  communications
  skills
  operations

To achieve the desired *values* it means:

- trust
- flexibility
- anticipation
- fast response
- high levels of capability
- shared and acknowledged pride in achievement
- cost effectiveness

OPERATIONAL CODE NO. 15

CUSTOMER CARE POLICY

Responding to our customers needs is the number one priority of the DSO Recreation, with all members of staff making it their personal responsibility to ensure these needs are catered for. Customers Care is only possible if all members of the staff team demonstrate a common acceptance of this number one principle. To achieve this a programme of training at induction and refresher level will be undertaken using the following statement as the aim of the training programme:

That all members of staff are employed to help our customers.

We will always listen and offer courteous, respectful, helpful attention and assistance.

The DSO Recreation want our customers to enjoy themselves.

Staff training will be based on the DSO Recreation Customer Care Training Pack.

Figure 3.6
Customer care policy

Above all it means professionalism

The *principles* identified require that staff:

- put the customer first
- work to the spirit of the contract
- adopt a professional and flexible approach
- are straightforward and easy to deal with
- achieve cost-effective performance.

The message in the Cardiff philosophy is quite clear and is symptomatic of a growing trend in successful leisure organisations which is 'closeness to the customer'. British organisations, including leisure enterprises, are beginning to heed the example of Japanese organisations who are totally customer-led in everything they do and sensitive to every discernible market trend.

From the quality perspective, the centre also ensures that customers receive a reliable and consistent service. The centre has not yet applied for registration to BS 5750 (it does not appear to need the perceived benefits of the kitemark at present) but it has installed an internal monitoring system based on BS 6001 'Sampling Procedures for Inspection by Attributes'. It uses the AXIS Quality Monitoring software package piloted with Bolton Metropolitan Leisure Services but now being used in a number of authorities and facilities. It involves three stages:

- the random selection of work to be inspected
- the inspection and assessment of the work for conformance with the agreed standards
- the calculation of the quality level achieved.

It is designed to randomly select items at a certain level of service to be inspected but can also be used for regular monitoring to check certain items on a pre-determined basis. It issues a spreadsheet with items to be monitored and their specification (for example when an area is to be cleaned) and is geared to an Acceptable Quality Level (AQL) – from the consumer's point of view – of, commonly, 90 per cent conformance. It can work at three levels and the number of items selected depends on the total number of possible attributes which may be inspected and the past performance demonstrated by inspection result.

'Philosophy of the quality responsive monitoring system'

Monitoring is a function of management to control the quality of a product or service by using inspection and other procedures as a means of assessing the quality of a product or service.

The monitoring procedure that has been developed to assess the quality of service delivery by the Leisure Management Contractor is based on the following principles:

- Client and contractor share the common goal of quality service delivery
- Formulation of a well documented procedure which is understood by both parties encouraging access and direct co-operation between all levels of staff
- Monitoring be used as a tool for both client and contractor to achieve the common goal
- The system be *responsive* to the needs of both the customer and the service.

The Llanishen package is set at an AQL of 90 per cent and level 3 with 32 items out of 1,000 to be inspected at random. It enables the client to inspect at a very detailed specification (determined by the contract specification) two or three times a month. It perhaps has a certain rigidity but provides a very objective assessment of service delivery at a pre-determined standard of service and has the advantage of focusing on outcomes and not simply inputs. With the appropriate relationship between client and contractor it can be a valuable management tool and a means of the contractor also providing verification of service being provided.

Key points

- ▲ *The centre's usage is very high in relation to its size.*
- ▲ *It appears to benefit from a coherent City Council corporate approach.*
- ▲ *Its marketing and advertising are well thought out and selective.*
- ▲ *It keeps in close touch with its customers.*
- ▲ *A high priority is given to customer care and staff training and development.*
- ▲ *It has not gone for registration to BS 5750 but has invested in a quality monitoring software package and feels that it is working well.*

Case study 3.2: Newham Leisure Centre – A year under contract

Key features

- *Recently built local authority leisure centre.*
- *Location in one of the poorer London Boroughs.*
- *Impact of Compulsory Competitive Tendering (DSO Contractor).*
- *Customer satisfaction measurement.*

Introduction

It is now over a year since the first wave of sports and leisure centres went out to contract. January 1992 was supposed to herald a new era for those leisure centres: an era when the focus would increasingly be on efficiency and cost-effectiveness; an era when the optimists felt customers would receive better value-for-money in the services they received ... when the pessimists felt financial pressures and an increased emphasis on the profit motive would result in cost-cutting and a deterioration in services. The pessimists' view was re-inforced by the belief that the Government's real agenda was not to increase value-for-money, but to reduce the level of expenditure on services funded by the Government and the local poll-tax payers.

Although it is only a year since the start of those contracts, it is possible to see some significant changes in the way Newham Leisure Centre (the subject of this case study) is being managed. This case study will show that some of the changes have been instigated by the Leisure Management Direct Services Organisation, the in-house workforce and others by the Leisure Management Client Unit. However, the aim of this case study is not to focus on where the stimulus for change occurred; but, rather, to assess whether these changes have resulted in a better or worse service to the customer. In other words, has the imposition of Compulsory Competitive Tendering legislation been of benefit to customers of a leisure centre that continues to be managed by an in-house work-force, after one year of the contract?

In attempting to answer this crucial question the case study will highlight the issues that have been of concern to the Leisure Management Direct Services Organisation (DSO) and to the Leisure Management Client Unit (CU), as well as the impact of those concerns on the way services have been delivered. It is worth stressing that the case study represents the client's view on both the issues of concern to the client and to the DSO (as perceived by the client). Although the case study was discussed with senior officers working for the DSO, it must be remembered that the study is essentially a client view of Newham Leisure Centre's first year under contract.

Background

Newham Leisure Centre which opened in May 1990, is a modern purpose built leisure centre building situated in Prince Regent Lane,

Plaistow. The leisure centre was built on a site already containing playing fields, a synthetic pitch and an athletics stadium. It was the management of all the facilities on the site (except the management of Grounds Maintenance services) that constituted the first Leisure Management Contract in the London Borough of Newham (see Appendix A for all facilities on the Newham Leisure Centre site).

The Leisure Management Contract was written during the leisure centre's first year of operation, putting enormous pressure on the DSO. They were expected to open and run a new centre and, at the same time, help prepare for Compulsory Competitive Tendering. In the event, senior officers from the DSO committed the extra time that was required, to help ensure that the contract adequately represented the services that the Council wished to see delivered at the centre.

In writing the contract a major consideration was obviously the political priorities of the Labour controlled Council. At the time the contract was written, the Council's main aim with regard to all services subject to competition, was to employ all legally acceptable means to ensure that contracts were won in-house and jobs protected. This was reflected in both the contract conditions and in the specification of the services, where there was a heavy emphasis on ensuring equal opportunities in service delivery. From the client's point of view, the writing of the contract provided an opportunity to focus on certain areas of equality in service delivery, which they believed the DSO should be delivering (although it is accepted that they weren't at the time the contract was written).

This has been a current issue since; the DSO believes that many of these areas of the specification represent an 'enhancement' of the service and are unachievable unless extra resources are made available; the client believes that a centre in an authority such as Newham should be prioritising such areas by better or different use of existing resources (and the fact that they were not being prioritised pre-contract is irrelevant).

The reason for the emphasis on equal opportunities can be found by both an analysis of the prevailing political culture and a range of socio-economic factors pertinent to the borough. According to a whole range of studies and statistical analysis, the London Borough of Newham is one of the most deprived boroughs in the country. Despite all the development opportunities associated with the Royal Docks and London City Airport, the proposed international railway terminal at Stratford, the proposed East London river crossing and improved road lines (all due to happen in the next 5–10 years), the London Borough of Newham currently has all the hallmarks of a depressed inner city borough (high unemployment, high levels of homelessness, high levels of crime, high levels of infant mortality, etc, etc). The London Borough of Newham is also one of the most racially and culturally diverse boroughs in the country, with the 1991 census showing that 43 per cent of residents came from one of the Asian, Afro-Carribean (and) Black and other Ethnic Minority communities represented in the borough.

The key aims of what is a Labour controlled authority are to achieve quality, equality and value-for-money in the services that it delivers to its local residents. The Leisure Services Department has these aims at the top of its agenda, as espoused in the Department's current leisure strategy 'Shaped for Success'. Although operational matters and isolation from other elements of the service can 'distract' managers of facilities from the core aims of the service, Newham Leisure Centre (along with all other discrete areas of the service) has a responsibility to deliver the Council's aims of quality, equality and value-for-money in service delivery. The client clearly has a responsibility to ensure that the contract defining the services to be delivered at Newham Leisure Centre, reflects these key aims. If the client were to fail in this responsibility, the DSO (whose main responsibility is to deliver the specification) might not be able to help meet those aims as much as they might like or the client would expect.

In addition to these 'local' aims, the Government (through its competitive tendering legislation) provided Newham Leisure with one further aim during its first year under contract: namely, to break even in financial terms. The requirement to set up separate trading accounts meant that Newham Leisure Centre, for the first time, could no longer be cross-subsidised by other services if it got into budgetary difficulties.

Newham Leisure Centre's key aims in 1992, its first year under contract, were to deliver the services defined in the specification (and, therefore, hopefully achieve quality, equality and value-for-money in service delivery) *and* to ensure that its trading account showed a break-even situation (at the very least). It is the degree to which the service at Newham Leisure Centre represented an achievement of these aims, in comparison to the period before the contract started, that is the ultimate test of whether the service improved during the first year of contract. Before the judgement can be made it would seem sensible to highlight the issues of concern to both the DSO and the CU which will have affected their ability to have jointly achieved the aims referred to above.

The word 'jointly' is used because it is not the preserve of the client or the contractor (in this case the DSO) to be solely responsible for services delivered to the customers of the centre. The client has, according to the spirit of the legislation, overall responsibility for defining the services that are required and for ensuring that the customers receive that service; the contractor (or DSO) has the responsibility to actually deliver the service. However, such divisions are inevitably less stark in a scenario where the in-house workforce continues to deliver the service (compared to a situation where a private contractor has taken over that responsibility). In the London Borough of Newham, the client–contractor split is at third tier level (under the Head of Recreation), making divisions in responsibility, as perceived by those involved (as well as those from the outside world), less easy to appreciate. The reality has been that in certain instances the client has had to rely on the advice and help of the DSO to define the service and the DSO has had to rely on the advice and help of the CU to deliver those services. In Newham the fact that the client and DSO have had to work closely together to make the contract a success is best shown by the voluntary involvement of both parties in a team-building course (held mid-way through the first year).

Overall judgements on the service have to, therefore, take account of the involvement of both the client and the DSO. That judgement is found at the end of this study, following an analysis of those issues of concern to the client and DSO, which have affected their ability to jointly achieve the aims of the centre during its first year under contract.

Issues of concern to the leisure management DSO

The start of the Leisure Management Contract at Newham Leisure Centre represented both the culmination of a period of rapid change and the start of a new era for the staff at the centre. The centre had opened barely a year and a half before the contract started: in that time staff had to open and operate a new building (in the manager's case, only a month after being appointed); prepare themselves for Compulsory Competitive Tendering; submit a bid (which turned out to be unopposed) and prepare themselves for the start of the contract. To say that this 18 month period was a period of change would be an under-statement. It has meant that there has been little time for consolidation since the building opened, let alone time to sit back and reflect on long-term planning, for the future direction of the centre.

The major change for the Leisure Management DSO has obviously been the requirement to operate to a contract and to deliver the required services within a tight financial framework. This has brought some advantages, accepted by the DSO: the writing of a contract has forced all concerned with the service to examine what they are trying to achieve at Newham Leisure Centre. The contract provides direction; the monitoring function of the LMCU has provided management with an opportunity to pressurise staff to improve certain areas of the service; the increased emphasis on marketing (in all its facets) has resulted in a more customer-orientated service; the requirement to break-even has encouraged tighter financial controls and the creation of a Member subcommittee to oversee all Leisure Management Contracts means that the DSO is more accountable for its actions.

However, from the DSOs point of view, the imposition of Compulsory Competitive Tendering has had its disadvantages as well. Although services have been defined for the first time, the contract has reduced the ability of the DSO to react in a flexible manner to issues and, to a certain degree, made the job less interesting. This is particularly true with regard to centre developments, where freedom has been restrained by a requirement to receive prior approval from the client. Operating to a contract is perceived to be more routine and therefore less motivating to certain staff. The increase in paperwork (record-keeping) and the requirement to respond to issues of concern to the client, is seen to be overly time-consuming and, in certain instances, actually preventing them from delivering services to the customers.

In certain areas, particularly the marketing requirements, the DSO views the contract as an enhancement of the service that was previously delivered and, therefore, unachievable given that extra resources were not available at the time the bid was submitted. Phasing has also been an issue, with the DSO believing they should be given long time periods to react to the changes required of them (for instance, programming requirements should be phased over a number of years, not delivered in year one of the contract). The DSO also believe the profile targets, with regard to the percentage of users from Asian, Afro-Caribbean (and) Black and other Ethnic minority groups; should have been phased over a number of years . . . not required in year one of the contract, which in their view is considered unrealistic.

The role of the CU has inevitably been an issue for the DSO. There is a view that Client Officers do not fully understand the 'local issues' and problems facing the staff delivering the service at the leisure centre and that little allowance is made of these issues/problems when the Client Unit assesses service performance. The degree to which the Client Unit has become involved in comparison to the 'arms length' management approach previously experienced by those working at the centre, has also been an issue. On some matters, though not all, the DSO believes the Client Unit has become over-involved in trying to resolve management issues which are of no concern to them.

Another important issue for the DSO, particularly in terms of motivating staff, is that now the contract has been won the DSO can only maintain its current position or go backwards. The DSO staff are now, in effect, on short-term contracts. This obviously makes staff feel vulnerable compared to other leisure services officers. To try to counter this the DSO have introduced a share surplus scheme which aims to reward staff for good attendance.

Aside from the requirements of Compulsory Competitive Tendering, the DSO has faced a number of difficulties in trying to meet its aims during the first year of the contract. This is particularly true of the financial aim to break even (and, if possible, to make a profit) which has been affected by a lack of appropriate financial information with which to plan, as well as a failure of the Council's financial systems on certain occasions (including a period at the beginning of the year when grounds maintenance staff were incorrectly being paid from the leisure centre budget). In practical terms, the amount of time that the DSO has had to spend on resolving financial issues has reduced the time available to address other priorities.

The DSO undoubtedly feels that it is being torn in two directions: the Government is expecting in-house workforces, where they win contracts, to behave more like the Private sector and yet the local authority does not allow the DSO to make the necessary changes that will allow such an approach. Although the DSO is expected to abide by established personnel procedures (including the recruitment process and disciplinary procedures) and by the Council's Financial Standing Orders (using contractors on an approved list, following the accepted tender process etc), such procedures are not easy to accept when they have an obvious financial cost and put the break-even position at risk. This remains one of the major issues facing the DSO (and to an extent the Client Unit), as they believe there is a link between certain 'constraints' placed upon them by the Authority and their ability to both deliver the contract and achieve a break-even position. Such 'constraints' will obviously become more of an issue as bids are prepared for the next contract period in 3–5 years' time.

Issues of concern to the leisure management Client Unit

Unlike many other local authorities, the London Borough of Newham did not transfer officers from the DSO to the client side. In the event, all client officers were appointed from outside the authority, bringing with them a range of management and sports development experience from other organisations (including the private, public and voluntary sectors).

One of the obvious results of this was that the client team had to work closely with the DSO, to ensure that the contract adequately represented the services required at Newham Leisure Centre. However, despite the enormous amount of time working alongside the DSO one of the main issues of concern to the client is that the DSO has not fully accepted the implications of the client role (as defined in the legislation). There is no doubt that the majority of the services at Newham Leisure Centre are satisfactorily delivered; the monitoring results show this clearly. There is also no doubt that the DSO has used the contract and the Client Unit's monitoring function as a vehicle for change in those areas of the service where *they*, as well as the client, wish to see change. It is true that many of those changes have been reactive but they have nevertheless been made. However, the client believes it is equally true that some key areas of service (which are detailed in the contract) have been largely ignored. The failure to offer a wider range of sessions target at the Council's priority groups, to meet the minimum levels specified in the contract, is the most obvious example. From the client's point of view, therefore, there has been limited success in encouraging the DSO to adopt a new approach – that of working to a contract. To the client, there appears to have been little change in attitude or in the work culture, despite certain changes in working practice.

The key issue to the client is that the DSO do not appear to have approached the obvious change in the circumstances in which they operate in a positive manner. At its simplest level the client believes there has been a failure to properly read and therefore grasp what is actually in the contract. Even allowing for the mass of text and the academic, legalistic style of writing, the DSO have obviously had difficulty in understanding and accepting some of the services they are now expected to deliver. As a result, the Client Unit have had to adopt a role they had not previously envisaged: an educating role. This in itself has caused problems as such an approach has been seen as being patronising.

Another difficulty for the client is that where problem issues have been understood by both sides, but there is a continued failure by the DSO to address them, the CU has only limited powers to effect change. The issuing of default notices, with the consequent loss of income to the DSO, has had an effect on relatively minor issues. However the major issues of concern to the client (eg failure to develop the programme according to specification requirements) are not easily addressed via default notices. One of the main issues facing the client during the first year under contract was how to react to a continued failure to deliver a specific aspect of the service, even in those cases when the DSO has been repeatedly defaulted for it. In some cases the DSO has allowed the client to become involved in management issues, the only realistic way of effecting change (eg catering issues); however, the majority of the time there has been an obvious reluctance from the DSO to allow the client to get too involved in resolving the issue of concern. The dilemma for the client is that it cannot get involved in management issues unless asked and yet it has to do everything it can to ensure services improve. The key obviously lies in the client–contractor relationship – if the contractor (DSO) trusts the client then that involvement is more likely to be encouraged.

During the first year of the contract the Client Unit have tried where possible to stress (orally and through its actions) that they are concerned to work alongside the DSO to improve services; so long as the DSO are prepared to commit themselves to achieving those improvements where it is reasonably possible. There has inevitably been disagreement about what is reasonably possible; ie what the DSO can realistically expect to achieve. This is particularly true when one looks at programming issues: the client expected an increase in the number of activities targeted at different sections of the local community (believing a centre in an authority such as Newham should be committed to such an approach); the reality was that the leisure management DSO changed the programme very little. Was the contract requirement to increase the percentage of programme time targeted at certain groups an enhancement or should a leisure centre in Newham be trying to achieve this anyway (ie should the fact that they were not doing enough before should be seen as failing, rather than any required increase in targeted programme time being seen as an enhancement)? The client and DSO had a different view for much of the first year of the contract; in the end a phased approach in the second year of the contract was agreed. Other issues, however, remained unresolved. Difference in perception of what is reasonably possible have undoubtedly affected the client–contractor (DSO) relationship, in varying degrees at different points during the year. From the client's point of view, only limited success has been achieved in terms of persuading the DSO that the client is not 'policing' them for the sake of it (or worse, to punish them); rather, that the purpose in all the CU work is to improve services delivered to the customer. The DSO's view that the involvement of the client sometimes hinders them from improving these very same services has been a factor in the client reacting less positively to the DSO than they might have on certain occasions.

Aside from the problems referred to above, the client–contractor (DSO) relationship has been generally a good one during the first year. Regular communication in the second half of the year has resulted in many issues being resolved and agreement on a number of service developments. From the client's point of view the major success has been the increased focus on customers. Despite the increases in customer attendances, the client believes that the centre cannot be said to be offering a customer-orientated service. There has, however, been an *increased* emphasis placed in responding to the requirements and needs of customers. A customer comments and complaints system has been introduced; two major customer surveys were undertaken (in May and

October); two customer forums were held and a significant amount of preparatory work has been completed for the series of outreach visits that are due to take place. To ensure the DSOs mind is equally focused on the customer, the CU link part of the payment that is made to the DSO to the results of two surveys carried out of the leisure centre. Eight per cent of the contract payments are linked to levels of customer satisfaction with the services at the centre and three per cent of the contract payments are linked to the customer profile at the centre (the percentage of Asian, Afro-Caribbean (and) Black and other ethnic Minority groups using the centre.

Although there are a number of mechanisms in place, in terms of the requirements of the contract and the way financial payments are structured, the client believes the centre still needs to become more focused on trying to meet the needs of customers. For instance, customer comments need to be seen in a more positive light and acted upon more consistently. Action also needs to be taken to address certain issues highlighted in the customer surveys, the merits of which are clearly not accepted by some officers working at the leisure centre (the CU is aware of at least one senior officer who has not even seen the contents of either of the surveys undertaken during the year).

Development of the service – To what extent have the centre's aims Been Achieved in the first year of the contract?

Despite the wide range of issues facing the client and the DSO, some of which remained unresolved at the end of the year, the first year of the contract has seen a number of improvements to the service. A number of specific examples can be highlighted including:

- The setting up and improvement of record-keeping and systems of operation (eg Health and Safety checks)
- Improvements to the catering services (eg standards of food presentation and service)
- Improved publicity at the centre
- Improvements to most aspects of cleaning
- The development of beauty/therapy treatment services
- Improvements to the 'Learn-to-Swim' programme
- The continued development of women-only activities.

One of the major developments has been the increased emphasis placed on providing a customer-orientated service. The customer comments system, customer surveys, customer forums and customer outreach visits (planned) are all evidence of the fact that the leisure centre is placing a greater emphasis on understanding and responding to customer needs. For the first time, the leisure centre is able to measure its performance in terms of customer satisfaction with the services and the customer profile at the centre.

The first year under contract has seen a significant increase in the total number of customer visits, with the surveys and regular monitoring of attendances showing a 25 per cent increase on the previous year. (This has obviously resulted in a significant increase in income on the previous year as well). With few extra resources at their disposal, the DSO can claim credit for maintaining customer satisfaction levels at a time of increased pressure on those delivering the service.

The results of the customer surveys, which highlight customer satisfaction ratings with various aspects of the service, show there has been a marginal improvement in customer views on specific issues, but a marginal deterioration in customer views on the service as a whole (see Table 3.1).

Table 3.1 Summary of levels of satisfaction with the centre

	Mean score June 1991	Mean score March 1992	Mean score Oct 1992
Friendliness of staff	1.11	1.00	**1.16**
Helpfulness of staff	1.08	0.99	**1.13**
Cleanliness of centre	1.00	0.82	**0.88**
Temperature of centre	0.58	0.85	**0.70**
Cleanliness of water	1.29	1.13	**1.13**
Temperature of water	1.06	0.92	**0.71**
Changing facilities	0.77	0.57	**0.61**
Showers	0.29	0.44	**0.52**
Cafeteria	0.54	0.79	**0.76**
Vending machines	0.49	0.66	**0.54**
Reception arrangements		0.43	**0.82**
Organisation of activity	1.08	0.99	**1.17**
Information and publicity outside the centre	−0.56	−0.09	**0.35**
Information and publicity available in the centre		0.93	**1.07**
Safety	1.50	1.42	**1.40**
Value for money			**0.98**
Overall satisfaction with visit	1.33	1.38	**1.28**

Note: The mean score is based on a value of +2 for very good, +1 for fairly good, 0 for average, −1 for fairly poor and −2 for very poor. People who had no opinion are not included in this calculation. A score of +1.25 thus means that on average the level of satisfaction is between very good and fairly good. Any positive score means on average people think a facility is good, a negative score means that people think it is poor.

October 1992 survey

In fact, the satisfaction ratings are so similar that the only conclusion that can be drawn from the results is that the service to customers has not significantly changed from the first survey (June 1991) to the final survey (October 1992). In effect, this means that the impact of Compulsory Competitive Tendering at Newham Leisure Centre, after one year of the contract, has not changed the customers' views of the service. However, given the significant increase in customer visits, these results could be said to represent an improvement in the results of the previous year. In terms of achieving the key aim of delivering quality services to customers, this data is the only information available that allows a 'before and after' analysis. The Client Unit has extensive records of its monitoring and of customer comments; but a comparison with the pre-contract period is not possible as such records are only available from the contract date.

One of the key aims of the client has been to establish the principle that Newham Leisure Centre should not be compared to other centres (in terms of measuring performance). The real issue, as far as the client is concerned, is whether the services at the centre are shown to be improving or deteriorating over a period of time. The implementation of the customer surveys has been a crucial mechanism for achieving this aim.

The customer surveys also show that there has been some increased success in achieving another key aim: to achieve equality in delivering services. Usage by women remained higher than men throughout the period and the October 1992 survey showed a slight increase in the number of Asian, Afro-Caribbean (and) Black and other Ethnic Minority users at the centre (although the overall percentages remain below the targets set by the Client Unit). The percentage of disabled users, however, remained relatively low compared to national population statistics and little 'remedial' action was taken by the DSO to redress this situation.

The third key aim was to deliver a service to customers that represented, in their view, value-for-money. It was felt that the only way to determine whether this aim was being achieved was to ask a specific question in the survey. This was asked for the first time in the October 1992/3 survey (see Table 3.2).

Table 3.2 Extent to which customers are receiving value-for-money

Very good value	30%
Fairly good value	44%
Average value	20%
Fairly poor value	2%
Very poor value	2%
No opinion	1%

Base = 507. October 1992 survey.

On average, customers at the leisure centre, believe they are receiving 'fairly good' value-for-money services (mean score is 0.98); with almost three-quarters of customers giving a positive response (ie stating they were receiving 'very' or 'fairly good value-for-money'). Although this represents a notable success the key issue is whether this level of customer satisfaction can be maintained or even increased. Unfortunately a before-and-after analysis cannot be undertaken as the 'value-for-money' question was not asked in the June 1991 survey, before the contract started.

The fourth and final aim of the centre was to end the year with the trading account showing a break-even position. The fact that the Council's financial year does not tie in with the first year of the contract, meant that the first trading account had to be completed after only 3 months of the contract (for the period January–March 1992). That trading account showed a surplus for the DSO and it is expected that despite some difficulties in the middle of the year that resulted in an expenditure freeze, the trading account for the period 1 April 1992 to 31 March 1993 is likely to show a break-even position. It would appear, therefore, that this crucial aim will be achieved by the DSO. It is interesting to note that the leisure centre overspent on its budget in the financial year before the contract started (1990–91); so it could be argued that Compulsory Competitive Tendering legislation has had a beneficial effect in terms of budgetary control.

Conclusion

The purpose of this case study is to examine the degree to which Compulsory Competitive Tendering has had an impact on the services delivered to customers at Newham Leisure Centre and whether the aims of the centre are now being better met under contract conditions. This assessment, which is essentially a client view, has to be seen in the context of a whole range of issues and difficulties faced by both the client and the DSO; not all of which can be attributed to the new legislation. There is no doubt that the client and DSO have struggled with their relationship, as new ways of working have put additional pressures on all concerned. However, during a time of change and increased pressure, there are signs that Newham Leisure Centre is moving towards a position where it can better meet some of its key aims.

During the first year of the contract, Newham Leisure Centre can demonstrate that there has been an increased emphasis placed on budgetary control and on meeting the needs of customers. The majority of customers responded positively to a question about whether they were receiving value-for-money (October 1992) and customer satisfaction levels have remained constant, at a time when they could easily have deteriorated. Furthermore, slightly more customers actually believe that services had improved rather than got worse during the six months prior to the October 1992 survey (ie during the year under contract), although it is true to say that the majority of people thought they had stayed much the same.

There has been a significant increase in the number of customers and improvements were noted with regard to the customer profile at the centre, (although the client would argue that a greater commitment to delivering equal opportunities in service delivery is still needed). Overall, therefore, the client would make a cautious assessment that the service at Newham Leisure Centre has slightly improved during the first

Table 3.3 Changes in previous six months

	%	
Improved a lot	8	23%
Improved a bit	15	
Stayed much the same	52	
Got a bit worse	4	6%
Got a lot worse	2	
No opinion	23	

Base = 507

year of contract. The extent to which this can be attributed to Compulsory Competitive Tendering legislation is more difficult to analyse, although the increased emphasis placed on budgetary control is most obviously linked to the legislation.

One can conclude by stating that an analysis of Newham Leisure Centre's first year of contract has resulted in some improvements to the service, with customer satisfaction remaining constant at a time of increasing pressure. At this stage, admittedly after only one year of a contract lasting a minimum of four years, it would appear as if the imposition of Compulsory Competitive Tendering has had some limited, but nevertheless positive effects on the service at Newham Leisure Centre.

Key points

- ▲ *The centre is situated in a challenging environment with implications for its mission and operation.*
- ▲ *The first year of the contract made under CCT has involved some reflective thinking by both client and contractor.*
- ▲ *There has been an increased focus on service delivery.*
- ▲ *Measurement of customer satisfaction has revealed little difference in customer perception since the start of the contract.*

Appendix A

The leisure centre building

The leisure centre building, which has full disabled access, was opened in May 1990 and has the following features:

Main Hall (32 m × 31 m × 10 m high)

The sports facilities include 8 Badminton Courts; 1 full size and 1 practice size Basketball Court; a full size and 2 practice size Netball Courts; 2 Volleyball Courts; Indoor Hockey Pitch.

The Main Hall also caters for Cricket, Archery, Short Tennis, Short

Mat Bowls, Table Tennis, Gymnastics, Trampolining, Roller Skating, and other sporting activities.

The Main Hall may be used for non-sporting purposes such as Entertainments, Exhibitions, Conferences etc, and has portable seating for 350, as well as a portable stage of 10.5 m × 8 m.

Swimming Pools

A Main Pool – (13 m × 25 m)

Six Lane Deck Level Pool with full access for people with disabilities.

A Learner Pool – (7 m × 13 m)

Both pools can be viewed from the nearby Spectator Area, which is 19 m × 3 m, and can seat 50 people. There is also an equipped First-Aid Room.

Sauna/Steam Suite

Consisting of 1 Steam Cabin and 1 Sauna Cabin, which together can accommodate up to 20 people at a time.

Fitness Room

An area of 16 m × 6 m containing 17 Schnell Resistance Machines, a range of cardio-vascular machines and a Disabilities Strength Training Machine.

Gill Gallery

A ground floor exhibition area of 100 sq metres available for art exhibitions and presentations. The Gallery has double sided, free standing display screens, and wall hanging space.

Supervised Play Area

An area approximately 52 sq metres in which children are able to play and learn while parents and carers use the centre. It has a range of creative learning toys, games and books.

Atrium

The focal point of the Centre which can be used as an extension to the Gill Gallery for exhibitions or to the Supervised Play Area. Covering an area of 188 sq metres the Atrium contains a Fig Tree as a special feature.

Regent Room

A large room (9 m × 20 m) available for a variety of purposes such as Fitness activities, Martial Arts, Dance and Movement, Parties, Receptions, Seminars and Meetings.

Cafeteria

Situated on the first floor, overlooking the pools, an area of approximately 272 sq metres. The Cafeteria serves food and non-alcoholic drinks.

Case study 3.3: Gran Dorado 'Port Zelande'

Key features

- *Commercial complex.*
- *Caters for tourists and local market.*
- *Business and product philosophy.*
- *Market niche.*
- *A model for survival.*

Background

Gran Dorado 'Port Zelande' is part of the larger enterprise Gran Dorado Leisure N.V. This complex consists of five different operating leisure centres and two still developing centres. The mission of Gran Dorado Leisure N.V. is to utilise holiday and leisure centres in Europe (currently four in Holland and one in Germany). Port Zelande is a facility built in the south west of The Netherlands near the border between provinces Zuid Holland and Zeeland. It is located near the North Sea and is built in a Mediterranean style; its facilities include 722 apartments.

The customers are encouraged to participate in an enormous variety of leisure activities. The way the organisation does this will be elaborated on in this section. Port Zelande has 230 full-time employees working in sports, recreation, catering, reception, shops, security, technical service and facility management. Gran Dorado tries to differentiate from other enterprises by mixing a leisure complex with a tourist facility; its combination of a diverse range of leisure facilities with a most attractive park setting has produced a synergetic effect – whether we see a blurring of leisure and tourism or the enhancement of one by the other. Furthermore, Port Zelande is aiming at a specific segment of the market; the target group are the people with more than average incomes. High standards of service and hospitality are seen as essential for attracting and retaining custom.

The organisational structure of Port Zelande reflects this commitment to customer service (see Figure 3.7). The customer is seen as the starting point from which Port Zelande attempts to reach the highest possible standards of service and quality, as the figure demonstrates.

Product

The product mix has three main components:

Accommodation
The accommodation for its tourists and business guests is an important factor in its quality reputation. By Dutch quality standards the total accommodation can be described as 5-star. There are 10 different types of living accommodation including 20 very luxurious VIP villas. Apart

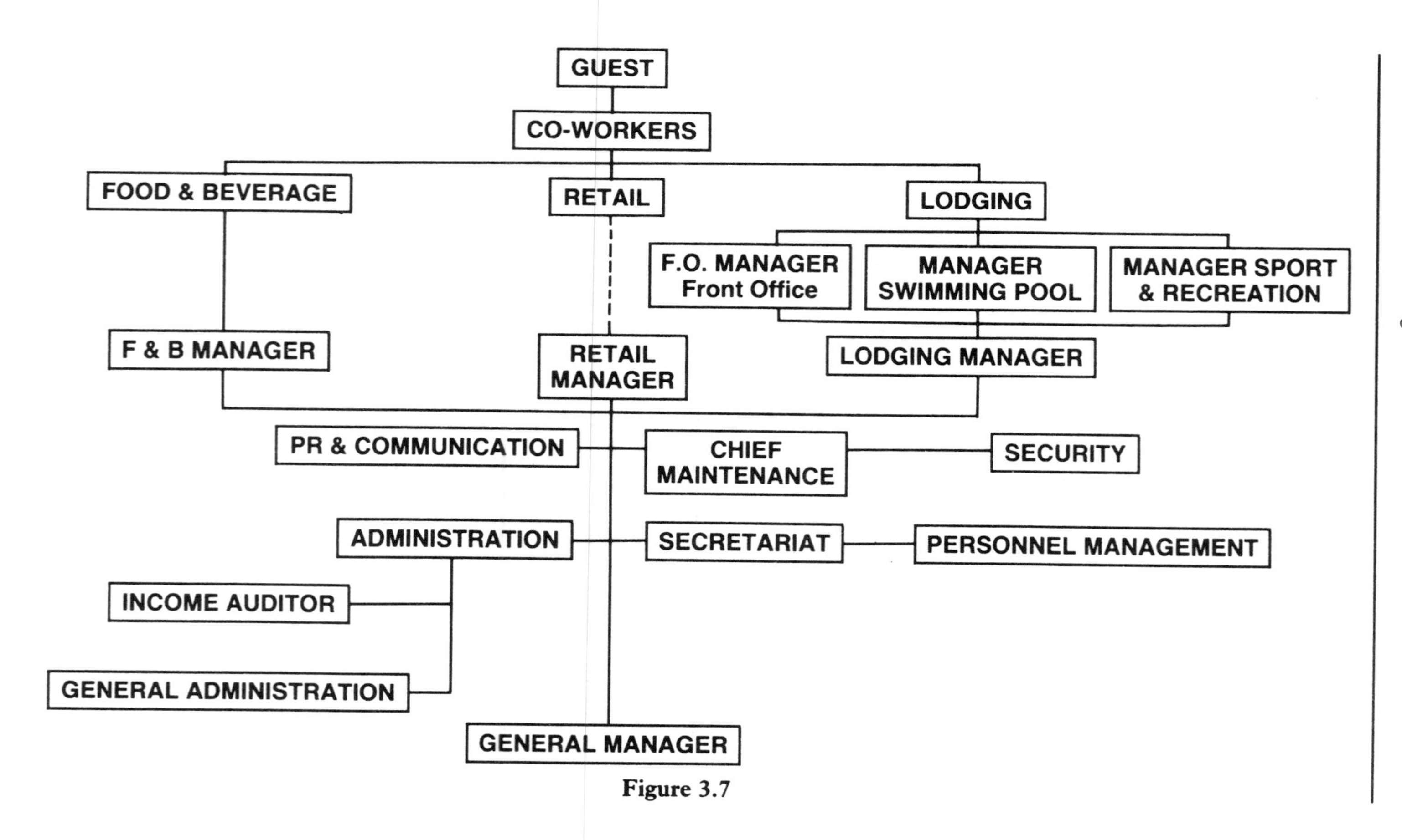
GUEST
CO-WORKERS
FOOD & BEVERAGE
RETAIL
LODGING
F.O. MANAGER
Front Office
MANAGER
SWIMMING POOL
MANAGER SPORT
& RECREATION
F & B MANAGER
RETAIL
MANAGER
LODGING MANAGER
PR & COMMUNICATION
CHIEF
MAINTENANCE
SECURITY
ADMINISTRATION
SECRETARIAT
PERSONNEL MANAGEMENT
INCOME AUDITOR
GENERAL ADMINISTRATION
GENERAL MANAGER

Figure 3.7

from being attractive to a certain niche market of tourists the standard of accommodation has also enabled the complex to break into the business conference and seminar market.

Aquatics
Port Zelande is located at the Kabbelaarsbank in the middle of Zuid Holland and Zeeland delta and between the North Sea and the Grevelingen lake (the largest salt water lake in Europe). It is an appropriate context for the aquatic facility 'Centre de Voille', which contains a luxurious yacht harbour for 650 boats. The main activities offered are sailing, surfing, canoeing, water-skiing, sea-fishing and diving. This impressive activity mix, together with its unique location between sea and lake, helps to explain appeal to all age groups.

Recreation and leisure centre 'Gran Place'
The indoor recreation facilities are located in two main buildings. The first building contains four tennis courts, four squash courts, a fitness room, a billiards and snooker room, a darts corner, a family games room, table tennis room, badminton courts and a volleyball field. There are also two opportunities for occupying children: a 3–7 year old creche; and an 8–13 year old meeting place.

The second building has a constant temperature of 27 degrees celsius which helps to explain the provision of the subtropical swimming pool with its wave-making facilities. It contains a sauna, Turkish steambath and Roman bathing hall as well as six tenpin bowling alleys and two skittle alleys. In front of both buildings an artificial skating track is installed every year between November and March. Finally, both buildings contain a variety of shops, restaurants and bars to cater for a range of groups.

Business and product philosophy

Its rationale and market position
The strategy of Port Zelande is derived from the corporate approach of Gran Dorado N.V. It aims at ownership, utilisation and development of a luxurious 5-star leisure centre in The Netherlands and Germany (new projects in Germany, France and the UK are under way).

The market positioning of these centres is reactive and influenced by the strategy of Gran Dorado Leisure N.V.'s largest competitor, Center Parcs (which has 60 per cent of the Dutch market). Gran Dorado tries to distinguish from its competitors in four ways:

- The attractiveness of its North Sea location. Facilities and architecture are adapted to the atmosphere of the location which is modelled on a Mediterranean (Cote d'Azur) style.
- The wider usage and open character of the centre. An important target group are the non-staying customers who are invited to use the variety of leisure facilities. In this way the facilities are used intensively in the off-season periods.

- The high standard of the accommodation – 'you pay a little more, but you get much more'.
- Its multivariate image offering choice of locations ('if you want sea you go to Port Zelande; if you want mountains and forest you go to Heilbachsee).

The business philosophy of Port Zelande

The staff of Port Zelande are regarded as the most precious asset of the organisation as it is through them that the product reaches the customer. Figure 3.8 shows the relationship between the most important stakeholders in the organisation.

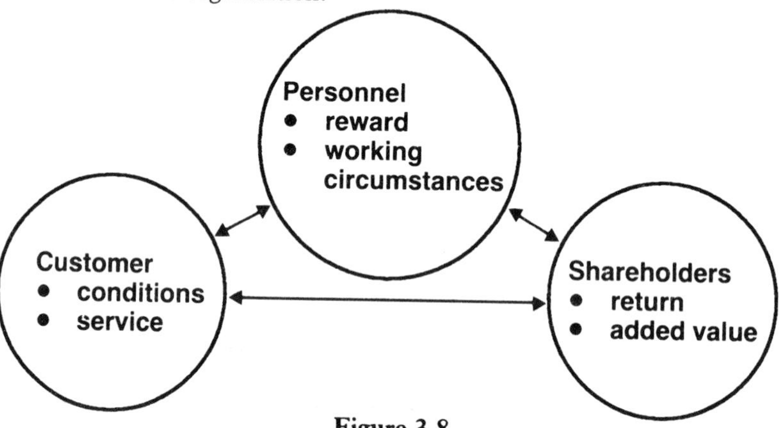

Figure 3.8
Business philosophy: balance between goals and interests of different stakeholders

Considerable resources are directed into training and staff development. Staff are expected to assimilate the philosophy and sense of mission of the organisation and much thought goes into providing rewarding and satisfying working conditions. Staff are encouraged to be creative and innovative; they are all given independence and responsibility and are given the opportunity for promotion or wider experience. It is significant that such a policy is firmly supported from the very top of the organisation.

The product philosophy of Port Zelande

Within the wider business philosophy of its holding company Port Zelande has a more specific approach towards its product or service concept. Its philosophy is encapsulated in the following 10 points:

1. quality in terms of value-for-money and meeting customer expectations

2. good communications
   - a clear message
   - clear signage
   - staff are visible
   - staff are seen as a source of information

3. a dynamic product
   - 365 days a year programme
   - a flexible programme
   - an imaginative product/activity mix
4. continuity of product
5. a differentiated product
   - style and character
   - a unique location
   - close, personal service
6. professionalism
   - knowledge and understanding
   - promises are kept
   - good customer care through well developed interpersonal skills
7. recognition (acknowledgement)
   - guests are treated as individuals
   - guests are made to feel at home
   - atmosphere is relaxed and informal
8. safety and security
   - security is visible
   - staff have had basic emergency training
   - staff are seen as competent
9. flexibility
   - anticipation of customers' needs and wants
   - everything is viewed from the customer's perspective
   - staff are there to solve customers' problems
10. openness and freedom
    - all nationalities welcome
    - a cosmopolitan atmosphere.

Quality and the staff/user interface

As the hierarchical organisational structure in Figure 3.7 implies, the customer is seen as the most important player in its operation. Staff are regarded as the most precious asset and the encounter between operational staff and customers as the most important transaction. In the context of this case study it is not possible to analyse the quality concept and the control methods of the organisation in any real depth; however, there are two particular features of Port Zelande's approach which merit some attention.

Firstly, quality through training and staff development:

- recruitment and selection of appropriate staff at all levels
- training to achieve and perform to consistent standards
- use of quality manuals
- high responsibility and authority at all levels

- close liaison and problem-solving through work co-ordination meetings.

Secondly, quality through extensive monitoring and evaluation:

- standard Gran Dorado questionnaires – general and accommodation
- verbal feedback based on spontaneous reactions from guests
- unannounced audits (with a specific brief)
- quality control of product and hygiene (eg food and beverage operations and water testing)
- invited panel of users (focus groups).

It is important to note that quality in The Netherlands has slightly different dimensions. Unlike BS 5750 and other quality systems which simply give assurance that standards will be adhered to, Dutch leisure centres can work to a benchmark or quality mark. The highest mark that can be awarded is a 5-star mark and Gran Dorado Port Zelande has achieved it.

Conclusions: Why Gran Dorado Port Zelande has achieved its quality mark

A simple model is used to illustrate the Port Zelande approach to quality (see Figure 3.9). It is called the FIT model and it implies that in order to survive, an organisation has to adapt to society on the one hand and to the individual (customer) on the other hand.

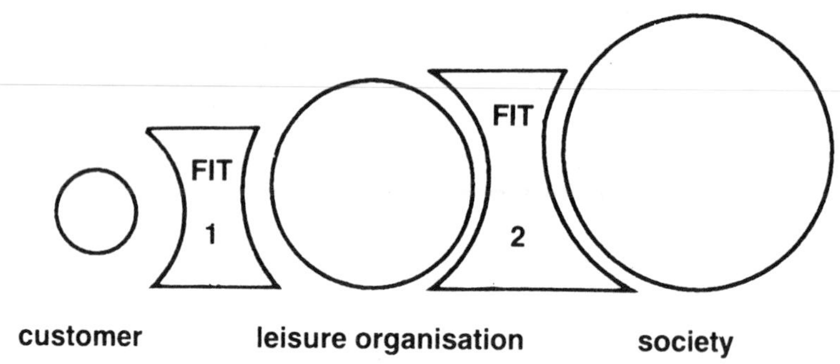

Figure 3.9
The FIT-model (Rubingh)

At FIT 1 a successful organisation has to fulfil individual customer requirements. At FIT 2 it has to be strategically alert to spot the trends in consumer behaviour and in society as a whole. The one problem for the organisation is that trends and individual needs can be at variance with one another from time to time. The history of Gran Dorado Port Zelande has told us that the need to be distinctive is vital in order for an organisation to survive. In the 1980s a trend developed in The Netherlands and other countries which has been described as the sportification of society. What is meant by this is that a number of social and cultural actions are transmitted through the means of sport and leisure. Dutch people were encouraged to take up new activities such as aerobics, snowboarding and other outdoor pursuits through the higher profile afforded sport. At the same time a number of new leisure centres rapidly emerged to meet the changing needs and motives of a more active population and to provide fairly inexpensive standardised opportunities. Gran Dorado Port Zelande searched very hard for a niche in the market as it, too, adapted to trends in society and endeavoured to satisfy individual customer needs.

Its marketing strategy embraced a wide range of potential customers but placed them in several market segments, with particular acknowledgement of the growing 'grey' market (a demographic trend in The Netherlands as in many other European countries). There are four main target groups together with their peak usage times:

- visiting families (children of non-school age)
  - holiday periods
  - weekends
- visiting families (children of school age)
  - Monday to Friday
  - out of season
- people with grown-up children
  - Monday to Friday
  - out of season
- people without children
  - Monday to Friday
  - weekends
  - holiday periods

Each target group is treated differently according to its needs and wants but with the highest possible standards of customer service. The essential characteristics of its products and services do not differ greatly from its competitors but the consumer experience can be distinguished by its unique location and its quality service delivery.

To summarise, the goal of quality customer service at Gran Dorado Port Zelande has been achieved through the combination of six key factors:

- attractive tourist environment
- attractive leisure environment also aimed at non-staying guests
- luxury standards of accommodation at reasonable prices
- good activity provision
- a sharply defined corporate image and message
- clear communication.

Port Zelande, as part of the larger organisation Gran Dorado Leisure N.V. has found a niche, dominated by its location, in the leisure centre market. It reflects societal trends and goes out of its way to satisfy individual needs. We saw how the structure of the organisation placed the customer at its head and how staff are regarded as the most precious asset the organisation possesses. Its management philosophy is the antithesis of a strict hierarchical approach that, perhaps, holds back individual enterprise and stifles flair and creativity. Gran Dorado Port Zelande has a flatter structure and a more organic and dynamic internal system. Empowered teams ('the total is more than the sum of the parts') have the autonomy to make their business units as successful as possible with every business unit manager responsible for his/her own budgets.

Personnel management aims at developing dependent, self-thinking and proactive staff who are equally responsible, with management, for company results. The concept of quality applies to both staff and the product; the customer is seen as the most important judge of that quality. The organisation can be typified as an organic, progressive one with a total quality management philosophy as its basis. The organisation is still very young and vulnerable. The prognosis, however, based on this analysis is a very positive and hopeful one.

Key points

- ▲ *The customer is at the head of the organisation structure.*
- ▲ *It has achieved a sharply defined market niche.*
- ▲ *There is much emphasis on customer feedback and internal monitoring.*
- ▲ *Empowerment and staff autonomy are important elements.*
- ▲ *Training and staff development are given priority.*
- ▲ *Product philosophy is well developed.*

Acknowledgement

The author is grateful to the following people who helped in the writing of this chapter:
Simon Parkinson Leisure Management Co-Ordinator, Newham Leisure Centre, London.
Hans Westerbeek Director, Sports Management Institute, Rijksuniversiteit Groningen, The Netherlands.

4 Health and fitness facilities

Dave Courteen

Introduction

The health and fitness industry has been one of the faster growing sectors of the leisure industry in recent years. Perceptions about facilities in the UK have evolved from the perceived seedy, back street, sweat shops attracting body builders to the prime site, fashionable clubs providing not only a range of exercise and relaxation facilities but also promoting health and education services to appeal to a broader sector of the community.

This chapter will investigate three health and fitness facilities in Europe, each serving a slightly different market niche. The *Thomas Cook Leisure Centre* in Peterborough is a corporate fitness facility developed to service the health and fitness needs of the employees. The *Livingwell Club* is based in Milton Keynes and is a stand alone private membership club geared towards providing a quality service for the local community. The final case study is the *Hans and Olaf Clinic* in Oslo, Norway, which is also a private members club but with a medical and injury rehabilitation bias.

The case studies of these clubs will look at the key areas of their philosophy, design and layout, operation, marketing and management and staffing.

Whilst each club has been analysed individually, it is hoped that it will be possible to highlight both the similarities and differences between the delivery of health and fitness facilities in Europe and the UK.

Case study 4.1: Thomas Cook Leisure Centre. A corporate case study

Key features

▲ *Corporate fitness facility.*
▲ *Staff well being.*
▲ *Vigorous commercial management.*

- ▲ *Lifestyle studio.*
- ▲ *Personalised service.*
- ▲ *Flexible membership.*
- ▲ *Extensive marketing.*
- ▲ *Quality circles.*

Origins

In 1987, when the chief executive of Thomas Cook announced to his staff at headquarters in Peterborough that the company was to develop a new corporate fitness facility, the most optimistic employee could hardly have envisaged the quality and size of facility that they now enjoy.

The Thomas Cook Leisure Centre opened in June 1989 and cost the company approximately £4 million to complete. Previously the employees had the use of outdoor playing fields, comprising football, hockey, cricket and tennis courts and a small social club with basic changing rooms and a bar. The headquarters building backs on to the Ferry Meadows Country Park enabling the employees to enjoy these additional extensive recreational facilities.

The company already owned the land on which the new leisure club was to be built and the new facility, comprising some 2,500 square metres, could be housed in an area that only affected the existing social club.

The leisure centre is primarily available for employees and pensioners of Thomas Cook, its parent company, Midland Bank, and their families; but in the past year a limited number of memberships have been made available through private or corporate subscription.

Philosophy

So, what were the motivating factors behind the decision to spend so much money on corporate fitness facilities? The potential benefits to a company of a corporate fitness programme are well documented but, perhaps, less well proven.

For Thomas Cook, the costs in developing the purpose built facility were reduced because they already owned the land on which it was to be built, but, nevertheless, the £4 million spent still represented a major commitment by the company. Like many corporate fitness projects the initial motivation and drive for the facility came from the highest level and Thomas Cook's chief executive was convinced of the benefits that the centre could bring to the company.

The decision to provide the facility is borne out by the Thomas Cook *mission statement*. This mission is simply to create the best and most profitable travel-driven service business in the world. The company recognises that to achieve this they have to have the best staff. The leisure facility, it hopes, not only helps to enable the staff to give of their best but also ensures that quality staff are attracted to, and retained by, the company. The retention of quality staff is particularly important in Peterborough, which enjoys relatively low levels of unemployment amongst the skilled, clerical workers that Thomas Cook require.

The company decided from the outset to apply a vigorous commercial management approach to the provision of these leisure facilities and services. The standards of service provided by the leisure centre are subject to the same commitment to excellence that applies to the provision of Thomas Cook's travel service for its customers.

The leisure centre is expected to break even on its operating costs and in order to meet this requirement membership has been extended to 'external' members, ie individuals who do not meet the criteria of being either an employee or pensioner of Thomas Cook or Midland Bank or part of their immediate families. Whilst the intention was always to offer limited external memberships, the number of members in this category has increased to approximately 800 two years after opening to help achieve the break even objective. The company maintains, however, that it will always attempt to keep the membership open primarily for its employees' benefit. To this effect, a significant number of external members are restricted to using the centre at 'off-peak' periods.

The leisure centre is also expected to achieve certain other goals. As discussed, fulfilling the aims of the corporate mission statement depends upon the retention of quality staff and the company hopes that the provision of corporate leisure facilities will result in a reduction of staff turnover at the Peterborough headquarters.

The centre is expected to improve staff awareness about the benefit of a healthy lifestyle and as such sees its role as a 'motivator' rather than 'provider' of leisure facilities.

Thomas Cook also want to create a sense of family involvement with the company whilst demonstrating to employees and to the outside world that it is a caring employer.

John Adams, the leisure centre director, reflects this aim when he states:

> 'We feel that we are here to care for people in the widest sense in that we provide for our employees to do what they want with their leisure time.
>
> It also allows us to focus in on the family. In most work situations the employee's family, spouse, children, have very little involvement with a company that may be the main source of income for the family unit. By involving the whole family in the leisure centre the company is able to acknowledge the contribution of the family unit to the success of the company.
>
> Our care also extends to the health and well being of our employees. Through the fitness studio we can tailor exercise regimes to the personal requirements of each individual.'

In order to realise these aims, the leisure centre personnel are set clear objectives:

- to complement the first class physical environment provided by the leisure centre complex through the provision of a first class service to users of the recreational leisure and social facilities
- to maximise the use of the facilities
- to maximise the public relations and promotional possibilities

provided by the leisure centre for the benefit of the company and especially in relation to staff recruitment policies
- to develop the facilities initially established in line with identified user requirements
- to ensure that the facilities are maintained in a top-class condition and are used safely.

As a non-employee it is difficult to accurately analyse how successful the leisure centre is in achieving its objectives. Certainly, the impression of the centre created when it is visited is of a clean and efficient environment. The programme range is guaranteed to offer something appealing to all, and the usage figures would indicate that at 'peak' periods the centre is close to full utilisation. The standard of service provided by the staff would match that of any successful private sector club operating to generate profit.

Design and layout

The facilities comprise swimming pool, fitness studio, sports hall, two squash courts, sauna, sunbed and also a lounge and bar area serving food and snacks throughout the day. Integral to the leisure centre is a purpose built day-nursery, conference rooms and an accommodation unit of three-star standard. A well stocked shop sells a range of sports and leisure wear.

The entrance to the centre leads into the bright and warm reception area housing a computerised membership and administration system. All members are admitted by a swipe card system which prevents abuse of the membership system and provides valuable management feedback on usage analysis, regularity of visits etc.

From the reception area the non-sporting members can head straight upstairs to the 'Pyramids' social lounge and bar. The standard of decor and furnishing would grace any three-star hotel with a bar that is both long enough and sufficiently well staffed to prevent queuing even at the busiest times.

Aside from providing the standard bar menu and pastries, the area also provides a full breakfast service for employees who want to workout early morning before commencing their duties at the office.

Entertainment and special events are a regular feature of the programme in the lounge which also has a secluded patio to offer summer barbecues.

The lounge also provides an 'under 10's den' – a safe play area for younger children which can be used as a creche while parents are busy pursuing their leisure activities.

The centre has three changing areas: for outdoor playing fields, for 'dry' indoor facilities, and for 'wet' facilities. All are well laid out with provisions for young children and babies in both male and female areas.

The 'Oasis' pool hall is located to the rear of the building and looks out onto the patio area and the country park beyond. The facilities comprise a spa pool, 10 m learner pool, sauna and 25 m main pool. The pools are deck level and treated with ozone to ensure bather comfort.

The centre also ensures the maximum level of safety by supervising the area at all times with fully qualified lifeguards backed up by closed circuit television monitoring and a radio paging alarm system.

Lifestyle fitness studio

On the ground floor of the building the sports hall and 'Lifestyle' fitness studio are housed. The latter contains over 30 pieces of exercise equipment, split almost equally between cardio-vascular machines such as treadmills, electronic exercise bikes, rowers and stair climbers and individual weight training resistance equipment. Although the vast range of equipment may at first seem a little daunting to the novice exerciser, the room is bright, carpeted, air conditioned and has mirrored walls to create a feeling of openness; this, together with separate stereo and colour video, ensures the emphasis is upon exercising for enjoyment and relaxation rather than portraying a 'sweat shop' image.

All employees and members wishing to use the 'Lifestyle' studio are given a pre-exercise screening with a medical questionnaire and fitness assessment, undertaken in a separate room nearby which also provides first-aid facilities. The assessment is used not only to provide information for the instructor to safely design an individual's exercise programme, but can also be used to motivate members in the maintenance of their exercise programmes or quantifying improvements in health and fitness that have occurred since their exercise programmes were first begun.

Once again, the centre's priority on safety is evident; the 'Lifestyle' studio is fully supervised at all times, with closed circuit television and radio paging alarm systems in line with the pool hall. The studio also has wall mounted heart rate monitors which can be used by everyone during their workout to ensure they are training within the safe, predetermined target heart rate zones.

Sports hall

Across the corridor from the exercise studio are the remaining sports facilities. A sports hall large enough to contain four badminton courts offers a programme of varied activities. A comprehensive range of dance, exercise and aerobic classes combine with volleyball, basketball, hockey, football, tennis, badminton, netball and long mat bowls. The hall can be divided into zones by netting to allow for simultaneous multi-activity use of the hall. An overhead canopy is also available to allow for projectile sports such as cricket or archery.

The hall is overlooked by a viewing gallery, but, again, the emphasis is on participation rather than spectating. The gallery houses both pool and table tennis tables and in the school holidays it is used for fun sessions for children on Saturdays.

Behind the gallery and the sports hall are two squash courts and a sunbed with a built-in stereo system helping users to relax to music while they tan.

Overall the centre is well laid out, clean and with adequate signage to ensure that facilities are easily found.

Operation

The leisure centre is expected to operate at break even. In order to achieve this, the employees pay for usage of the facilities. It could be argued that, irrespective of whether the facility has to break even or not, the policy of charging for corporate leisure facilities, albeit at below market rates, is of benefit. If something is given away for nothing it is perceived to be of no value yet if the facility is charged for then the value becomes appreciated.

The membership structure of Thomas Cook Leisure Centre is designed to suit the varying needs of employees. Initially membership was divided into four distinct categories. These categories have now been extended as the varied needs of members have become more apparent, and it was felt that employees required more choice.

As can be seen from Table 4.1, the bronze membership is free from any monthly fees. It is available to all employees, pensioners of Thomas Cook and Midland Bank and their families, who simply pay for the facilities as they use them.

The silver membership requires payment of a monthly fee which is debited from salary. It entitles members to reduced session fees on most facilities.

The gold membership is the most expensive in terms of monthly fees. It is aimed at individuals who use the club on a regular basis as use of the swimming pool, fitness studio and aerobics classes are free. Gold membership has been further subdivided to provide employees with more choice and to maximise the selling potential of gold membership. Employees can now buy a type of gold membership that only gives them free access to one or two named facilities out of the fitness studio, swimming pool and aerobics. Thus, if the fitness studio usage becomes maximised then the 'gold fitness' membership is closed, but the centre can still sell gold memberships giving free access to just the swimming pool or just aerobic classes.

Currently, two years after opening, the centre has 3,800 staff and family members with approximately 50 per cent on bronze membership, 22 per cent on silver membership and 28 per cent on the various gold memberships.

The 'external' memberships available to non-employees are offered on the same basis but at a higher price. The membership tariff is, on average, 230 per cent of the tariff for employees. The centre has about 800 external members with a further 400 on a reserve list waiting for a place to become available.

Whatever the category of membership, all administration is controlled by the reception team located at the centre of the building. It is from here that all bookings are taken for the various facilities. Whilst all facilities are well used, it is perhaps the sports hall and fitness studio which are in most demand.

At present the various exercise classes, which are extremely popular, are held in the sports hall thereby reducing the capacity for other popular sports such as badminton etc. The centre is currently planning to alleviate this problem by converting the gallery overlooking the sports

THOMAS COOK LEISURE CENTRE

MEMBERSHIP FEES AND SESSION CHARGES 1990

CATEGORY	PRIVILEGES	MONTHLY CHARGE		SWIMMING POOLS SAUNA, SPA POOL	SQUASH COURT PER 40 MIN	BADMINTON COURT PER 1 HOUR	LIFESTYLE FITNESS GYM	AEROBICS	INDOOR BOWLS PER MAT 1 HOUR	TABLE TENNIS PER TABLE PER 1 HOUR	SOLARIUM PER 20 MIN	SPECIAL EVENTS
BRONZE	Access to social lounge, Use of outdoor changing	ADULT STAFF	FREE	1.50	2.00	2.00	3.00	2.00	2.00	1.00	4.00	SEE NOTICE BOARD FOR DETAILS OF SPECIAL EVENTS & DISCOUNTS
		2ND ADULT CARD	FREE	1.50	2.00	2.00	3.00	2.00	2.00	1.00	4.00	
	STANDARD RATES	CHILDREN	FREE	0.70	2.00	2.00	1.50	1.00	2.00	1.00	-	
SILVER	Access to social lounge, Use of outdoor changing, Six day court booking	ADULT STAFF	1.00	1.00	2.00	2.00	1.50	1.50	2.00	1.00	3.00	
		2ND ADULT CARD	0.50	1.00	2.00	2.00	1.50	1.50	2.00	1.00	3.00	
	SILVER DISCOUNT RATES	CHILDREN	FREE	0.50	2.00	2.00	0.70	0.70	2.00	1.00	-	
GOLD	Access to social lounge, Use of outdoor changing, Six day court booking, Free swimming, Free Gym Free Aerobics	ADULT STAFF	10.00	FREE	2.00	2.00	FREE	FREE	2.00	1.00	3.00	
		2ND ADULT CARD	5.00	FREE	2.00	2.00	FREE	FREE	2.00	1.00	3.00	
	GOLD DISCOUNT RATES	CHILDREN	2.00	FREE	2.00	2.00	FREE	FREE	2.00	1.00	-	

Table 4.1 Thomas Cook Leisure Centre. Membership fees and session charges 1990

hall into a new, larger fitness studio. The existing fitness studio area can then be used for exercise classes freeing more time for other sports in the sports hall.

Thomas Cook has an active sports and social club operating many teams, such as volleyball, basketball, badminton and table tennis, competing in local leagues whose facility requirements and fixture commitments must be met; this can obviously slightly compromise the availability of the sports hall for casual use by leisure club members. In general, the policy pursued is to try and fit club bookings into 'off peak' times, but, undoubtedly, some conflict of interest does occur.

The *fitness studio* is operated on a highly personalised basis. Each user is given an individual one-to-one introduction to the fitness studio. This introduction comprises a medical questionnaire, discussion of personal exercise objectives, prescription of personal exercise programmes followed by the client being guided through the prescribed workout. The leisure professional responsible for the introductory workout then becomes that person's personal tutor. The use of the personal tutor creates an atmosphere of mutual participation between instructors and client who should feel that someone is taking a special responsibility for them. It also helps to spread the work of monitoring usage and updating clients' programmes.

The instructor in the fitness studio will aim to talk to each client a minimum of three times during each workout:

- when they arrive to analyse their programme and decide what they are doing that day
- while they are working out to ensure that they are happy with the programme
- as they leave to collect their programme and make any changes as necessary.

A computerised fitness assessment is also offered as part of the fitness studio service. Assessments are usually carried out at six-monhtly intervals and are intended to be motivational in terms of quantifying an individuals fitness improvement.

The fitness studio also tries to keep exercisers motivated through a regular series of promotions and events. These promotions are designed to record regular exercise. Included in this are events such as 'member of the month' to reward a specific personal exercise objective/goal that a member may have achieved, and a 'race' from Peterborough to Santa's grotto in Lapland held at Christmas and related to distances covered on cardio-vascular equipment.

The level of attention given to members in the fitness studio is difficult to criticise. The fitness personnel seem able to relate well to all clientele and it is this skill, coupled with the high operational standards, to which one can attribute the high number of previously sedentary people who are now exercising successfully and regularly in this area.

The *swimming pool* is perhaps the most universally popular facility at the centre. The facility is fully supervised at all times by qualified lifeguards. A range of swimming lessons and fun sessions are arranged throughout the week according to demand but at least two lanes are left available for casual swimmers thereby preventing a conflict of interest. The only occasion the pool is closed off for exclusive use is at off peak times for the water polo club and for adult beginners swimming lessons.

Marketing

At first hand, the marketing of a corporate leisure facility may appear fairly straightforward. The entire catchment population, ie the employees, are in the same place over the same period of time and will literally pass by the club's doors every working day. However, there is an inherent danger that a significant proportion of employees will actually do just that – pass by the facility and not use it.

At the development stage of the facility, the leisure centre management researched other existing corporate fitness facilities and highlighted the fact that one of the major problems was converting sedentary employees into regular users who would in turn provide the company with the benefits of a fitter workforce. Many corporate facilities it seems only provided cheaper and more convenient exercise facilities for employees who would be exercising irrespective of whether corporate leisure facilities were provided or not.

Market research

The company, therefore, decided that the first stage of marketing must be to attempt to outline the specific needs of the workforce, their current exercise habits and their health interests and concerns. To achieve this a questionnaire was circulated to every Thomas Cook employee. A copy of the questionnaire is shown in Figure 4.1. Apart from providing the required feedback on employee needs, the questionnaire also achieved two other goals. Firstly, it gave employees a sense of ownership of the leisure centre. They did not feel that the new facility was something being imposed upon them by authoritarian management, but rather a project for them and in which they had a direct influence to suit their particular needs. Further to this, the questionnaire also made employees aware of the potential benefits they could individually enjoy from using the centre. To many sedentary employees, the leisure centre had been seen as a project for 'fit' people and not a place where they could seek relief from stress, back pain, obesity etc.

The message

From the outset it had been decided that the employees would contribute to the operating costs of the facility. This policy would ensure that there was a two-way commitment between the company and employees – the company had shown its commitment to provide the facility and the employees were demonstrating their commitment by contributing to its upkeep.

Obviously a key initial marketing concept was to promote the payment aspect in a positive way. This was partly achieved by regular distribution of information leaflets to all staff detailing all decisions that had been made and explaining the reasons for imposing charges. One of the most successful messages to be put across revolved around the

THOMAS COOK LEISURE CENTRE

As part of our planning for the Leisure Centre we are sending the enclosed questionnaire to all staff. I would be grateful if you could complete and return to me by 27th April. Thank you.

Ian Thompson

IAN THOMPSON
SPORTS SERVICES MANAGER

QUESTIONNAIRE

1. PERSONAL DETAILS

SEX

Female ☐
Male ☐

AGE ____________

LOCATION

Thorpe Wood	☐	Other Peterborough	☐
Coningsby Road	☐	Midland Bank	☐
Aragon Court	☐	Other	☐

2. DO YOU CURRENTLY TAKE PART IN ANY ACTIVE SPORT OR CONTROLLED EXERCISE OR USE SOCIAL FACILITIES REGULARLY.

	SPORTS			SOCIAL FACILITIES		
	Self	Partner	Children	Self	Partner	Children
Three or more times a week	☐	☐	☐	☐	☐	☐
Once - three times a week	☐	☐	☐	☐	☐	☐
Once a fortnight	☐	☐	☐	☐	☐	☐
Once a month or less	☐	☐	☐	☐	☐	☐
Never	☐	☐	☐	☐	☐	☐
Don't Know	☐	☐	☐	☐	☐	☐

Figure 4.1

4. PLEASE INDICATE, IF YOU INTEND TO USE THE SPORTS FACILITIES, WHICH ACTIVITY YOU WILL MOST LIKELY PARTICIPATE IN?

INDOOR		OUTDOOR	
Workout in fitness gym	❑	Team Sport	❑
Team Sports eg,basketball/netball	❑	Tennis	❑
Exercise class eg, aerobics	❑	Bowls	❑
Squash	❑	Cycling	❑
Swimming	❑	Running/Walking	❑
Badminton	❑	Croquet	❑
Indoor Bowls	❑		
Table Tennis	❑	I am not interested in the Centre	❑
Sunbed	❑		

5. IF YOU ARE NOT INTENDING TO USE THE CENTRE PLEASE STATE THE MAIN REASON WHY?

____

____

6. PLEASE INDICATE ANY OF THE FOLLOWING WELLNESS PROGRAMMES WHICH MAY BE OF INTEREST TO YOU. YOU CAN CHOOSE AS MANY AS YOU LIKE.

Weight and fat loss	❑
Stress relief	❑
Nutrition/dietary control	❑
Back care	❑
Smoking cessation	❑
Alcohol control	❑
Healthy heart/blood pressure	❑

7. HOW BENEFICIAL DO YOU THINK THE NEW LEISURE CENTRE WILL BE TO YOU AS PART OF THE BENEFITS OF EMPLOYMENT WITH THOMAS COOK?

NO BENEFIT				VERY BENEFICIAL
1	2	3	4	5

8. PLEASE LIST BELOW ANY SUGGESTIONS YOU MAY HAVE FOR THE OPERATION OF THE LEISURE CENTRE.

____

____

Figure 4.1 (continued)

principle that those who used the centre the most should pay the most for it was important. By helping to fund the operation of the facility through paying for usage, the subsidy from the company would be reduced. Any subsidies the company put into the centre would attract a taxable benefit in kind applied to each and every member of staff, irrespective of whether or not they used the centre. This argument also helped to appease those employees opposed to the development of the centre, objecting on the grounds of company money being invested in a corporate perk that they felt would not benefit all employees.

Marketing plan

As the opening of the centre approached, a specific marketing plan was put into action. Its goals were as follows:

- to educate employees in the benefits of using the centre
- to develop awareness of all services the centre was offering
- to create desire to use the centre
- to convert as many employees as possible into the paying membership categories, ie silver and gold.

The plan was put into action over the 10 weeks preceding the opening and used a number of tactics to achieve its objectives.

A poster campaign was operated whereby posters were placed around the offices displaying the number of weeks left to the opening of the centre and announcing a benefit of regular exercise. The posters were changed on a weekly basis. Along with the educational message, the posters were intended to stimulate a feeling of anticipation and expectation as the opening day approached.

A series of fitness promotion days were held in the main foyer of the office building. The promotion comprised a stand displaying information on the centre which was staffed by leisure centre personnel. This enabled them to build up a rapport with employees and answer directly any queries or misgivings that employees may have had about using the centre. Employees were also given the chance to workout on a hi-tech exercise cycle from the fitness studio and have their heartrate monitored. This highlighted to some not only how unfit they were and how much they could benefit from exercise, but also the high levels of safety and care that they would receive while exercising at the centre.

Following on from the fitness promotion days, a series of tours were arranged for employees in small groups to be shown around the centre by one of the leisure personnel. This provided a direct selling opportunity and was the most effective way of demonstrating the quality of both product and service that the centre would be providing. It was particularly useful in helping to remove any fears or misconceptions about the fitness studio that sedentary employees may have had.

The pre-opening marketing plan was fairly simple to implement, but nevertheless appeared to be effective given that after four months of operation the centre had enrolled 2,420 members onto the 'gold' and 'silver' membership categories. These were the categories to which employees contributed a monthly subscription and exceeded budget projections, forming 74 per cent of the total membership.

Information
Despite the relative success of this plan, the centre continues to market its services to employees through a number of media. A display board is allocated specifically for the use of the leisure centre in a strategic position in the foyer of the main office building and all news of forthcoming events and programmes are displayed there.

A regular newsletter is also produced and distributed to all staff containing articles on health and fitness information together with details of programmes on offer.

The centre continues to promote the benefits of a healthy lifestyle through various courses and promotions linked into national campaigns, eg smoking cessation advice tied in with the national no smoking day. These courses are run by leisure centre personnel with the assistance of external advisors where necessary and, it is hoped, will help entice sedentary employees to visit the leisure centre and commence a regular exercise programme.

It could be considered that the most important marketing programme would be to attract external members to the leisure centre. In fact, it appears that this is not the case. Although the centre now has 800 external members, it has done no specific marketing to attract them except for holding basic promotional leaflets and information brochures at the centre reception. All external members have been generated by referrals, local awareness of the facility through local press reports, and Thomas Cook sports teams competing in local leagues against private clubs. Indeed, such is the demand for membership that the centre currenty has 400 people on a waiting list hoping to secure a place as an external member.

Management and staffing

The leisure centre employs just over 40 staff divided into three distinct teams: a bar and catering team, a management and supervisory team, and an administration team based at the centre's reception.

The whole operation is overseen by a Leisure Centre Director and below him are three managers for each of the three teams previously described. Thomas Cook, as a company, assigns its employees differing role levels according to ability, performance and responsibility, on which salary scales are based. This precipitates a *cluster or team organisational structure* rather than a definitive hierarchical system, a policy borne out by the leisure centre and the staff where a good camaraderie and sense of teamwork exist.

Initially the team system did have its problems, however, with the three teams being insular and protective of their own responsibilities. The communication between teams was not good and this led to misunderstandings, particularly between the leisure management and the administration teams. The problems appear to have been resolved by the introduction of centre team meetings involving all staff and, more significantly, the formation of a quality circle. This quality circle contained representatives from each team and met primarily to discuss methods of improving the quality of all of the centre's services. The open forum also led to a greater understanding of each team's responsibilities and difficulties and to better staff relations. Furthermore, staff turnover amongst the leisure personnel has been low.

It is interesting to note that the recruitment of leisure personnel was mainly done internally. This was done partly to keep the total payroll numbers down but also because the management felt that the centre should be operated by individuals who had an understanding of the company, and also with whom potential employee users could relate. This factor could have significantly contributed to the successful conversion, at the initial stages, of so many sedentary employees into regular users.

One problem of this, however, was that the leisure personnel had to undergo significant *retraining* to be able to undertake the duties required, especially in relation to supervising the fitness studio and poolside. This training was administered in a five week period prior to opening and involved achieving an RLSS Bronze Medallion, First-Aid at Work qualification together with significant exercise prescription training. The initial training was supplemented with both internal and external training once the centre was open; indeed, some staff are now attending day release leisure training courses at local colleges.

Whilst it may be questionable whether the quantity of training was sufficient, it can only be judged by the outcome: from opening, the centre has been noticeably successful in converting sedentary employees into regular exercisers and, to date, there have been no accidents or injuries attributable to poor advice or unsuitable exercise programmes. These factors suggest that the staff team are well trained.

Summary

The Thomas Cook Leisure Centre is a facility which, in terms of both quality of provision and quality of staffing, must compare favourably with any corporate leisure facility in the UK. It represents a massive commitment to the welfare of its employees. The company sees its commitment as ongoing and is continually looking at ways of improving the service; not only through such basic steps as employee surveys, suggestion boxes and complaints books, but also through research. As this case study was being undertaken the company, in conjunction with the University of Sheffield, has embarked on 'Project Step Up', a research project aimed at proving the benefits of the leisure centre to both employees and the organisation as a whole.

It is perhaps appropriate to conclude with Thomas Cook's own slogan, which the leisure centre certainly does reflect: 'a new concept in corporate care'.

Key points

▲ *The facility is run commercially but is designed to enhance the well-being of members.*

- ▲ *The centre prides itself on keeping as close as possible to members needs and wants.*
- ▲ *It offers a good mix of facilities, activities and a one-to-one service.*
- ▲ *Many staff are recruited from within the Thomas Cook organisation because of their empathy for members needs.*
- ▲ *They benefit from specific training and open communication.*

Case study 4.2: Livingwell Health Club – Milton Keynes

Key features

- ▲ *One of seven in an American chain.*
- ▲ *Distinctive philosophy.*
- ▲ *Membership only.*
- ▲ *Customer-driven approach.*
- ▲ *Flat organisational structure.*
- ▲ *Training.*

Origins

Just over three years ago the taste of health and fitness came to the UK, American style. 'Livingwell' was one of the first American owned and operated health clubs to be established in the UK. At present, the company now has seven clubs in this country; the others are in London and Manchester and are within four Hilton hotels.

Livingwell UK is a wholly owned subsidiary of the Livingwell Company in America, where the company operates the 'Houstonian', a massive health and fitness club in Houston, Texas, which the company claims is the most profitable in the USA and employs the holder of the IRSA Fitness Director of the Year title.

It is, perhaps, appropriate that Milton Keynes was chosen as the location for the first club as it is about the most Americanised conurbation in the UK. Built in a grid pattern, Milton Keynes is a series of satellite developments all linked by roadways and paths, revolving around a central business, shopping and entertainment area. It is in this central area that the Winter Gardens are to be found. Aside from the Livingwell Club, the Winter Gardens house a number of other outlets including restaurants, a nightclub and a bar all controlled by Livingwell UK.

The Winter Gardens have an impressive wedge shaped structure and a glass lift which takes the prospective visitor from the central concourse to the health club entrance on the ground floor.

The health club comprises about 22,000 sq feet of facilities designed to appeal to a broad spectrum of the local community, both business and residential.

Philosophy

Livingwell believed in bringing American ideas on fitness to the UK market. It is widely acknowledged that the boom in fitness facilities occurred earlier in America and, as such, their methods and standards of operation have been generally more advanced than those in the UK.

The size and scale of the operation was, initially, larger than any other health and fitness facility provided by a UK operator. The club has three main areas that are the foci of its operation: selling membership, the consistent achievement of high standards of client service and care, and a commitment to improving the health and fitness of its members.

1. The club's attitude to *selling* is certainly very professional. It has a dedicated sales force whose sole responsibility is selling membership. The sales strategy revolves round the personal selling skills of its sales staff and their ability to make potential members aware of the benefits of joining.

2. The customer care programme permeates the whole of the club, from its reception team to its fitness instructors. The club sets down clear customer care guidelines and then gives staff incentive programmes to motivate them to keep those standards.

3. Livingwell believes it is not just sufficient to provide the health and fitness facilities but sees its role as a 'motivator' to assist exercise adherence. This is borne out by the company's mission statement: 'to supply health and fitness to improve the quality of life'. To this end, the club operates a comprehensive education and seminar programme on health-related topics to supplement the programmes and exercise advice provided in the fitness studio.

Livingwell's philosophy is based on an *holistic* approach. The provision of health and fitness facilities is only a small step towards improving the quality of an individual's life. Livingwell attempts to go beyond this to address the other issues such as diet and stress management, for example, which are of equal importance in achieving a quality lifestyle.

The importance of the Livingwell staff in delivering their philosophy is not to be underestimated. The company refers to its employees as associates, implying a sense of partnership between the two. The Livingwell philosophy is perhaps best explained in the four goals it issues to its 'associates':

- to anticipate, listen and respond honestly to members' needs, so that their expectations may be met or surpassed in the most efficient, effective way possible.
- to have a positive long-term effect on members' 'Life Quality' by increasing the perception of the value of exercise, nutrition and self-image through education, support, quality programming and the provision of the highest quality facilities.
- to create and support the ultimate professional environment by encouraging personal and professional growth. To place the

highest value on those associates who demonstrate consummate standards of honesty, dedication, creativity, integrity and innovation in the performance of any job related action. To encourage a focus on a balanced work experience that is both rewarding and enjoyable.

- to produce the most profitable return possible on the investment of time, energy and capital that is associated with the development and operation of our business.

The Livingwell vision therefore is clearly one of 'making life better'.

Design and layout

The Livingwell Health Club is based in the Winter Gardens at Milton Keynes. The *entrance* to the club is below the main concourse of the complex and is reached by either a glass lift or staircase. Whichever route is chosen, the visitor has to walk through an indoor 'botanical' garden with fountains and ponds. The effect of this accentuates the different ambience between the hustle and bustle of central Milton Keynes, that has just been left behind, to the relaxed atmosphere of the club. Irrespective of whether this was a deliberate policy, it is certainly an effective means in ensuring that the visitor's first impressions are of a relaxed, healthy environment. The foyer of the club is light and airy with the reception area to the left. A long reception desk ensures minimal queuing enabling customers to walk up to the counter where there always appears to be at least two receptionists on duty. Behind the reception area is a glass window which overlooks the 23 metre swimming pool. This is an effective piece of asset marketing as the first-time visitor cannot help being impressed by its luxurious appearance.

The *foyer* area also houses a pro shop, the bar and lounge in open plan style. This design gives the club a 'busy' atmosphere. By being near the entrance, the bar and lounge become a natural place to meet for a pre- or post-workout drink. There is a limited menu of snacks and a salad bar available together with soft drink and alcoholic beverages. The lounge is comfortable with a TV and selection of daily newspapers available to read.

The *pro shop* offers sports clothing, sports shoes, swimwear and together with other operating accessories provides the club with a significant profit centre. Although only small in size, it is undoubtedly its location in the main foyer, by the entrance, that ensures significant passing trade is serviced.

Once through reception there is a 2,500 sq foot fully air-conditioned *exercise class studio* to the right, with mirrored walls and a cushioned floor. Like the pool it is clearly visible from the main walkway helping to create a positive impression with the first time visitor. The club opens out at one end to a 6,000 sq foot gymnasium containing a proliferation of exercise equipment. There are about 30 pieces of resistance equipment from various manufacturers and about 50 pieces of cardio-vascular equipment, including treadmills, rowers, cycles, steppers and climbers. Circling the workout area is a 100 m indoor running track. The gym is divided into two by an open plan staircase which takes the visitor from the walkway to the workout floor. The floor is carpeted and the workout area is surrounded by plants to perhaps add to the 'Winter Gardens' feel. An area of the gymnasium is given over to free weights and it is possible for the club to appeal to body builders and serious trainers as well as sedentary individuals.

The *wet area* comprises a 23 metre swimming pool with two saunas, steam room and spa bath on poolside. There is a poolside relaxation area and this whole area appeared to be kept very clean and was certainly well used.

The *changing areas* are large and sumptuous. This is a key area in a membership based club, as it is one of the few areas that the members will visit twice each time they use the club. There appears to be plenty of lockers available and the club provides complimentary towels, shampoo, body wash and deodorant.

A purpose built *creche* area is provided so that members have somewhere to leave their children while they exercise. The creche is available for under seven-year olds and has qualified staff on duty. There were a range of stimulating toys, games and activities on offer to ensure that quality time was spent at the club by both parents and child.

The Livingwell club offers a series of treatment areas which provide professional services for members. These services include a hair and beauty salon including two sunbeds, fitness assessment room, aromatherapy area and a sports injury clinic.

In general the club is well laid out with the open plan style making it easy to travel from one area to another and giving the club a friendly and busy feel to it. The designers have clearly ensured that all the facilities are well marketed to people in the club; the pool is visible from the reception, as is the dance studio from the main walkway which ends in a gallery overlooking the excellent fitness studio. The decoration uses warm, pastel colours to give the club a warm, relaxing feel.

Operation

Livingwell operates as a *membership only club*. Its profile of members varies greatly in age banding from over 21 through to the 60+ age bracket for whom there is a special 'evergreens' membership category. The average age of its members, though, is 39 and at the time of writing the club had approximately 3,000 of them. When the club first opened, its membership had an average earning of £28K per annum but this has now fallen to between £18K–£24K per annum, presumably through the need to market to the lower income earners to achieve the required membership levels.

The principle of the membership system is that on joining the club a one-off joining fee is payable and then a subscription is paid monthly, usually by direct debit, to validate the membership. The main categories of membership are 'gold' and 'off peak', with the 'gold' membership entitling full usage of the club throughout the opening period, while 'off peak' restricts usage to between 9am and 4pm Monday through to Friday and between 6pm and 9pm at weekends. These membership categories are further subdivided into individual, joint or corporate bands as shown in Table 4.2.

Further to this the club also offers special categories of membership to certain groups. Reference has already been made to the 'evergreens' membership which is a club for the over sixty-year olds. Evergreen membership is based on off peak membership at a reduced rate, targetting the age groups needs by including special exercise classes, tea dances and seminars directly related to their interests and capabilities.

The 'recession buster' membership was introduced as a result of the awareness by the club that the joining fee was a significant factor in preventing people from joining. The up-front lump sum payment was proving to be too much for people to find in the harsh economic climate of 1992. The 'recession buster' membership therefore offered a reduced joining fee but higher monthly dues. A stipulation on the membership had to remain valid for a minimum of a year. This policy proved successful in attracting just under 200 members to the club.

The membership 'Freeze' epitomises the club's attitude to customer care. It allows members who are unable to use the facilities for various reasons, eg temporary relocation of work, illness, etc, to freeze their membership, paying a nominal monthly due, to guarantee their place when they wish to return to full membership whilst not having to pay another joining fee.

The administration of the membership is handled by an administrative team based at the club's reception area. Within the team are four full-time dedicated sales staff, responsible for all sales and marketing initiatives and for conducting tours of the club for prospective customers.

Livingwell believe that the essence of their club is a *customer driven approach* coupled with the quality of their staff. This approach is shown in their employment of a retention manager whose sole responsibility is to monitor and ensure the retention of members. Responsibilities of a retention manager include dealing with all complaints, following up membership cancellations, analysing the reasons behind cancellation, and dealing positively with all bad debt letters. By recording each member's visits to the club, the retention manager is able to highlight current members who are not regularly attending the club and will then be able to send a letter to see if a problem exists behind their lack of usage. The club also run a series of special events and parties to provide added value to the membership. The success of this policy can be borne out by the 20 per cent attrition rate the club has, which is fairly low when compared with the size of the membership and the industry norm.

Obtaining customer feedback is also an important part of the client care ethos. To this end the club sends out a 'Commitment to Excellence' brochure style questionnaire to all members on an annual basis. On an on-going basis staff are encouraged to feedback customer comments to the appropriate manager whilst there are suggesttion cards available for the member to complete. Livingwell claim their policy is to respond within 24 hours by phone to a completed card.

Educating the member is seen as a crucial role for Livingwell. The club run a series of programmes that the member can take advantage of

Table 4.2 Livingwell membership information as at June 1992

Description	One-off joining fee	Monthly dues
Gold Individual Full membership for one person	£395.00	£43.00
Gold Joint Full membership for one person, partner and children under 18	£595.00	£60.00
Gold Single Parent Full membership for one person and children under 18	£395.00	£54.00
Corporate Individual Full membership for an individual with a corporate that has 6 total memberships	£300.00	£40.00
Corporate Joint Full membership for an individual partner and children under 18 with a corporation that has 6 total memberships	£500.00	£57.00
Off Peak Individual Membership for one person from 9.00am–4.00pm Mon–Fri 6.00pm–9.00pm Sat–Sun	£190.00	£29.00
Off Peak Joint Membership for one person and partner	£380.00	£42.00

varying from a low-back clinic, cholesterol screening, weight reduction, control your own life, to beauty seminars and aromatherapy for men courses. These seminars are backed up by information leaflets that are produced in-house and include advice on healthy eating, avoiding heart disease, etc.

Two programmes offered are called *Be-well* and *Living Light*. The 'Be-well' programme proves to be particularly successful and runs for a 10 week period costing the member £100. It comprises a series of lectures on eating, exercise and coping with stress, together with a one-to-one consultation for an hour with a fitness instructor to discuss dietary habits and exercise programmes. The clients on the programme are encouraged to keep food logs and many have noted significant improvement in body weight and body fat levels over the duration of the course.

Whilst these education programmes are important, it is the delivery of service in the fitness studio that most members are paying their membership for. Livingwell believe in a *highly personalised approach*. Each member receives a one-to-one consultation before beginning their programme of exercise in the fitness studio. This consultation includes completing a questionnaire covering health, nutrition, stress and a check on blood pressure and body composition levels. If there are any significant contra-indications to exercise then a standard letter of referral is sent to the members' GP, with their prior permission to ensure the prescribed exercise programme meets with the GP's approval. This policy builds up trust between the clients' doctors and the club, demonstrates the level of care to the member and, perhaps, encourages further referrals for the club.

Once written, the programme is assessed every six to eight weeks to allow for any necessary alterations. Regular reassessment is needed to keep the client motivated. Fitness motivation programmes are also run regularly in the gym and, at the time of writing, the club had recently held an indoor superstars event using the gym equipment and a 'Try for Fun Triathlon' on the exercise bikes, treadmills and rowers.

To complement the fitness studio, a programme of over 60 exercise classes are held weekly ranging from High/Low Impact Aerobics, Step Aerobics to a special 10 minute abdominal workout. Exercise classes are also held in the swimming pool together with a programme of lessons and coaching on swimming technique.

Marketing

The membership catchment area of the club is considered to be within a 20 mile driving distance of the facility for people working or living in and around Milton Keynes. The well developed road system in this area enables the club to market to a fairly large area.

The usual marketing media of radio and press have been used. The club offered a free membership to a DJ on the local independent radio station in return for 'on-air' mentions. The station also gave a free week's pass to the club for its competition winners, while another promotion saw a Livingwell fitness instructor offer health advice on the radio's phone-in show.

Livingwell undertook some local advertising mainly geared around enticing people to visit the facility. The sales strategy is based around getting prospective members to visit the club where the sales staff can then offer them a tour, free trial use of the facilities and then hopefully close the sale.

Initially when the club opened the joining fees were introduced in stages: the first 100 members at no joining fee, then the next batch were admitted at half-price etc. This strategy is based on the knowledge that new members will sell on the facility to friends etc, enabling some initial members to use the club when it opens, whilst simultaneously generating leads for new members. The strategy obviously works as 70 per cent of membership sales at Livingwell are achieved through referrals and point-of-sale information.

Direct mail and leaflet drops have been used and the club buy in local mailing lists. The 'evergreen' and 'recession buster' memberships were marketed in this way. An over sixty year old sales person was hired to sell the evergreen membership as the club felt that older prospective members would be happier buying from someone of their own age. Another neat marketing ploy with this membership category was to offer a discount of £1 for every year of the person's age.

One problem that has been encountered with offering special deals to new members is that existing members feel the club is not doing anything for them, so the club try to offer promotions for members in addition to new members' promotions. One such promotion was to offer a camera to existing members for introducing a friend to the club who subsequently joined.

It is particularly noticeable that the club produces separate *leaflets* for each of the different offers and memberships that are available. A corporate leaflet is produced to sell corporate memberships, a fly sheet is produced to promote the recession buster promotion and so forth. A common theme across all of these leaflets is that they all describe benefits to the target audience of the membership and not just the features. Undoubtedly, the best example of this is the tariff sheet which lists the benefits to the potential member of each of the facilities the club has to offer.

Reinforcing the *benefits* of membership to existing members in order to stimulate membership retention is another marketing tactic. Regular newsletters are produced containing information on exercise, forthcoming events, and club news whilst a booklet is distributed to members explaining the benefits of regular exercise.

Mangement and staffing

Livingwell employs 60 staff to run its Milton Keynes club. The club is headed up by one manager who oversees the whole operation. The manager believes that it is the staff that set Livingwell apart. The management style is very much 'hands on' with the club manager being very visible to both staff and members. Although Livingwell is part of a chain of clubs, the site manager has a fair degree of autonomy. It would appear that once the budget is agreed with head office, the manager is left to his own devices providing he is able to hit targets set. The clubs obviously operate to a system so there is some head office involvement, particularly in staff training for example, but the manager still feels he has the freedom to manage the club without too much close scrutiny.

The *organisational structure* is very flat with the manager supported by an assistant whose function is that of fitness and aerobics co-ordinator. Beneath these two the staff team is divided into departments each headed by a senior member of staff. The club has nine departments as follows: catering, administration, membership retention, sales, fitness, creche, beauty and hairdressing, pro shop and services. The services department are responsible for the cleaning of the club, its maintenance and the treatment and dosing of the swimming pool.

Communication between the teams would seem to be acceptable, although without first hand experience this is difficult to judge. The club attempts to have weekly staff meetings between the heads of department to discuss budgets, customer care and other management issues. It is then left, it would appear, to the discretion of the heads of department to disseminate this information down to their employees.

The club visibly attempts to make the staff feel involved and to appreciate the importance of the role they each play in its operation. Although there is no performance related pay, the club do run a rewards for excellence scheme and the manager strongly believes in seeing staff 'doing things right'. A recent company-wide promotion was held where staff were awarded stars if they had performed a function particularly well. Over a pre-determined period of time the 10 staff to have received the most stars were sent to EuroDisney, with special awards going to a further 10 employees.

Livingwell do seem to place a great deal of importance on *staff training*. Upon joining the company, an employee goes through a 30-day starter programme; once succcessfully through this they are then put on a six-week course with training given for four hours per week. At the end of this there is an in-house exam where the instructor must reach a minimum standard.

Ongoing training is given through a continuing education credit system. Staff have to attain a certain number of credits by attending certain seminars, training days, workshops, analysing newsletters, and reading material sent out by the company's training manager. In all the club looks to provide six to seven hours of training a week.

In terms of formal qualifications, the food handling staff are required to attain the relevant catering and health and safety qualifications, while three of the services staff must have the IBRM pool plant operators qualification. For fitness personnel there is the need to have the RSA Exercise to Music award and the company like them to have a relevant BTEC or City and Guilds qualification. The principal quality looked for, however, when recruiting staff is the ability to possess the communication and people skills required to deliver the customer care ethos of Livingwell.

Summary

On reflection, the Livingwell Health Club is an admirable facility. From the investigation undertaken, the management have a proactive and forward looking approach to health and fitness provision and, judging by the membership totals achieved, they are also successful in their delivery.

The level of customer care and the education they provide combined with the commitment to staff training and development will be valuable weapons in the battle to succeed.

The name Livingwell certainly seems to encapsulate the nature of the club.

Key points

- ▲ *Its American philosophy is designed to encourage exercise adherence and education about health and fitness.*
- ▲ *The club offers a highly personalised service based on one-to-one consultation.*
- ▲ *It places high priority on membership retention.*
- ▲ *It targets new members through word of mouth and 'point of sale' marketing.*

- ▲ *It combines autonomous management with much staff involvement and training through rewards and 'education credits'.*

Case study 4.3: Hans and Olaf Clinic – Oslo, Norway

Key features

- ▲ *Private health and fitness club on prime site in Oslo.*
- ▲ *Close involvement of owners.*
- ▲ *One of Norway's most successful health and fitness clubs.*
- ▲ *Sequence exercise.*
- ▲ *Philosophy of rehabilitation and prevention.*
- ▲ *Large membership with high percentage of corporate members.*
- ▲ *Customer care and staff care.*

Origins

The Hans and Olaf Clinic in Oslo is now one of Norway's most successful and renowned health and fitness facilities. It began in 1967 when Hans Gunnari and Olaf Evjenth opened a physiotherapist practice. They were based in a rented room within the Torgatta Baths complex, a prime site in the city centre.

The clinic began purely as a physiotherapy practice but as their client base widened, and business grew, Hans and Olaf wanted to develop exercise prescription rather than just recommend the type of exercise a patient should be undertaking for their rehabilitation. In 1984, the converted baths were acquired and the physiotherapist practice was extended to involve a fully equipped fitness facility selling memberships to the local public.

In a city with a population of half a million people there are a plethora of health and fitness facilities. Hans Gunnari believes that there are over 70 physical therapy clinics and 20 health clubs. By reputation, location, expertise, competitive pricing and developing their own exercise equipment, the Hans and Olaf clinic has been able to position itself as a market leader in Norway.

Philosophy

The philosophy of the Hans and Olaf clinic is very much one of rehabilitation and prevention. With a majority of their clients arriving with a specific sports injury, muscular or skeletal problem, the first priority is either treatment or healing. The second stage is to prescribe a programme of exercise that will prevent the problem from reoccurring.

The exercise programme will involve working out on fitness equipment designed and developed by the gym owners. Indeed, a significant part of their business is now involved with the marketing of their equipment throughout Europe and America.

The exercise prescription recommended by the gymnasium is perhaps a little simplistic but has nevertheless been successful. Known as *sequence exercise*, it is similar to the circuit training principles we are familiar within the UK. A sequence exercise circuit will involve five exercises, each one working a different major muscle group sequentially. There are three sequences for the client to progress onto, the second and third groups working smaller muscle groups in a more specialised way to the first. There is no rest between exercises so if the heart rate has been elevated prior to beginning the sequence exercise routine, it is feasible to maintain an elevated heart rate and hence reap cardio-vascular training benefit. Sequence exercise is therefore the foundation on which the Hans and Olaf Clinic has developed. It is a very simple approach and a particular emphasis is based on appealing to ordinary, sedentary individuals. Bodybuilders are actively distracted from joining, particularly as the total weight on the resistance machines is kept very light.

The Hans and Olaf *mission statement* does not translate well from Norwegian but can best be described as 'we will show you how you can help yourself'.

Design and layout

As has already been stated the club is located in a prime site in the centre of Oslo. Although the building is an old baths complex the facility does not contain a swimming pool at present.

The building in which the fitness studio is located, and which is owned by the gym operators Hans and Olaf, contains numerous other businesses including a health food shop, newsagents, restaurant and a suite of offices. These additional facilities are, of course, very useful in attracting passing trade.

The club has three squash courts, a hairdresser and beautician with the main area divided into 30 physiotherapist treatment rooms. These treatment rooms are then hired out to qualified therapists who refer their patients on to the fitness studio.

A reception fronts the building, where all enquiries are handled and where guests, members, patients and prospective members are greeted. The club or 'clinic', as the owners tend to refer to it, comprises 1,400 square metres with the main feature being the gymnasium housing 60 pieces of resistance equipment, laid out in the groups of five sequences as earlier described. In addition to the resistance equipment are two treadmills, 15 exercise cycles and a selection of light free weights. Although well arranged, clean and tidy, the standard of decoration and furnishing in the fitness studio does not appear to be as exclusive or up-market in comparison with the Livingwell club. The appearance of Hans and Olaf's gymnasium is more functional.

The changing rooms also provide a similar feel; they are clean and functional but reasonably basic. The members are not provided with towels nor complimentary toiletries.

It is not an easy task to analyse whether the clients' expectations of a facilities quality, in terms of design and layout, are lower in Oslo than in Milton Keynes. Any difference between the two clubs could of course be attributed to factors such as pricing policy and the target market which will now be discussed.

Operation

To join the gymnasium is quite straightforward. The club has a single membership category which allows usage of the gymnasium throughout the opening period with no additional or session charges. The fee must be paid annually in advance and, depending on currency fluctuations of course, equates to £200. There is no joining fee to enter the club and no facility to spread the cost of the membership via a direct debit system. It seems that this system was introduced as one person is responsible for all membership administration and therefore the simpler the system the easier it is to administer.

The club has fairly recently introduced an off-peak membership for OAPs which allows usage during the quieter times between 9am and 4pm, but this is the only variation on the one membership system described.

The club seems to revolve around a referral system with the 30 physiotherapists treating their patients – who need not be members of the club – on a session fee basis. Once the initial treatment is complete they then recommend a programme of exercise in the fitness studio, a positive way of increasing membership.

Usage

There is an average of 500 members working out each day with, at times, 70 people working out in the gymnasium at the same time. Although the membership total does tend to fluctuate, it is usually around the 5,000 mark, which means that on average a member will use the club once in two weeks. This is not a particularly high ratio and would imply that there are a number of 'hidden' members, ie members who use the club very infrequently despite having a current membership.

This may be because 60 per cent of members are joined through corporate membership schemes. Here the membership fees are paid by the employer to the club and then deducted at very favourable rates from the employees' salaries. As the fees are paid by the employer at a discounted rate there is therefore an embarrassment factor perhaps preventing the employee from informing the club and their employer of their desire to cancel.

The club is open from 7am–9pm Monday through to Friday but is closed at the weekends. This decision is made as the owners do not feel that there is sufficient demand to justify weekend opening. This is unusual when compared with the UK market, but could be attributed possibly to residential patterns in Oslo and the city centre location of Hans and Olaf's clinic.

Another slightly surprising feature is that the clinic closes completely for the month of July. This is the peak holiday season in Norway and provides the owners with the opportunity to redecorate the club and maintain the equipment. Some physical therapists remain on site for consultation and emergency treatment. The policy of closing for one month certainly seems strange on the surface. The risk is surely run of members getting out of the habit of visiting the club and not returning or renewing membership when the facility reopens in August. It does, however, explain why a monthly direct debit payment system is not offered, as it would be difficult to justify collecting any dues in the month when the club was closed!

The gymnasium is fully supervised by at least one instructor, or 'therapist', as the Norwegians refer to them. Further instructors will be on duty at peak times, ie after 4pm. Despite the heavy usage of the club, the owners feel this cover to be sufficient as all members receive full instruction when they first begin their programme together with instruction pamphlets on the use of the equipment. The principle of sequence exercise, where there are only five pieces of equipment in each programme, may also mean that technique is easier to remember and the client requires slightly less supervision.

Although there appears to be no formal customer care policy, the owners believe that *customer satisfaction* is achieved through ensuring that staff are rewarded according to the success of the facility. In this case all reception and gym staff are remunerated with a relatively low salary but high commission rates based on members renewing.

The success of this policy in delivering customer care is difficult to assess as no customer feedback is actively sought. If clients cancel their membership or fail to renew, the club will either telephone or write to determine the reasons why; but the results of the survey are not formally analysed. The membership records are not computerised and therefore it is difficult to generate management information. The club is not able to calculate membership retention or attrition rates but do believe that the majority of members tend to be with them for a long period of time.

Marketing

A significant amount of promoting Hans and Olaf's clinic is done for them through referral from the 30 physical therapists based within the club. The owners are proud of the fact that they have never advertised the facilities except for an entry in the local phone book.

The club receives considerable coverage from local press and media and its name is also spread by encouraging members to take pens, chocolates and other various gifts to friends and relatives.

Both Hans and Olaf had established a good reputation as physiotherapists to the extent that they would have clients waiting for up to eight weeks for treatment. When they established their fitness facility they carried this reputation with them, and their membership has grown accordingly.

The club does not employ any sales staff, so new 'leads' as such are not generated. It is impossible to calculate, therefore, the conversion level of enquiries into members that the club achieves. Free trials of one or two sessions are offered by the club and then the prospective member has the opportunity to join.

The club appeals to a wide age range and has never had a difficulty achieving high usage of the gym either early morning or after 4pm. It was more of a problem maximising usage in the off-peak period but this was partially alleviated by offering discounted membership to OAPs. This is the only time that the club has specifically targeted a market segment.

Management and staffing

Hans and Olaf, the two owners of the club, are the dominating forces behind this operation. Olaf still practices physical therapy whilst Hans tends to concentrate on the administrative side of the business. Three receptionists and a separate team of full- and part-time instructors work for them. There are no middle managers so all the information is passed straight down from Hans and Olaf. The management style appears to be fairly autocratic with little opportunity for the junior staff to express their ideas or influence decisions.

No great emphasis is placed on training as the owners recruit instructors who are all graduates in physical therapy and are therefore believed to be suitably qualified for the responsibilities that they have. The receptionists do undergo in-house training in customer care from Hans, with the key recruitment criterion being possession of good interpersonal skills.

Summary

Hans and Olaf's clinic is certainly based on a different operating style to the others investigated in this chapter.

The success of the club seems to have been driven by the quality and dedication of the two owners, Hans and Olaf, and the referral system achieved by the location of the physiotherapists within the complex.

The concept of the facility seems to revolve more around the volume market, ie high levels of membership, than it does with the quality of service it provides its members.

There can be no doubting, however, the success of a club that has never actively marketed its facilities through paid advertising but has still secured 5,000 members.

Footnote

Whilst completing this case study, Hans Gunnari and Olaf Evjenth have sold the business. They still remain the owners of the building but four therapists now operate the facility and pay a rental to the two founders.

Key points

- ▲ *The club is part of a wider complex owned by Hans and Olaf.*
- ▲ *They market the club as a clinic.*

- ▲ *A key concept is the referral system with the 30 physiotherapists.*
- ▲ *The club combines a high volume approach with the personal commitment and philosophy of the two owners.*
- ▲ *Customers care is firmly linked with staff care.*

Conclusion

As stated in the introduction, each of the clubs analysed are serving slightly different sectors of the health and fitness industry and, therefore, direct comparison is always difficult.

The greatest similarities occur between the two UK clubs. Both are concerned with a high quality of service, high levels of customer care, motivation of the customer to ensure exercise adherence and the delivery of a health promotion message.

All three clubs have, however, been successful in their own right. The question that this study really raises is whether the Norwegian public are better motivated to exercise and more aware of the benefits of regular exercise, so that they do not need the same level of attention and motivation as their UK counterparts. It is doubtful, for example, whether a fitness club in London could achieve the same level of success as Hans and Olaf's gym in Oslo whilst spending as little attention on marketing or customer care. This could also be attributable to greater competition in the UK or a more discerning customer.

A common feature amongst all three clubs is the growing importance of the relationship between fitness and the medical services. The value of referring a patient from a physiotherapist to the gym cannot be better demonstrated than by Hans and Olaf's clinic.

May be the vision of the health and fitness facility of the future is one which offers both medical advice and the opportunity to exercise in a customer care orientated way with a commitment to quality of sevice.

5 Theme parks
Professor Terry Stevens

Introduction: development of theme parks

As the theme park industry has developed and diversified over the past 20 years, so an adequate definition has become more complex. Theming has become a recognised concept in its own right and is now widely used in many visitor attractions including heritage presentations. Elsewhere, theatrical techniques are increasingly applied to retail and merchandising operations to theme presentations. The term 'theme park', according to Brown and Church (1987), originated in the USA following the opening of Disneyland in California. The North American park developers would be the first to acknowledge the vital contribution to the concept made by early European recreational provision.

The Tivoli Gardens in Denmark with its landscaped gardens, Japanese pagodas and Mediterranean architecture, influenced early theme park designers. Walt Disney, in preparing the conceptual material for Disneyland in the early 1950s, is known to have been positively influenced by a visit to De Efteling in Holland – a park that remains a market leader. Grover (1991) has highlighted the synergy between the Disney theme selections and the European traditions, particularly folk and fairy tales.

Brown and Church (1987) argue that the term 'theme park' has a specific meaning this being

> 'a large scale amusement or leisure park incorporating rides and attractions grouped into areas, each having a specific theme which dictates the nature of the amusements and the decor'.

This definition broadly conforms to that used by the Landmark Entertainment Group (Christopher, 1992) who point out that there may be one or more themes in a recreational facility in which

> 'fantasy, fun, education and adventure become reality and guests knowingly escape to lands and places unlike their own in a period of suspended reality . . . within these worlds they experience other cultures, time periods, other peoples, and other ways societies live . . . and every age group experiences it within a framework of multiple attractions and entertaining activities.'

The American Marriott Corporation endorse this definition regarding a theme park as 'a family entertainment complex orientated towards a particular subject(s) combining the continuity of costuming and architecture with entertainment and merchandise to promote a fantasy provoking atmosphere'.

The English Tourist Board in its recent *Handbook of Tourism Products* (1991) resolves the difficulties inherent in defining a 'theme park' by examining their functions and features. The ETB, in line with others, confirm that whilst many recreational and leisure parks exist, some with themed elements, the actual number of themed visitor attractions is limited. Although the scale of the supply-side may not be extensive, the size of their markets and their overall contribution to tourism development is significant. These factors are explored later.

A number of recent reports, including the ETB review (ETB 1991, Projection 2000 1991, Tourism Research and Marketing 1990, Lyon 1987) agree on the main features that characterise a 'theme park'. These are:

- a distinctive overall or series of discrete themed areas with complementary rides and associated decor
- a strong aesthetic appeal based upon manicured amenity landscaping, and generally in a parkland setting away from an urban area
- high capacity, large volume, site with a variety of rides (including large scale white knuckle rides) and entertainments to meet the throughput and load demands of relatively high visitor attendances
- heritage and education objectives are secondary to rather more hedonistic or experiential ideas or activities
- the product offers visitors the potential for full-day length of stay generally with a pay-one-price (POP) admission scheme
- provide a range of rides, amusements, entertainments, catering and other facilities to cater for a broad market
- operate integrated transport systems for the efficient distribution of visitors into and around the site.

In this context there are relatively few parks based upon a single, discernible, theme. Examples of these single theme operations are:

- Asterix (France) – Gauls/Romans
- Camelot (UK) – Arthurian Legends
- Big Bang Smurf World (France) – Smurf Characters (now Walibi Schromph)
- OK Corral (France) – Wild West
- EuropaPark (Germany) – Europe
- De Efteling (Netherlands) – Hans Christian Anderson Tales
- Futurescope (France) – Moving Image Technology

The majority of parks, however, are more likely to offer visitors a series of inter-linked but individually themed areas that may include: historical or cultural tableaux from the host or other countries; traditional fairy tales or futuristic cameos; or themes that relate to a specific natural environment, such as a jungle, or the ocean. Recent investments in existing parks reflect this concept of mixed theming which is a function of the way the park has evolved over time.

Using these criteria to form a broad definitional basis, it is clear that

Exemplar 5.1

The Tussauds Group

On 30 March 1992 the Tussaud's Group opened a revitalised Alton Towers, Staffordshire, UK. During the previous season the company assessed the potential of the park and the need for new attractions. At the same time they invested in the refurbishment of existing rides and the upgrading of the general environment of the park. A £10 million investment package focused upon two new rides and the creation of three new themed areas.

The first of the new rides, the 'Haunted House', is located in 'Gloomy Wood' themed area. Regarded as the showpiece of the development, the 'Haunted House' was designed by John Wardley and manufactured by Mack of Germany. The ride is an amalgam of traditional dark ride features enhanced by a wide range of special effects. The second new ride, also constructed by Mack, is the 'Runaway Train' in the 'Katanga Canyon' themed area – based upon an African colonial village – includes themed merchandising and catering and is targeting the family market. The third new themed area is 'Thunder Valley' in the White Knuckle area of the park which is geared to the young, thrill-seeking market. Rides include the 'Alton Beast', and the 'Thunderlooper'.

there are relatively few theme parks in Europe. The English Tourist Board recognise 10 such parks. In the rest of Europe, there are acknowledged to be a further 25–35 parks, whilst in the USA Lyons (1987) estimates there to be 50 parks, of which 30 have in excess of 1 million visitors per annum.

In Europe, although spread over a number of countries, the parks exhibit a number of similarities which, interestingly, make them comparable to their US counterparts. Whilst there has been in Europe a long tradition of pleasure parks and seaside resort funfairs, the phenomenon of a boom in theme park development over the past 15 years does, however, find its roots in a similar but earlier movement in the USA. The majority of US parks are owned and operated by major corporations: Six Flags has eight parks, Kings Entertainment four, and Anheuser-Busch two. In the main, European parks are often owned and managed as single operational entities; often as a family enterprise. However, increasingly international corporate activity is emerging. In the UK the total market for the top 10 theme parks is approximately 10–12 million visitors per annum. The market is dominated by six parks operated by the Tussaud's Group, Leisure Sport Ltd and the Granada Group.

Although, as we have seen, there are relatively few theme parks in Europe their market share is significant with an estimated total market of between 24–26 million visitors per annum. The most heavily visited of these parks being De Efteling in Holland, which originally opened in 1951, and now attracts over 2 million visitors per annum. These figures do not include the 8–9 million visitors to EuroDisney during 1992 (expected to rise to 11 million pa by 1995).

Brown and Church (1987) stress that in Europe theme park development has, to date, been a northern European phenomenon, with a particularly strong representation in the Netherlands, Germany, Belgium and the

Table 5.1 UK park operators

	Opened	Holding Company	Operator/ Owner	Park	1991 visit m	%
1	1992 (refurb)	Pearson	Tussauds Group	Alton Towers	1.9	33
2	1987 (refurb)	Pearson	Tussauds Group	Chessington	1.4	
3	1979	RMC	Leisure Sport	Thorpe Park	0.9	9
4	1987	Granada Group	Granada Gt Ad	American Ad	1.0	24
5	1983	Granada Group	Granada Gt Ad	Camelot	0.7	
6		Granada Group	Granada Gt Ad	Granada Studio Tours	0.7	
7	1979	Lightwater Valley	LV	LV	0.4	4
8		Flamingoland	Flamingoland	Flamingoland	1.1	11
9		Drayton Manor	D Manor	Drayton Manor	0.99	10
10		W Midlands Safari	WMS Park	WMS Park	0.9	9
					10.00 m	

Source: Author.

UK. There has, however, been recent activity in Northern France prompted by the EuroDisney development. A number of these parks including Mirapolis near Parkis and Zygofolis in Nice, as well as some well-recorded proposed developments in the UK (notably Britannia Park in Derbyshire, Wonder World in Corby and Battersea in London) have either failed to materialise or struggled and closed. Several observers, particularly Lavery and Stevens, (1990) ascribe these failures to a number of reasons, that reflect the high risk, specialist business of theme park development. They include:

- a lack of understanding of the concept and the market
- insufficient data and comparative performance information
- under-capitalisation
- the impact of seasonality, and
- sheer size and scale of the operations.

Speigel, the President of the International Association of Amusement Parks and Attractions in 1989, in an interview with *Leisure Management* ascribes the failure of parks in France for the following reasons: 'It is the people who designed the parks and the people who operate the parks who had the problems. They didn't know what they were doing . . . (they) didn't understand what makes a park function successfully' (*Leisure Management* 1991).

Significantly, new theme park development in Europe, and indeed elsewhere in the world, is being increasingly undertaken by existing, successful operators. The owners of Phantasialand in Germany have now opened a park in Brazil, whilst Disney's global expansion now embraces three continents. Future developments are likely to see an extension of existing operational interests, with park operators collaborating with investors, rather than a new generation of theme park companies emerging. For example, US-based Anheuser-Busch Corporation are combining with the Barcelona park operators Tibidabo to build a $300m theme park complex in Catalunya, Spain for 1995.

Despite the global representation and recent growth of theme parks, there remains relatively little written analysis about them, which may help to explain Speigel's comments. The President of the Landmark Entertainment Group recently described theme parks as being at the 'verbal stage of development' (Christopher, 1992). There are a number of trade publications which report primarily on operational aspects of park management, notably *Park World* (published monthly by World's Fair Ltd); *Fun World* (published monthly by the International Association of Amusement Parks and Attractions); and *Leisure Management* (published monthly by Dicester Ltd). Elsewhere, strategic matters affecting theme parks have been reviewed in *Travel and Tourism Analyst* and *Tourism Management*, whilst the 1992 edition of *World Travel and Tourism Review*, for the first time, carries a feature on the attractions sector.

There are a number of significant reasons for this relative dearth of published analysis which reflect generally the nature of the theme park industry. Firstly, there has been a tendency for the 'art' of running the 'business' to be handed-down rather in the tradition of the traditional showman's craft. Theme parks have evolved from, and have definite generic roots, in the world of the travelling showman. As a result many parks remain family-owned and operated, especially in Europe, whilst the design of many of the rides and the entertainments in the parks closely reflect their funfair, music-hall or circus predecessors (Wardley 1989).

Secondly, and in the spirit of the family business, the sector as a whole remains a close-knit community. The actual size of the sector in terms of the overall number of parks is relatively small; the geography of parks is, to a degree, self-selecting, due to the need for high levels of capital investment and access to catchments with large centres of population. Until recently, therefore, the sector was not as competitive as other areas of leisure.

Increasingly, and to a certain extent inevitably, this somewhat cosy self-supporting relationship is being challenged as multinational and international developers review global opportunities for their theme park product. As a result, a competitive edge has entered the sector. This, in turn, is making operators adopt a guarded approach to divulging operational information. The opening of EuroDisney near Paris in 1992, and the proposals by Anheuser-Busch to open a theme park near Barcelona in 1995 reflect the growing US interest in the new market opportunities created by the Single European Act 1986, which was enacted on 1 January 1993. Within Europe, the past five years have seen a similar extension of interest, as happened in the US in the 1980s; notably the development of multiple park operations by international holding companies. This trend is likely to continue in Europe and elsewhere during the next 10 years.

Finally, the paucity of information available is due to the industry's keeness to demonstrate that it's products are individualistic with unique components or features. This, combined with the present domination of the sector in Europe by single owner-operators, makes it difficult to have agreed measures of performance between parks or any central point of collection. Indeed, disclosure of information, even with regard to paid admissions, is inconsistent. As a result, comprehensive and comparative analysis within the sector is difficult to find. The most comprehensive database is that collated by IAAPA from its members and only available to its members.

Product development

Whilst operators strive to market the uniqueness of their park, there are a number of inherent dilemmas which threaten to undermine this proposition. Firstly, there is a growing but nonetheless limited range of providers of rides and shows for the industry. The IAAPA '1991 Director and Guide', for example, lists 62 categories of products and services, of which just six categories relate to the provision of these core theme park products. Although there are over 500 entries in these categories, the primary source of ride technology remains vested in a limited number of companies, notably Vekoma International BV, Mack Inc, Zamperla, and Togo International Inc. The use of laser technology and the advent of other new technology creating simulation with virtual reality experiences has added new dimensions and opportunities for parks with a fresh range of specialist companies entering the market such as the 'Showscan Corporation', Omnimax Iwerks and Laser Fantasy.

Given the prescribed range of types of rides available park developers have to place great emphasis upon their theme designers to create the unique environments around a basic ride, skeleton or show. This skeleton may be similar to that used in other theme and leisure parks. There is, therefore, a heavy dependence upon the cosmetics of theming and landscaping to give the park its distinctive qualities.

In the search for appropriate theming, many parks have struggled to create adequately differentiated products. As a result, there has been a tendency for parks to adopt similar theme characteristics, either wholly or in part. For example, 'Wild West' presentations based upon late 19th century North American Western towns feature, to varying degrees, in a number of parks throughout Europe, including: Phantasialand (Germany); OK Corral (France); American Adventure (UK); and, EuroDisney (France). Similarly, replica features of streetscapes of European cities constitute theming in Thorpe park (UK); Europark (Germany); Bellewaerde (Belgium); and in Brupark (Belgium). The ride design and conceptualisation within the Tussaud's Group represents refreshing diversity and creativity. John Wardley, the ride designer and architect, stresses the need for formal and informal research in this important process. He, along with other leading figures in the industry, emphasise the importance of riding-the-rides and incognito queuing with visitors (Murphy 1992) in order to understand customer perspectives. In the constant search for new product development the importance of the theming process to create the appropriate balance of authenticity and fantasy cannot be over-emphasised. A number of parks have, over the past few years, strategically decided to strengthen the theming within their parks, through enhanced design, rather than invest in expensive new rides. This has brought continuity and clarity to the visitor experience helped broaden market appeal, as well as proving a relatively cost-effective investment.

Design

The design of a theme park, or even for themed areas within a park, involves four essential elements. The total process can take between six months to four years to bring to the operational phase depending upon the scale and complexity of the development. Those involved in the engineering of the human experience stress the need to design for a specific location and for a particular guest experience.

Influence of EuroDisney on the theme parks industry in the UK and mainland Europe

Just as Disney, and particularly the opening of Walt Disney World in Orlando, proved a watershed for many positive changes in these park operations in the US theme park industry, so it is hoped that EuroDisney will have the same effect for UK and European parks. The general response to EuroDisney prior to its opening amongst theme park operators was generally positive. The consensus was that there would be a heightened awareness of theme parks in general; higher expectation of standards of service; together with an evolving willingness to pay the market-related entry fee (Larner, 1992).

The perceived challenge by EuroDisney stimulated a flourish of investments by theme parks in the UK and the rest of Europe (Larner, 1992). In the main the investments were geared to extending the parks appeal to a broader market range. Consequently, with one or two well publicised exceptions such as Lightwater Valley, Yorkshire, UK, £5m 'Ultimate' roller coaster, there were few multi-million pound thrill ride investments. Diversification of product, markets, and sources of revenue has characterised recent investment activity. In part, this slow down in the scale and the shift in the nature of investments reflects the fact that expansion that increases revenue and attendances is only relevant if it increases profits. The US based Economics Research Associates have developed a model for theme parks to analyse the impact of investment strategies called 'The Attendance Re-

Exemplar 5.2

The Landmark Group

Three levels of experience are referred to by Landmark in their multi-disciplinary approach to the design process:

- Emotional (laugh, cry, romantic, scary)
- Intellectual (think, stimulate, learn, rationalise)
- Physical (sensory, active, participation, movement)

The design process itself then begins with the concept – a story, theme, idea or vision which is tested against a range or variables in the context of an initial feasibility study. This review will cover:

- establishing aims and objectives
- market analysis and assessment
- evaluation of alternative and competing provision
- master planning and the determination of circulation, capacities, infra-structural parameters
- budgets and programming
- awareness of rides and entertainments suppliers, availability, installation and operational requirements.

Phase two of the process is the refinement of the concept linked to preliminary engineering drawings, detailed budgets, and proving the initial assumptions about both the market and the concept. Phase three shifts the process towards scripting, commissioning and the invitation to tender for the fabrication and supply of rides. Finally, following selection, there is the process of installation and implementation leading to the hand-over to operational staff and the on-going monitoring of visitor reaction.

gression Model'. Increasingly, such tools are being used to establish vigorous criteria upon which to base the investment decisions.

Fears that EuroDisney will directly compete with the existing European market for theme parks appear ill-founded. Gratton (1992) identifies the clear difference between the visitor profiles of the Disney market and those visiting other theme parks. The latter appeal primarily to the domestic day visitor market with lower socio-economic profiles and travelling by car from within a 150 mile catchment. The Disney concept, including Disney World in Florida and EuroDisney, is orientated to an overnight tourist market with a higher socio-economic profile. Consequently, Gratton (1992) predicts that, if the 'European market behaves like the US market, existing operators need not worry too much'.

The opening of EuroDisney has, however, focused the thinking concerning many facets of the development and management of UK and European theme parks. Firstly, EuroDisney has made other park operators recognise the potential of the overnight tourist market. The resort concept, applied by Disney, has been adopted elsewhere with various forms of overnight accommodation being provided, ranging from caravanning and camping sites to hotels.

Secondly, the importance of secondary spending within the attraction as

- Drayton Manor, Staffs, developed 'Pirates Cove' for the 1992 season involving an original £3m water ride from 1990, a soft play area, themed trails, a pirate swing ship and the Buccaneer themed food area.
- Thorpe Park, Surrey, has spent £½m developing the theme of the sea around an earlier £1.5m 'Fantasy Reef' investment. Octopus Garden is a play area for young visitors which integrates with Neptunes Kingdom, a dark slide, and the swinging seashells ferris wheel.
- Pleasureland, Lancs, has used Morocco as the theme base for two new attractions: a two acre children's play area and an adventure miniature crazy golf course.

Figure 5.1
UK investments 1991/92

a means of generating revenue is developed to a sophisticated level within the Disney operation. Other parks are rapidly recognising the full range of benefits derived from appropriate retailing activities (food and beverage, merchandising, event/venue leasing).

Thirdly, Disney has demonstrated that alternative sources of capital and revenue finance can be accessed for product development. These opportunities, still in their infancy in European parks, range from sponsorship and corporate advertising, to ride concessions, leases and franchise activities. Parks provide many and varied vehicles to carry adverts, logos and promotional messages to large captive markets thus creating interesting opportunities for target marketing by sponsors. For example, Eastman Kodak Ltd have recognised the photo opportunities which exist in theme parks and have developed a range of sponsorship packages. These include simple sign posting schemes identifying 'photo locations' around parks to endorsement of merchandise products and advertisement on rides such as the Vampire ride at Tussauds 'Chessington World of Adventure', Surrey, UK.

Finally, the Disney experience is a carefully contrived balance of 'unskilled' and 'skilled' consumption. The skilled consumption is based upon varying levels of visitor involvement and participation. As Gratton (1992) points out, 'thrills and white knuckle rides tend to provide low skill experience'. In contrast, the development of interpretive exhibits, interactive displays and educational facilities has a 'skill' requirement. Such facilities, a feature of EPCOT in Orlando, are being successfully introduced in other leisure attractions. For example, there are now a significant number of 'hands on' science centres (Heureka in Finland, Xperiment and the Exploratory in the UK and Evulon in Holland) that are introducing visitors to the concepts of physics or chemistry; whilst a number of recreation parks have skill-based sporting activities. It is generally predicted that theme parks should look to these opportunities for new areas of product development rather than the thrill ride features.

This latter trend offers a number of benefits, particularly in an increasingly competitive market in which there will be a significant decline in the

Exemplar 5.3

Futurescope, Poitiers, France

'The rapid and spectacular development of communication technologies and information processing has modified all aspects of daily life' . . . The idea of Futurescope was to introduce people to these concepts. At the same time the theme park – The European Park of the Moving Image – was conceived as a tool for regional development in the, predominantly, rural department of Vienne. In the period 1985–1992 over which Futurescope has been developing, some 7,500 jobs have been created in the region as a direct result of the attraction – representing some 50 per cent of all jobs created. The park opened in 1987 with 225,000 visitors, in 1991 over 1 million paying guests were received with turnover increasing from 7.5Fr m to 125Fr m during the past 5 years.

The park consists of 15 special media shows produced by the Worlds leading companies including Kinemax, Omnimax, Iwerks 3D Cinema, Showscan, Imax 'Magic Carpet', and the interactive 'Cineamtomate'. In addition, there are a series of interactive exhibits and children's world. The park, which is operational from March through until November has been supported by the Vienne General Council in partnership with the State Regional Council and the EC. The innovative scheme has, to date, received an investment of 600 m francs.

A key aspect of the project is the diversification taking place around the concept of the theme park. In addition to the expected provision of restaurants (6 on site with a capacity of 3,000) there is the development of a resort complex with a range of accommodation and entertainment. There are 2,500 rooms available in 1 to 3 star hotels including 570 rooms on-site in 6 hotels, and a 1,000 capacity conference centre.

A particularly interesting aspect of diversification is the focus of development on business, research and study around the themes presented in the park. The theme park has become the popular expression, the interface, of this technological innovation. By 1995 the site will host 800 researchers, representing 10% of the French research potential in physical engineering. Critical to the success of this programme is the high school and University developments, the establishment of a Training Centre for Future Technologies, the National Centre for Long Distance Learning, and the International Centre for Long Term Forecasting.

'Futurescope' is a model of the use of a theme park to stimulate regional development through a diversified and interrelated set of technological activities. In many ways, therefore, Futurescope is advancing the original concept of Disney's Experimental Prototype Community of Tomorrow – better known as EPCOT.

number of 16–24 year olds in Europe over the next 10 years. As a result of this changing demography, parks will have to broaden their market appeal, orientating particularly towards family groups and, within the niche markets, to educational group visits.

Exemplar 5.4

This Great Game Ltd

This Great Game Limited is an international sports attraction company based in the UK. The attraction called, 'This Great Game' has been designed specifically to operate within sporting venues such as stadia and arena. The attraction combines traditional presentational and display techniques with a multimedia show which tell the story of the heroes, legends and great events associated with the sports played in the Stadium. The innovative components of the attraction are a range of interactive exhibits which allow visitors to experience the virtual reality of competing, to participate in TV commentaries, develop their sporting skills, and become involved in computer simulation activities.

It has already been stated that available comparative data is limited. From the information which is available, primarily the published Annual Reports or independent market surveys, it would appear that the current users of theme parks exhibit the following characteristics:

- catchments are generally regional from within 100–150 miles
- attendances range from 0.4 million to 2.5 million visitors per annum
- visitors on holiday represent 25–35 per cent depending upon the location of the park
- group business rarely exceed 15 per cent of the total
- overseas visitors to inland parks rarely exceed 5 per cent of the total; however, parks located close to international frontiers (EuropaPark, Phantasialand, De Efteling) record 30–40 per cent international visitors
- repeat business can range from 20–30 per cent of the total business
- children 4–14 years represent between 30–40 per cent of all visitors
- parks are dominated by socio-economic groups C1/C2.

Significantly, in the US it is estimated that the two Disney parks represent approximately one-third of the total annual market for theme parks. In Europe, assuming EuroDisney achieves its fully operational 17 million visitors per annum, this will represent a similar proportion of the European theme park market. Early indicators are, however, that EuroDisney's management are scaling down the estimates of annual visitations following an initial below expectation performance in 1991.

It is essential to recognise, however, that there are distinct operational differences for theme parks around the world. For example, per capita visitor spending on merchandise at Tokyo Disneyland is twice that of the US Disneyland at Y9,000; Nagasaki's Holland Village gets Y5,000 (about $36) compared to Colonial Williamsburg's $14. Similarly European parks have been generating per capita spending of about 60 per cent of the US performance, for example, De Efteling's $15 equivalent compares to £25 in US.

Key operational considerations for UK and European parks

1. Seasonality has a significant impact upon visitor numbers, their distri-

bution. The use of events and other methods of programming can be successful in extending visitation into the traditional shoulder and low seasons. Despite the sophisticated use of events, including Christmas activities, demand remains seasonally focused to the main school holiday periods in the summer months. Many parks expect 60 per cent of visitations in the period July–early September.

2. Staffing regimes need to reflect appropriate operational levels and visitor demand. Although visitor numbers may fluctuate by a factor of 10 between high and low season, clearly there is a minimum level of staffing required to provide the core service of rides and facilities operational throughout the period of opening. Generally parks maintain a core, year-round, staffing of 100–120 complement, which is gradually increased as the season progresses, so that at peak times between 500–600 total staff may be involved in the park – representing 20–25 per cent annual operational costs. Just as the demographic structural changes are affecting the visitor market, so theme parks are having to explore fresh methods of recruiting staff. The indications show increased collaboration with higher level educational institutes (especially those offering tourism-related courses) as well a shift towards older age groups, including seniors, and incentives to ensure high levels of return amongst seasonal employees.

3. The selection of rides and entertainments – together with their configuration, location and inter-relationships, is a fundamental consideration. These factors are key determinants of practical issues which will affect the success, or otherwise, of a park. These issues centre upon the contribution of individual rides or facility to the park's overall capacity. Each ride, or entertainment, plays a specific role in the construction of the visitor experience. Rides with a high volume throughput, need to be balanced with high capacity, low throughput, facilities. Parks need entertainments to suit a wide range of audiences; quiet areas for rest and relaxation; adequate corridors and routes to link features; and sufficient covered provision for shelter (from rain or sun). The success of the functional relationship between the entertainments distorts consumer reactions. Visitor management, particularly the efficacy of queuing systems and overall customer care considerations, is proving to be a major operational feature. Once again, the standards set by Disney in these aspects are causing existing operators to reassess their parks.

4. Peaking of visitors – this is a widespread phenomenon throughout European parks. Peak days occur outside of the main season, at Easter and early May, thus exacerbating the problems associated with seasonality (see 1 above). Peak operational days, of which there may be 30–35 in April–October in a seven month opening period, are likely to generate 30–35 per cent of total attendance. It is interesting to note that throughout the attraction sector, a peak day attendance is generally 1 per cent of the total annual level of visitation. A peak day will generate 3.5–4 times the normal average daily attendance in the main season. Peaking creates a number of operational concerns relating to facility provision, staffing and other resourcing criteria which need to be addressed.

Exemplar 5.5

Tourism Quality Services Limited, Wales

TQS Ltd is a company established to operate quality assurance and associated inspection services. It was established in association with the Wales Tourist Board in April 1990 with an independent board. Initially TQS was contracted, on an ongoing basis, to inspect 5,000 accommodation units in Wales ranging from large hotels to self-catering complexes. Over the past two years the company has become fully involved with the British Standard for Quality Assurance as inspectors and consultants and today operate in a number of countries around the world.

During 1989 the English Tourist Board piloted a scheme for the inspection of visitor attractions in the West Country Tourist Board Region. After a number of refinements the ETB adopted the inspection scheme for England in 1991. At the same time the South Wales Tourist Board's Attractions Advisory Committee involved TQS as a pilot project in Wales.

The response by attraction operators to these schemes has been positive and in 1992 a quality assurance inspection programme was introduced by TQS in Wales on behalf of the tourist board. The inspection process involves independent, trained, inspectors making anonymous visits to judge a wide range of agreed operational and presentational criteria. Very often the inspections are made as part of a family or social group thus giving the inspector feedback from a broader range of consumers.

The inspectors score the attraction for provision of service and standards of cleanliness, presentation, and safety on a reporting form. An important function of the inspection process is the debriefing by TQS Ltd, with individual operators. This helps ensure that issues are addressed and standards maintained, or hopefully, improved.

Attraction operators pay a nominal fee for the inspection process and are rewarded with a certificate. It is the long-term intention of the scheme that only attractions inspected and verified by the Wales Tourist Board through TQS Ltd will be promoted in Board literature.

5. Operational standards and the quality of the product is being given increasingly high importance. The standards established by Disney, particularly in relation to cleanliness, safety and customer care, are being emulated throughout the industry. Quality assurance procedures are now being introduced in a number of areas. In Scotland, the Scottish Association of Visitor Attractions (Graw 1992) have commenced an inspection scheme, whilst the Wales and English Tourist Boards introduced an attractions accreditation scheme in 1992. At this stage IAAPA and Europarks, the two leading representatives of theme park operators, have not indicated a move towards such assurance mechanisms.

6. Profitability and methods of stimulating revenue have become key issues. Parks are increasingly following the Disney model of developing opportunities for secondary spending within parks for day visitors (pri-

marily through retailing of food and beverage and gift merchandising). Other methods of extending the commercial potential of the parks are through the leasing of facilities for event, conferences, incentive business filming and product launches. Kings Dominion theme park in Virginia (USA) has a 10,000 seater multipurpose auditorium which regularly hosts concerts by top name musicians, whilst the Mountbatten Pavilion at Thorpe Park (UK) is the venue for a myriad of conferences and business events.

It should be re-iterated at this stage that information on operational profits is limited. Table 5.2 uses published annual reports for two parks in the UK indicating that profit as a percentage of turnover may be expected at between 20–25 per cent.

Table 5.2 Comparative performance of two UK theme parks 1987

	Park X	Park Y
Visitors 000s	2.30m	0.813m
Turnover	£16.5m	£4.8m
Employee Cost	£4.4m (26.5%)	£0.97m (20%)
Depreciation	£1.9m	£0.28m
Operational profits	£3.7m	£1.1m
Profit as % turnover	22.5	23.7

Returning to the issue of retaining visitor spending within a theme park, operators recognise a wide range of benefits which accrue from these activities in addition to the simple feature of enhanced spending. Evidence suggests that in UK and European parks, expenditure on food and beverage may represent up to one third of total receipts from admission charges whilst retailing of souvenirs and gifts generates 20–25 per cent of gate receipts. These figures as we have seen are low compared to the anticipated 80 per cent of combined secondary spend on food, beverage and merchandise at the Disney operations and are about 60 per cent of levels of per capita secondary spend expected in US theme parks.

Secondary spending can be regarded as the per capital expenditure from visitors that takes place in a park once the primary products (entry fee, parking, access to rides) have been purchased – a kind of discretionary disposable income. There are a range of secondary spend activities. Secondary spend opportunities may include merchandise, food and beverages, momento-type souvenirs (eg themed photographs), service hire (eg cameras, baby buggies, telephones), donations, or fees for special or exclusive use of facilities or events. These activities, if undertaken successfully and as an integrated feature, serve a number of functions, besides generating income, including:

- they add value to the visitor experience, meeting demand and extending the length of stay, thus they enhance visitor satisfaction
- they increase the variety of facilities available, extend the capacity of the park and provide additional covered areas

- the facilities are services that can be used effectively to develop theming through stylised menus, costumed staff, authenticated souvenirs
- the merchandise in particular complements and reinforces the marketing activity. Gifts bearing the park name or promotional logo (T-shirts, pens, hats, postcards) are efficient promotional tools

and, finally

- retailing activities increase the personal contract between the park, its staff and the visitor. This can usefully (i) serve to develop referral marketing within the park (ie staff suggesting rides to visit); (ii) be used to gather market research about visitors; and (iii) stimulate further sales or repeated business but basis customer care.

Theme parks have developed the secondary spend activities to varying degrees of sophistication, scale and quality. At Alton Towers, Thorpe Park and Drayton Manor in the UK, entire 'streets' of merchandising activity have been developed. In Phantasialand and EuropaPark in Germany discrete, theme-related retailing takes place supported by peripatetic 'carts' selling merchandise. Phantasialand is a good example of themed catering with a series of appropriately focused restaurants, snack bars and bars reflecting the themed areas of Chinatown, the Wild West, Petit Paris and Berlinstrasse.

In the main, these secondary spend services and facilities are managed in-house by the park operator. There have been limited attempts to introduce concessions at a number of parks. Clearly, however, the purpose of providing the retailing is to stimulate income, and there is little proof that the fees received from a concession outweigh the profit from a self-operated outlet. The issue of franchising and concessionary activity will become an increasingly important operational consideration over the next 10 years.

One of the most enduring of recent trends has been the integration of themed entertainment and amusements into retailing, food and beverage operations. As development companies and retailers compete for customers there has been increasing innovation in ways shopping malls and centres can gain a competitive position. As we have seen, parks have fully embraced the concept of themed retailing and catering to enhance their revenue performance due to higher consumer expectations. The same demands are at work in the retail environment.

The traditional demarcation between entertainment and retail is being rapidly eroded (Wade, 1992) as highly themed restaurants (eg Hard Rock Cafe Inc, Daryls Inc, and The Hollywood Bowl) together with high profile resort destinations, raise public awareness of the attractiveness of theming. The West Edmonton Mall in Alberta, Canada, and Metroland in Gateshead, UK (with 10 rides) have pioneered large scale retail complexes with integrated theme–posh style amusements. 'Increasingly specific retail stores are using small attractions and cost-efficient theming to enhance the retail environment' (Wade 1992).

It is significant that primary entertainment companies including Disney and Warner have firmly entered the retailing industry – Disney with over

130 Disney Stores worldwide. In the UK the heritage attraction charity, the National Trust, has for a number of years translated its attraction-based trading operations into the high street. Perhaps the most successful example of the transition between retailing and the concept of theme park entertainment is that adopted by the 'Sanrio Company of Tokyo, Japan. In the mid 1970s Sanrio expanded its retail operations into the USA and now operates 126 stores (16 wholly owned, 110 under license) handling 3,000 themed product lines. The next logical step was to apply the park concept in the development of the Sanrio Ginza Gallery in Tokyo which opened in 1987. The critical aspect of the success of the gallery is the integration of interactive technology entertainment and merchandise.

Future prospects for the industry

The management of the theme parks is seen, therefore, as an increasingly complex and multi-faceted skill. Although it is forecast that the day visitor market in Europe will continue to increase, and scope exists for theme parks to increase upon their current penetration of the market, there will be relatively few new theme parks developed. Scope exists, as has been identified by Anhauser-Busch for park development in Southern Spain, and there is some activity in Southern France. Opportunities in Eastern Europe will remain limited for the foreseeable future, at least until personal incomes and mobility achieve reasonable levels.

Consequently, theme park development is likely to remain a northern European and UK phenomenon in the context of Europe, with limited developments close to the main tourist destinations of the Mediterranean. Elsewhere around the world, developments are set to continue at a pace, particularly in the Pacific Rim region, South America and South Africa (Stevens, 1992). It is predicted that the predominant features of the European theme park industry over the next 10 years are likely to be as follows:

- on-going improvements, upgrading and extension of existing operations
- the development of integrated holiday resort complexes in association with the theme park
- investment in quality and assurance of standards
- increased orientation to the family market and product development aimed at encouraging visitor participation and involvement
- the development of an entertainments, including live music, base for new market activity
- the potential for independent holding companies or investors to use existing park management expertise to operate parks, and
- the further investment in Europe by American theme park companies who are aware that the US market has plateaued out.

De Efteling in Holland is a particularly good example of these recent phenomena at work, as well as being an example of good practice in a number of developmental and operational aspects.

Exemplar 5.6

De Efteling

De Efteling, located at Kaatsheuval in Holland, is within a 90–120 minute drive of the major population centres of the Randstadt, Belgium and Western Germany. Despite this international catchment, Efteling's visitors are predominantly Dutch 87 per cent with 60 per cent returning within a three year period.

Opened originally as a sports complex in 1933, then developed into a nature park and playground in 1951, Efteling officially opened with the 'Garden of Fairy Tales' in May 1952. Efteling has long-term claims, therefore, as Europe's premier theme park, influencing Disney and continuing to lead in product development. The park's management consider their product to be complementary to EuroDisney, but recognise the need for further expansion, diversification and improvement to ensure their continued success.

Throughout its 40 year history, Efteling has judiciously invested in order to offer a fresh product to its core market. The original fairytale garden, designed by Anton Pieck and animated by Peter Reijnders, continues to provide a solid attraction for families with young children. The current park covers 72 ha, one-fifth of the land available (380 ha) for development, and embraces forests, lakes, rivers and high quality landscaped areas. The floral displays and amenity horticulture are a major attraction for the park, as well as creating a pleasant environment in which to develop the themed areas.

Throughout the 1960s and 1970s, additional fairytale themes were added to the forest areas. In 1981 the park added its first white knuckle ride – the Python – a corkscrew roller coaster and forerunner of a series of thrill rides designed to broaden the market appeal. These ride investments included the Halve Maen, a swing pirate ship (1982); the Pirana, a white water rafting experience (1983); Carnival Fiesta (1984); and The Bob, a bobsleigh run (1985).

In 1986 the Arabian Adventure of 'Fata Morgana' opened after 5 years' planning and an investment of 15m Dutch guilders. This major themed attraction comprises a water boat ride through an Aladdin's cave and a series of audio-animatronic figures in a series of tableaux. During the late 1980s the management of Efteling concentrated upon enhancing the park's infrastructure: introducing 50,000m^2 of floral displays, upgrading and extending restaurants; developing intra-park transport systems; and extending the original fairytale concept.

By 1990 the park had secured 2.5 million visitors per annum, extended its peak operational capacity to 40,000 per day (6,500 car parking spaces, 150 coach spaces); and was well advanced on an ambitious programme of diversification and expansion for the 1990s. This expansion programme has a number of key components:

Exemplar 5.6 (continued)

1. Consolidation of the park as Europe's premier traditional theme park with the opening of the wooden roller coaster, Pegasus; the addition of the Great Efteling Summer Circus and Summer Ice Show, and the fortieth anniversary attraction 'Dream Flight'.
2. The phased creation of a year-round resort based upon a range of overnight accommodation. The Efteling Hotel, a 12 room 3 star hotel to meet demand for extended visits to the park, opened in June 1992 as phase 1 of this programme, at a cost of 15.5 million, designed by Meeuwis of Holland. Phase two, scheduled for 1996, is a themed holiday village with 650 holiday apartments.
3. Diversification is focused upon the development of an 18 hole golf course in 1993, to be extended to 27 holes in 1996, and the construction of a multi-purpose entertainments complex by 1994.

Efteling's opening season is mid-April through until late October. A pay-one-price admissions policy is applied with discounting available for groups and for a two-day ticket. A range of innovative visitor services have been introduced, including wheelchair and pushchair rentals, and advance purchase vouchers for group use in the park's restaurants and retail outlets. Picnic areas, novel litter gobblers (Holle Bolle Gijzen) and regular live entertainment throughout the park are further examples of good practice by one of Europe's oldest theme parks.

Conclusion

Theme parks, whilst being embraced by national tourism policies and often receiving significant levels of assistance towards their development, primarily service the day visitor markets. Only the US Disney parks and EuroDisney attract a strong overseas tourist element. However, several theme parks operating close to international frontiers in Europe, not surprisingly record high levels of 'international' day visitors activity – for example, the Belgian Parks together with Phantasialand (Koln) and EuropePark (Rust) in Germany estimate that 40–60 per cent of their day visitors are from neighbouring countries – and all parks are looking to develop their tourist potential. Brown and Church (1987) do make the legitimate point, however, that theme parks stimulate the short break market and positively contribute to the general tourist awareness of a region. Trends to develop integrated accommodation associated with parks will reinforce these attributes.

The overall number of theme parks in the whole of Europe, totalling less than 40 in 1992, is unlikely to increase significantly. The overall size of the day visitor market will continue to show growth; however, it is predicted that supply will continue to match demand. Consequently, average attendance figures are unlikely to show significant changes. These predictions are made on the assumption that parks continue to invest in their product development, and that future investments take account of the changing demography and market demands. Survival will be dependent upon reposi-

Exemplar 5.7

Big Bang Smurf World

In 1990 Sorepark S.A. the then owners of Big Bang Smurf Theme Park recognised the potential of the UK market particularly in the post-Euro-Tunnel period. The theme park, which opened in 1988, is strategically located in the North East close to the borders of Germany and the Benelux countries.

The park's marketing campaign aimed at the UK market, launched in 1990, has three main strands:

- package arrangements with major coach and tour operators
- sponsorship and associated short-break activities for one-off events
- joint promotional campaigns

Big Bang Smurf theme park's initial visitor numbers of 700,000 in year one exceeded expectations, however, heavy operational losses were reported to the share holders who included Parilsas, Society General and Groupe Suez. The park has 100 rides and three theatres spread throughout four main themed areas which originally focused upon the Age of Civilisation, the Art of the Future, the Village of the Smurfs and the Wild Continent. Critical to the marketing approach is the fact that the park is being promoted as a 'European Theme Park'. A concept which recognises the initial tide of reaction in France against the imposition of American storylines and themes in a growing number of European parks. Later in 1990, however, the Walibi Group (Belgium) purchased the failing park and re-opened it as Walibi Schromph.

tioning towards the family, and revenue enhancement. The impact of Euro-Disney will focus attention upon improving the quality of the product and enhancing the operational aspects of park management. Richards (1992) suggests that market penetration by theme parks in Europe is still low with only 17 per cent of the population visiting compared to 60 per cent in Japan or the USA. Whilst cultural differences are likely to account for these variations it is also apparent that an investment in quality, weatherproofing and diversification for many theme parks in Europe and the UK is essential.

References

Brown, J. and Church, A. (1987) 'Theme Parks in Europe. Travel and Tourism Analyst', February, *The Economist*.
Christopher, T. (1992) *The Theme Park Experience*. Landmark Ent.
ETB (1991) *The Handbook of Tourism Products*. London.
Gratton, C. (1992) 'Is there Life After Disney?'. *Leisure Management* **12** 4.
Graw, L. (1992) *The Scottish Association of Visitor Attractions*. Bord Failte, January.
Grover, R. (1991) *The Disney Touch*. Business One.
IAAPA (1991) *International Directory and Buyers' Guide*. Virginia.
Larner, C. (1992) 'Shaping Up to Disney'. *Leisure Management*, May **12** 5.
Lavery, P. & Stevens, T. (1990) 'Attendance Trends and Future Developments at Europe's Leisure Attractions'. *Travel and Tourism Analyst* 2.

Lyon, R. (1987) 'Theme Parks in the USA. Travel and Tourism Analyst', January, *The Economist*.
Murphy, C. (1992) *Investing in the Future Park World*, June.
Projection 2000 (1991) *Theme Parks Report*. London.
Richards, B. (1992) 'Themed Trends'. *Leisure Management* **12** 12.
Stevens, T. (1992) 'Trends in the Attraction Industry'. *World Travel & Tourism Review* **2**.
Wardley, J. (1989) 'An Interview with Terry Stevens'. *Leisure Management* **9** 3.
Wade, G. (1992) 'Upscaling Merchandise'. *Funworld* May 1992.

6 Heritage centres

Siân Johnson

Introduction

Visitor attractions perform a critical role in the tourist market; they add character to a destination area, and are capable of generating tourist traffic in their own right.

The 1980s saw a rapid development and sophistication of the visitor attractions market. The UK market now comprises some 5,000 attractions of which only 1,000 achieve visitor figures of more than 1,000 visitors a week. The market growth has been brought about partly through the increase in day visiting activity as car-ownership has grown, and partly through technological advances in display techniques. The strength of the demand for visiting attractions is illustrated by time series analysis from the Touche Ross Leisure Attractions Database, which holds records on the sector going back to 1985. Such analysis shows that not only did commercial sites, ie those that charge admission, register a 10 per cent volume increase in attendance figures between 1986 and 1990, but that admission prices increased in real terms by 44 per cent over the same period.

In 1991 however, visitor figures for commercial attractions declined against 1990, as recessionary forces affected leisure spending power. Meanwhile new developments in the market, conceived during the leisure boom of the 1980s chose 1991 as their launch year.

This chapter examines two UK attractions and a new French entry into the visitor attractions market across the channel at Boulogne which attracts 105,000 visitors from the UK alone. All three were conceived during the leisure boom of the 1980s, but their launch coincided with the onset of the recession in the UK. Two of these, Tullie House and Nausicaâ, represented significant investment from the public sector, seeking the economic benefits of inward tourism expenditure. The third, Cadbury World, is a purely private sector investment in the visitor attractions market, and offers a fascinating insight into how marketing professionals have addressed the attractions sector.

Case study 6.1: Tullie House, Carlisle

Key features

- ▲ *Adapted local authority visitor attraction site.*
- ▲ *Training and team building.*
- ▲ *Marketing and promotion.*
- ▲ *Management style.*
- ▲ *Local usage.*

Development history

Tullie House in Carlisle is an example of a municipal museum which has turned into a visitor attraction, and in so doing has become a cultural venue to serve local residents, day visitors and tourists alike. The name Tullie House is a collective name for the attraction, which includes the original Jacobean Tullie House, a state of the art visitor experience called the Border Galleries, as well as an art gallery, an exhibition gallery and an impressive gift shop and restaurant.

The development came about as a result of a planning gain deal negotiated by Carlisle City Council with Asda, which allowed the Council to achieve its objectives of creating a venue capable of offering an interpretation of the City's heritage as well as providing space for the Museum's collections which had outgrown the space provided in Tullie House and its Victorian extension. The main period of development was from 1988–90 when the shell of a modern wing was built, consultant designer John Ronayne appointed to design the interior, and the new Director, Nick Winterbotham, appointed. The director's task was to liaise with the project development team and develop a management and operating system for the launch and post-launch running of the attraction. The original museum at Tullie House was closed for a full year for the construction, during which time pre-launch planning and marketing was undertaken by a core team. The initial capital budget of £3.5m set at the concept development stage in the mid 1980s, fell foul of the inflationary costs spiral of the development boom at the end of the decade. The final cost was £5.3m, of which £1m was spent on the Border Galleries. The new attraction opened in January 1991.

The components of Tullie House

The total floorspace for the complex is 18,600 square feet, of which the display area, excluding the art and exhibition galleries, is approximately one fifth. The shop is relatively large at 900 square feet and the catering area at 2,400 square feet allows 160 covers and is adequate for functions business. There is a 100 seat lecture theatre which has a dual use for education and for corporate hire. Access is free to the ground floor area which includes the art gallery and the Jacobean House. Admission charges are made for the Border Galleries in the upstairs area, where visitors can spend over an hour in an attraction which manages to combine the many disparate themes of Carlisle as a Border City into a varied and stimulating experience. By means of different display and audio-visual techniques the Border Galleries cover the themes of archaeology, the Roman heritage and Hadrian's Wall, medieval siege warfare, the Border raiders, the Civil War, the Jacobite rebellion and Carlisle's railway heritage, as well as the natural environment of the rural areas surrounding the city.

Pricing policy

Admission charges at launch were £2.80 per adult and £1.40 for children and concessions, and prices have risen to £3.30 (adults) by the third year of operating. However, admission prices are not charged to the 100,000 residents of Carlisle who, by means of purchasing a 'Tullie Card' for 75p, have free access to Tullie House for life.

Performance against plan

Tullie House declared 300,000 visitors in its first year, and 280,000 in 1992. Of these, only 140,000 in 1991 and 120,000 in 1992 paid admission to the Border Galleries, and it is this area where performance has been below expectations. Given the relatively isolated position of Carlisle, the timing of the launch year with the 1991 recession, and the fact that the immediately surrounding population need not pay admission, it is not too surprising that the paid admissions figure is below 200,000. The City Council is pleased with the overall performance of some 300,000 visitors and in particular with the fact that 30,000 Tullie cards have been issued, which is a very high penetration figure and demonstrates that Tullie House is reaching its primary objective of serving the community.

Visitor management

Tullie House experienced congestion at entry during its first week, and is busy on wet Bank Holidays, but it has not found it necessary to adjust its visitor management policies other than by staffing more tills. It has however altered the shape of the reception area so that the visitor flow through the shop is improved. Although there are days of light visitor flows, management policy has been to maintain its opening policy of 364 days a year.

Management structure

The management structure comprises a Director and six department heads. These are:

- Services, which includes all front of house activities, licences, technical services and catering
- Curator

- Education
- Arts
- Marketing
- Contract management

The last department involves the management of the catering contract, and it is in fact the contractor's manager who is a member of the Tullie House management team.

Financial management is the responsibility of the Director who draws on the central services of the Council for payroll, management accounting and purchasing.

Staffing

There are 43 people on the Tullie House payroll which is £470,000 pa, but the total number of paid and unpaid (ie volunteer) jobs is 80, including the catering staff. All payroll staff, whatever their function are on a salary-based remuneration package, which means they are all members of the same union. It also means that the salary-scale for the main front of house staff is much higher than would have been the equivalent under a wage-based system, and therefore Tullie House benefits from a number of high-calibre staff who have in the main been employed since inception. This front of house team speaks five languages between them and is trained in:

- till handling
- first aid, disabled support, fire and bomb-scare evacuation
- interpretation and guiding
- exhibit handling; and
- shop management.

Management operation

The main departmental managers meet once a week for an operations meeting and for a management meeting. In addition, Tullie House has a number of teams with specific tasks, such as education, marketing, events. The teams are cross-departmental and meet regularly. Full staff meetings are held monthly.

Every member of the management team serves on the seven-day duty-officer rota, whatever their main discipline, which means that each obtains the experience of hands-on management.

Each department is a cost centre, and department managers run their own budgets. In addition, there are eleven sub-departmental cost centres.

Training

New front of house staff undertake a two-week induction training in tandem with a staff member, and on the job training is continuous. There is a formal training period every second Monday, when the Museum is late in opening its doors, and this training is carried out by the management team and sometimes by outsiders. Staff are trained in certain topic areas within their cross departmental teams. The topics emerge from the different disciplines encompassed by the staff and include such areas as archaeology, education and teaching skills, sponsorship, team management and managerial skills.

Tullie House has won a regional award for its training programme; it is the Lady Inglewood award and has always in the past been won by private sector companies.

Quality management

The quality management system at Tullie House is based on team building. The management team investigated the possibility of a system based on BS5750, but felt it was inappropriate and unnecessarily costly, especially in terms of the maintenance after implementation. Instead they have opted for a system called Team Improvement Review, or TIR, which is a form of group appraisal. Under TIR team meetings have a behavioural agenda which sets out team personal objectives as well as the business of the day. A team member is appointed to take notes against the behavioural agenda, and at the end of the meeting reports on the behaviour of the team leader and members. Recurring issues are:

- whether management listens
- do certain team players dominate by interrupting, and
- do all who might contribute do so.

It is felt that TIR gives meetings and staff a sense of purpose and meetings have become more structured and businesslike since its inception.

Other aspects of quality management is the training programme, as described earlier, and a system of individual appraisal which is not salary-related. It is a voluntary scheme and involves an informal, one-to-one interview between boss and staff members. The interview is investigative, but no 'carrot and stick' techniques are employed to seek improvements. No formal records are kept on the central personnel file, although a pencil and paper record is made and each has a copy, which is destroyed/returned when the employee leaves. By keeping this appraisal system separate from the performance monitoring and salary review systems the management feels it achieves a more truthful feedback from employees on how the management is performing, as well as how individuals are developing.

Marketing activity

The marketing budget is only £30,000 which is some 7 per cent of turnover. There is extra marketing resource through the tourism marketing officer for Carlisle, however Tullie House does not have a dedicated part of the city's tourism marketing budget to develop the tourist market more directly.

The in-house marketing activity has tended to concentrate on trips

originating from within 60 minutes, which management believes represents a residential catchment of only 500,000 people.

In its pre- and immediately post-development period the marketing effort was to build awareness of Tullie House locally and through the educational sector, so as to build business through word of mouth referrals and repeat visits. The marketing team has monitored the visitor profile by visitor surveys, sampling 800–1,000 visitors a year over three or four periods, and management feels it has achieved success through return visits by children bringing parents after a school trip, and by Carlisle residents hosting visiting friends and relations, whom they introduce to Tullie House. The majority of paying visitors are either on a day trip from the North West and West Yorkshire, or are tourists on a day trip from a holiday base such as the Lake District or Northumbria.

Promotional activity has included co-operating in coupon-redeeming promotions where these are offered, and contributing on a co-operative basis to a Christmas TV commercial promoting books, one of which is exclusive to the Tullie House shop which thus ensured Tullie House being featured in the advertisement. The management has also developed a software package based on key stages 2 and 3 of the National Curriculum Discovery of Sources. This package has been successfully sold to several education authorities throughout England and Wales, and by being based on Tullie House, is regarded as fulfilling a marketing function on a self-liquidating basis.

Marketing plans for the future include developing the Scottish market, such as to participate in Scottish Travel Fairs.

Funding

Tullie House was funded as a result of a windfall capital receipt from a retail deal. Ninety-six per cent of its capital budget was met by the City of Carlisle City Council, and 4 per cent by one of the last Section 4 tourism grants from the English Tourist Board. Its revenue budget also requires a subsidy from the City of Carlisle as part of the museum service. With free entry for some 180,000 visits a year from holders of the Tullie card, the museum has an operating deficit of £800,000. The 1992 turnover was £420,000. A deeper penetration of the tourism and destination day trip markets would reduce the deficit through increased revenue, but it would not be eliminated without a substantial drop in operating costs. Tullie House after all is a museum as well as a visitor attraction, and needs public sector support to serve its educational and curatorial responsibilities.

Key points

- ▲ *Tullie House has made the successful progression from traditional municipal museum to a sophisticated visitor attraction complex.*
- ▲ *It benefits from a quality approach based on team building and a successful training programme.*

- ▲ *It is distinguished by its mix of high calibre staff and unpaid volunteers.*
- ▲ *Its management team all take their turn in the seven day duty officer role.*

Case study 6.2: Nausicaâ, Boulogne

Key features

- ▲ *Mixed public and private sector visitor attraction.*
- ▲ *Its theme is the sea.*
- ▲ *Interactive and educational service concept.*
- ▲ *Primary catering.*
- ▲ *Visitor management.*
- ▲ *High usage*

Nausicaâ stands on a prominent position beside the harbour at Boulogne, on the site of an old casino. It is an exciting visitor attraction on the theme of the sea, and comprises aquaria and audio-visual displays as the main visitor experience.

Nausicaâ was the inspiration of three marine biologists, one of whom, Philippe Valette is the Director-General today. It opened in May 1991, after nine years of planning and development, much of which was taken up with the negotiations for the £16m capital budget. The architect Jacques Rougerie won the contract after an international competition, and the designer was Le Conte-Nairot. From the start, Noirot Nausicaâ has worked to its stated mission:

> 'To inform by all possible means the need to manage the Sea, its resources and environment, and to persuade that each of us is responsible for so doing'.

The components of Nausicaâ

Nausicaâ occupies 150,000 sq feet of gross floor space, and includes tanks of a capacity of 600,000 litres. It offers the visitor the means to touch, see and listen to the sea, starting with a 60 foot wall of plankton, to tanks and displays of fish and other sea creatures. There are 5,000 fish altogether. The theme embraces every aspect of the sea and its creatures, covering pollution, the dangers of commercial fishing, predators, wrecks, a coral lagoon and a touch pool. The tanks are dramatically displayed, one as a suspended diamond swirling with tuna fish, and another giving the impression of being surrounded by sharks. There is a walk-on audio visual set in the form of a trawler, where sound, light and temperature changes simulate the effect of battling against the elements at sea. The length of stay for the whole attraction is up to two hours.

Nausicaâ has a shop which is run by the management, but the difference between Nausicaâ and an equivalent British attraction lies in its catering. Where in Britain a self-service cafeteria is the typical end of

stay catering offer, Nausicaâ has a full-service prestigious fish restaurant, with views over the harbour and a capacity for 300 covers. It was awarded two Michelin forks in its first year and is operated by a concessionaire; it is open at lunch-times and in the evening after the attraction has closed. In addition to the display areas there is a marine resource centre and library, called the 'Mediathéque', and a cinema and educational suite which is also used for corporate functions. There is an active educational programme, including an out-reach distance learning package for schools sponsored by Findus, which reaches 130,000 primary school classes.

Pricing policy

The admission price at launch was 45ff for adults and 30ff for children. A modest increase to 48ff and 33ff respectively in April 1993 may have taken into consideration that the significant proportion of visitors who are British had already faced a larger price increase through devaluation. Group discounts are not particularly generous at approximately 5 per cent, and parties have to book in advance to qualify.

Performance against plan

Low discounts for party-bookings and a policy of restricting groups to low season periods are a sure sign of a successful attraction, and Nausicaâ is no exception. During the development period two market appraisal studies were conducted by Paris-based business consultancies, and visitor figures were forecast at around 350,000 pa. The promoter's own forecast of 500,000 was initially regarded as optimistic, but in the event the 12 months from May 1991 saw 700,000 visitors through the door, and in September 1992 Nausicaâ announced its first million.

Visitor management

Nausicaâ's management experienced congestion from 2,600 visitors on its first day, when a queue formed from the boulevard up the steps and into the foyer. The initial problems were solved by expanding the number of till points and creating a separate entry system for groups. However they have problems with capacity on more than peak days, and have developed a timed entry system. It is based on a computer programme developed by a Lille-based software company. Maximum visitor flow is based on allowing 50 people to spend five minutes at each display point, which means they have an acceptable capacity of 1,200 people on site. The flow of visitors is monitored by the front of house staff, each of whom carries a walkie-talkie radio. A signal system at the till flashes up three levels of flow:

- green = light
- orange = 800–1,000 on site
- red = 1,000 or more.

Management and structure

Nausicaâ is owned by a private company whose corporate status in French law is known as a 'Societé anonyme d'economie mixte'. Eighty per cent of the ownership is by public sector agencies, representing the original funders of the project, and 20 per cent is owned by private sector companies. These include the ferry companies, Eurotunnel, and local French firms and entrepreneurs who have an interest in the benefits of Nausicaâ to the local economy.

The management team comprises the Director-General and six department heads, namely:

- Marketing
- Communication
- Aquariology
- Cultural Animation, which covers education, exhibitions and programming
- Development
- General services, which includes finance, administration and personnel.

The average age of the management team is 34.

Staffing

There is a core payroll of 50 at Nausicaâ, with extra staff in the summer. The back of house team includes eight aquariologists, as well as people involved in the education programme, the mediathèque and administration. The back of house team includes 10 'hostesses' who are involved in customer handling; the number rises to 16 in the summer months. The qualifications for the job are education to the level of 'A' level equivalent, and fluency in English. After interview the team is selected for having a positive attitude towards the sea and the environment, and for general appearance. Originally, both young men and women were appointed to this team. There has been a staff turnover of 30 per cent per year, and the team is now all-female, and, typically, young and attractive. The hostesses wear a casual uniform of tracksuits in the winter and shorts and T-shirt in the summer, with a large Nausicaâ logo on the back. Name badges are worn by all front of house staff, and language skills are being extended to include Dutch and German.

Quality management

Nausicaâ's quality management system works in two ways: by identifying quality indicators and setting standards, and by running quality circles. Examples of quality indicators are:

- the life-span of the fish
- speed of paying suppliers (less than 30 days is the target)
- cleanliness

- number of equipment breakdowns
- the 'welcome quality' (defined in consultation with staff).

The exit survey questionnaires are used to monitor quality by feedback from the public.

Quality circles are organised through section meetings which are held once a month. Staff are encouraged to be self-determining in developing quality improvement; this means that they are active in developing quality management rather than simply working to imposed systems.

Training

Before it opened, Nausicaâ's head of general services had hired the full complement of staff, who underwent five weeks pre-launch training. Such training is now conducted on the job, with staff who join the front of house team, for instance undergoing a trial period. The front of house team is trained in:

- till and ticketing procedures
- security, including evacuation, first aid, fire drill
- equipment breakdown
- customer handling, including guiding groups
- self-presentation, and
- the welcome and smile.

Training is done by a supervisor combined with work shadowing a team commando.

Marketing

The marketing budget is set at 10 per cent of shop and admission sales, apart from the pre-launch marketing activity. During the development period the marketing strategy identified a number of visitor targets, and performance in reaching them was monitored post-launch through exit surveys. The catchment was defined as 50 million people living within 160 miles, which includes London, Paris and Brussels. Fifteen per cent of the first year's visitors were British, a proportion which was rising in the first half of 1992, but which probably settled back after devaluation. Five per cent of the business is from group bookings, and a third of the visitors are children under 12 years.

The main medium for building awareness in the launch year was advertising, starting with French regional press such as Voix du Nord. The campaign was extended to posters on 1,200 sites including the London Underground and Paris. Travel trade directories and guides were used, and exhibitions such as World Travel Market. The ferry companies, who have a stake in Nausicaâ, have been used for promotions and leaflet distribution. £400,000 was spent on advertising and promotion in the first 18 months; this figure includes the cost of a

London based PR consultancy briefed to handle trade enquiries and obtain press coverage in the UK.

Funding

The capital costs of £16m for Nausicaâ was entirely funded by the public sector. The percentage breakdown of contributions are shown in Table 6.1.

Table 6.1

	%
European Community (ERDF)	44.6
French Government	9.8
Regional Council, Nord/Pas de Calais	16.3
General Council, Pas de Calais	8.5
Boulogne-sur-Mer Town	9.3
Chamber of Commerce and Industry	2.5
IFREMER (French Institute for Research and Development of the Sea)	5.0
Others	4.0
	100.00

The assembly of the stakeholders took many years, and undoubtedly was finally achieved after the announcement of the Channel Tunnel, which was seen as posing a threat to the ferry business which is the main source of income to Boulogne. Indeed the Folkestone–Boulogne ferry service has recently been discontinued.

The first year's turnover was £2.9m, with operating costs of £2m. With no debt finance, the resulting operating surplus has enabled them to finance the first new investment, a mini-farm for cultivating sturgeon, from revenue. The operating surplus has resulted from exceeding forecast visitor figures by 200,000. Nausicaâ is using the surplus to support its educational institution and to develop new projects in France and elsewhere.

Economic impact

With such a large investment by the public sector, the economic institute l'Insée has been commissioned to undertake an economic impact study of Nausicaâ. The management is very aware of its role in the local economy, hence its determination to pay local suppliers promptly. Nausicaâ began to develop the functions and entertainment business after the first year, but the management is opposed to social functions such as weddings and birthday parties, preferring instead to support local businesses and educational establishments.

Key points

- *It combines education, the environment and entertainment in the experience it offers.*
- *It has also established a reputation for its cuisine which is very rare for a leisure facility.*
- *It has had to tackle the healthy problem of high usage through careful visitor control.*
- *Its staff are carefully selected and are encouraged to be autonomous yet involved through quality circles.*
- *It has a huge potential catchment area and is set to benefit further from the opening of the Channel Tunnel.*

Case study 6.3: Cadbury World, Birmingham

Key features

- *Private 'factory' visitor attraction.*
- *Rapid success.*
- *Development of its service concept.*
- *Visitor management.*
- *Approach to quality.*
- *Market-led philosophy.*

Development history

Cadbury World opened in August 1990, and within a year became the most successful 'factory visit' attraction in the UK. Its achievement in adjusting both the product and the marketing techniques to bring about this success is a tribute to the professional, market-led approach to a new business area adopted by its parent company, Cadbury Ltd.

The concept for a dedicated visitor attraction arose from a review of Cadbury Ltd's public relations in the mid 1980s. It emerged that the decision to close the firm's popular factory tours as a result of concern over health and hygiene, combined with increased mechanisation in the production process, had created a void in public relations in terms of communicating the message that Cadbury is 'the first name in chocolate'.

Thousands of requests for factory visits were still being received, so the company commissioned a feasibility study in 1987 to examine the potential of a stand-alone visitor attraction on the Bournville factory site, the heartland of Cadbury's corporate heritage. The purpose of the project was to create a marketing resource to reinforce public perceptions of the Cadbury name, but at the same time to be self-financing.

The capital cost for all external and internal works was £5.3m.

The concept and its evolution

The umbrella concept for the attraction was to project the central message:

'Cadbury means chocolate means fun'

The main components of the visitor experience which emerged from the development plan were:

- interpretation of the history of chocolate
- the story of the Cadbury history
- the history of the Bournville site
- a demonstration of chocolate making
- interpretation of Cadbury today, and its advertising material
- a shop with a catering outlet.

From the moment the product was previewed by the trade and press, and over the initial trading period, the management monitored and measured consumer reaction. As a consequence, considerable adjustments were made to the displays and experiences on offer. The changes came about partly as a result of public demand, and partly as a result of capacity problems as the popularity of the attraction grew. For although visitor figures were greatly above projected levels, the company took the long-term view that it should seek to maximise customer satisfaction and secure the corporate PR benefits set down in the original purpose.

Examples of the changes made were:

- more sampling of chocolate during the visit
- the addition of a 'real' factory tour, by opening up a packaging line to public viewing
- development of the advertising story, especially the Milk Tray TV commercial
- adjustment of the Cadbury heritage display, so as to optimise visitor flows
- a change in the pricing strategy in the shop, to cater for the principle of 'weaver-to-wearer' discount expectations of the visitors
- the alteration of the catering policy in the restaurant, by simplifying the menu and speeding up food-service delivery.

The company still monitors visitor satisfaction, but is more confident that it has developed a new brand in the company portfolio which matches up to the quality of the other Cadbury brands. Moreover Cadbury World fulfils a promotional function in communicating both the corporate and the other brand values to the public and trade, and it now constitutes a key part of what Cadbury call 'presence marketing'.

Pricing policy

The original tours were free, on request for a booking. Cadbury World has charged admission from launch of £3.75 for adults and £2.75 for children. Prices rose to £4.00 and £3.00 during 1991 and 1992. In 1993 adult admission rose to £4.50, but the children's admission price was frozen. Senior Citizens are admitted at £3.95, Monday to Friday only. A family Ticket (2 + 2) offers a £2 reduction.

The company has a well-organised group discounting policy in that it ensures pre-booking on the part of groups, thus mitigating its visitor flow capacity problems. It adds extra privileges to multiple-visit groups, thus securing loyalty and repeat business in this important sector.

Performance against plan

In the last year that factory tours were available, 160,000 people visited the Cadbury chocolate manufacturing plant. The Business Plan projections for the new concept Cadbury World, as a stand-alone visitor centre with an admission charge, were for the first year's visitor figures to be 250,000. In the event they were 414,000, and 400,000 visitors per year is now regarded as the settledown rate. As a result of its gift-giving connections, Cadbury World benefits from having a strong Easter and Christmas holiday trade, as well as Mother's Day and Valentine's Day in a period which other attractions would regard as low season.

Visitor management

As previously mentioned, a major constraint on visitor numbers has been the capacity problem. The Design Day is 2,400, while the site has actually handled 3,000 on certain days. Such a high throughput is not satisfactory, however, and the management has concentrated on various techniques to alleviate the problem. These include deflecting group bookings away from popular arrival times, and selling timed admission tickets to the independent visitors who arrive during peak periods. The Cadbury World leaflet now warns potential visitors of the risk of being refused entry at very busy periods, and the company has used local radio to put people off coming when they are nearing peak capacity. In 1993 the company introduced an advanced booking system for independent visitors, and also benefited from the extension of their opening hours to include Sunday morning, for which they had to apply for permission from the planning committee which had approved the original application with Sunday afternoon opening. Finally, adjustments to the product were made with maximising capacity in mind.

Management structure

The management of Cadbury World is a sub-cell of the Cadbury Ltd Marketing Department. The General Manager is the same level as a marketing manager within Cadbury Ltd, and reports into the Marketing Director.

Under the General Manager at Cadbury World are three managers:

- Sales and Marketing, responsible for the functions of public relations, booking office, key account management and marketing, each of which has a managing executive

- Commercial Operations, responsible for retail, catering, development and all front of house operations
- Finance, responsible for day-to-day cash handling and budgets.

Staffing

There are 80–100 staff depending on the season, and further casual help hired on peak days. Staff are mainly women, with 70 per cent working front of house. All staff and managers wear first-name name badges. All staff wear uniforms.

Management operations

Management planning and systems are mainly in line with Cadbury Ltd's corporate activities. Each manager including senior managers takes a turn as duty manger, including covering weekends, as part of their management development.

Quality management

Quality Management systems are partly the same as the rest of Cadbury Ltd, but other systems have been bought in. The main system is CMQ (Cadbury Means Quality), in which the staff are divided into three teams:

- Front of House
- Back of House
- Management.

Each team has a representative from the other two and a quality facilitator, and meets fortnightly. The team leaders and the quality facilitators, who are trained quality management executives, meet separately. The system encourages a 'bottom-up' approach to quality awareness.

In addition to CMQ, Cadbury World has bought into 'MQA', a Marketing Quality system, which standardises their operations and procedures.

Training

Training is the remaining element of the quality management system. Each member of staff has a full day's training before starting the job, and up-dating training sessions are held during closed days (in periods such as mid January and early February Cadbury World does not trade seven days a week). Cadbury World have bought in a Customer Care training programme from an external tourism training consultancy, but otherwise draw upon Cadbury Ltd Personnel Department for in-house and external training programmes for managers. Cadbury World's management believe the emphasis on training ensures a welcoming smile to visitors, good staff relations and team spirit.

Marketing activity

Cadbury World is the product of a marketing philosophy based on nurturing and maintaining long-term brand values in a highly competitive market. The management has transferred the skills and disciplines of fast-moving consumer goods marketing to the visitor attractions market. It uses the whole range of marketing tools, including market intelligence, consumer and trade research, key account management, promotions, advertising and public relations. Its marketing budget is 11 per cent of turnover, a figure which is associated with successful attractions such as Jorvik, and above the norm for a sector of the leisure market which is known for low investment levels in marketing.

The marketing support for Cadbury World began in 1989, allowing for an effective pre-launch campaign as well as the build up in year one. Group bookings were the first target, and 2,000 had been achieved before Cadbury World opened. Groups account for 45 per cent of the visitor volume. Customer research in the form of exit surveys was undertaken so as to identify the visitor profile and develop the market more effectively in future campaigns. A full educational programme was developed, working in line with the educational work already established for Cadbury Ltd. Consumer advertising was used in the launch year as part of the primary task to develop awareness, but it soon became apparent that it should be confined to local press and radio commercials and used tactically to fill off-peak periods, and also as part of the visitor management strategy. Every source of business at each time of the year has been identified, and a marketing strategy designed to develop it.

Funding

Cadbury World has to meet the same financial criteria as any other new venture developed by Cadbury Ltd. The business performance criteria are confidential, but clearly it is recognised by Cadbury that an investment period is necessary to establish a new product, and it is this corporate patience and willingness to continue to support the venture which has allowed the management to develop the product further, rather than resting on its laurels as soon as it achieved its original plan in terms of visitor figures. The rewards have been reaped in increased secondary spend levels in the second year of trading, and a well-established new attraction despite being launched in the recession.

Key points

- ▲ *Cadbury has substituted their free visit scheme with what has quickly become the most successful 'factory' visitor attraction in the UK.*
- ▲ *It has created a very popular leisure experience but also has wider benefits for its core products.*
- ▲ *Its marketing strategy is sharply defined and attracts a healthy budget.*
- ▲ *It has adopted a bottom-up approach to quality.*
- ▲ *Like Nausicaâ, it has had to deal with the problems of peak visiting times.*

7 Conference centres

Martin Kinna

Introduction: the development of conference centres

The recession of the late 1980s and early 1990s and the impact of the Gulf War had the effect of reducing travel and consequently the number of delegates at meetings. By 1993 the incidence of meetings, conferences, seminars, rallies and congresses was on the increase and the delegate numbers showing a slow but definable growth.

National Tourism Offices have long recognised the importance of the 'delegate spend' and surveys on the financial impact of meetings and exhibitions on the economy of a town or region (and indeed, on a country) have focused the attention of local, regional and national authorities on the potential gains in invisible earnings of this type of business.

Gone are the days when a city had to have its cathedral before it could have confidence and self-respect among others. Today it is the conference centre that provides the municipal focus and shows its citizens what Town Hall politicians are doing with their taxes to attract more life to the area as well as provide more public amenities.

Northern Europe has seen a great change in holiday and recreational habits over the past 40 years. The hotels of the old traditional resorts have found it hard to compete with package holidays which increasingly have taken their regular and national clients to sunnier climes at advantageous prices.

Furthermore the need to extend the season in which it is profitable to keep the hotels and restaurants in operation has forced proprietors to look for alternative sources of business. This often began merely by altering the Ballroom sign to read 'Conference Room' but even that was a start. It did not take long for the meeting planner to obtain the removal of the chandelier that obscured anything projected onto a screen.

In resort towns the need to maintain tourism infrastructure, to preserve and create jobs and to attract other revenue has led municipal authorities to create conference sales and business tourism sections within their public relations and visitor promotion departments.

National associations began to see the need to travel their meetings round the country to address their regional and more demanding memberships, political parties needed to show the local nature of their interest by being available at grass roots, and in some cases there was an incentive element to delegates, which increased attendance simply by holding the meeting away from the main cities in more relaxed surroundings. As the meetings business began to grow and the needs of the organisers became more clearly focused so, at the same time, came the understanding in Town Halls of the extra value of 'delegate spend' over that of the traditional tourist. Thus the need to compete, by offering an improved conference infrastructure, became more and more a necessity and especially so in those cities and towns with an existing holiday business facing shrinking seasons in the face of overseas competition or where there was a pressing need for urban regeneration.

In many cases this led to an understanding of market forces and a perceived need for a conference centre. The benefits of such a building were thought to be the ability to attract the larger meetings events as well as to offer an extra amenity for public entertainment purposes in the town.

As it turned out, often the greatest benefit a centre has brought to a town is that it demonstrates the area is serious about having a conference capability. The centre itself, whilst being the figurehead and providing the marketing impetus, has actually attracted many more meetings to other facilities in its area, the most notable beneficiaries being the hotels, which already benefit from the bed-nights.

Today there is much more understanding of how to look at both the feasibility and the viability of such projects and where to go to obtain the necessary marketing advice. Managers of conference centres, especially the newer ones, are all too familiar with the regular visits of ill assorted groups of municipal worthies, engineers, money men and architects which tramp round their facilities asking all the questions that will lead, in time, to the creation of further conference facilities, at home and abroad, all able to act competitively with the very facilities being visited.

Before looking at some examples of well conceived and well run facilities it is necessary to look at the conference market and the way it operates.

The market for conference centres

The market breaks down into regional categories, Local, Regional, National, European, International etc. It can be further divided into Association, Corporate, NGO, Political, Religious and still more categories. Thus it is possible to have the conference of the National Association of Cardiologists, as well as the European and International meetings of the same type of specialists.

Each of these will differ in size and structure and the balance may vary from the amount of business of the association to be transacted to the number and scale of the social functions as well as the educational element of the meeting and whether an exhibition is held alongside.

The association market

The Association market is much favoured by those who market conference venues, services and facilities as it is the easiest market segment to research and in which to find the decision makers. The activities of International

Associations are well documented by the Union of International Associations (UIA) in Brussels, and the International Congress and Convention Association (ICCA) in Amsterdam. The UIA keeps statistics on the frequency and pattern of association meetings and ICCA tracks their movement and provides marketing information to enable suppliers to approach the correct people within the associations to solicit their business.

The corporate market

The corporate market is much harder to define and the decision makers harder to locate. There is the *Times* Top Five Hundred companies, many of which have an in-house meeting planner or organising department. However, most companies do not retain such a luxury and it can be extremely difficult for the conference salesman to locate the true decision maker in a company.

Indeed, it is often suggested that as the manager of a successful conference will probably be promoted and the manager of an unsuccessful one will probably be dismissed, so most managers probably only run one conference in their lives and then disappear from the sight of the conference sales department.

This is significant since it determines the eventual staffing structure of the conference centre and its likely success in the future sales operation. A good venue will have sufficient resources, both human and technical, in its research and marketing function because it is this that will generate the lifeblood of the building, the meetings and their delegates.

How the delegates view the building, and are able to use it, really determines its success or otherwise in fulfilling its outward aim of attracting revenue both directly to the building itself and to its environs.

A badly maintained, staffed or managed building will swiftly receive a poor reputation in the market-place and local authorities would be well advised to look at the effects of proposed management re-structurings, changes in policy and the privatisation of services before agreeing to them. Grandiose projects with many millions invested in them can, in the wrong hands, become terrible day time wastelands if the committees and directors do not understand the industry their buildings were built to serve.

Furthermore, it is necessary to understand the differences in booking practices and reliability of the various sectors. An international conference may decide 10 years in advance on its destination. The manager of a new facility, taking his post on the first day of operation of his new building, will be unlikely to attract any international association business for at least three years and may be even more.

In contrast the corporate meeting books closer and closer to the date of the event itself and this can create enormous planning difficulties, especially in the multi-purpose hall.

The difficulties faced by those buildings which share their meetings facilities with resident orchestras (as London's Barbican Centre), are legion. Without a clear policy set out beforehand a constant warfare between the Arts and Conference Departments can become part of the daily existence of the building.

Orchestras prefer midweek and weekend dates in clearly defined seasons depending on location, and the larger international association meeting tends to have its welcome reception on a Sunday and to run through to the following Thursday or Friday, again at certain very inflexible times of year.

Provided the meeting can be booked sufficiently far ahead it can be accommodated but if the orchestra has been promised a five year tranche of dates and is hiring soloists well in advance this can still lead to difficulties and conflict.

In summary there is no such animal as a typical conference but many different types of event (large, small, regional, international, scientific, educational etc). The booking patterns of these events and their differing lead times, delegate numbers and duration can also differ widely and the decision makers vary from being very easily identifiable to almost invisible.

The accommodation requirements both for the conference itself and for the rooming of the delegates can vary also from five star and de luxe properties to university and bed and breakfast accommodation.

The three case studies

With this background it is interesting to look at three contrasting venues, one in Britain, The International Conference Centre, Birmingham, The Scanticon Centre in Elsignor, Denmark and France's Acropolis Centre in Nice.

It depends a great deal on the type of construction and the type of funding as to whether a conference centre ever makes a profit. Some claim to do so, most local authority built and managed centres do not, though great efforts are made to make the figures look as close to an operating surplus as possible. The argument goes that the money and life and jobs attracted into an area by virtue of the existence and the activities of the building justify the expense and the charges on citizens' taxes.

Privately owned conferences do not have this luxury so it is perhaps appropriate that we first examine one of the most successful conference concepts in the world, the Scanticon, privately owned and dedicated to providing a high standard of design, comfort and service for meeting planner and delegate alike and all, as one might assume, at a profit.

Case study 7.1: Scanticon

Key features

- *Privately owned.*
- *Combination of conference centre and modern hotel.*
- *Sympathetic design.*
- *Wide range of events.*

The *concept* of the Scanticon centres was born in Denmark where the daily focus and concentration on design and performance is second nature. No other European country has such an understanding of the functionality of furniture and household objects in daily use. Danish Design became an expression of caring thought and successful production immediately after the Second World War. Colour research and the suitability of everyday objects for different tasks was questioned and developed. A good example is how SAS, Scandinavian Airline Systems, designed a special coffee pot to enable its stewards to pour more easily and with less fatigue at the unnatural angle necessary when standing in aircraft gangways.

Meeting customer requirements

It was therefore, natural that the Danes considered the needs of the delegate and the meeting convener when considering the development of a conference centre. From the point of view of environment, the learning experience and entertainment, the aim from the start was to provide all the necessary constituents for a productive exchange of ideas among the participants at a meeting.

The idea behind a Scanticon is to blend a professional conference centre and a modern hotel to combine quality and comfort with hospitable efficient service. The Scanticon ambition is to see people meeting across professional, cultural, political and national boundaries and, at the same time to produce an atmosphere and a setting that are conducive to problem solving.

To achieve this the designers, led by Piet Hein, were exemplary in holding back any of the natural arrogance of the artistic architect who likes to play god. First asking the end users of facilities for meetings what it was that worked for them and where they would like to find solutions to everyday meeting problems, they gradually developed the Scanticon concept.

Not unnaturally, the professional conference organisers, and the delegates were quick to respond. All the things that had irritated in the past (the sound of catering being set up outside a meeting, poor lighting, no access to natural light, different catering needs, the lack of any facility by which the speaker could control the ambient light and the audio visuals) were aired and discussed and prioritised before any type of design solution was attempted.

Some special events are arranged each year, such as midsummer banquets or national celebrations, and there is an important trade in wedding receptions.

Denmark's Scanticon facility is run with a minimum of staff, 4 permanent technical staff, an in-house catering operation, cleaners etc and two marketeers responsible to a general manager. Scheduling is never a problem as there is no arts or entertainment element here. The building can operate as well for holidaying families as for seminars and the two can overlap with impunity. The nearest equivalent is that of an hotel.

Scanticon's success has stemmed from its original concept of enquiry. '*Find out what the clients need and then supply it*' is as good a way as describing the initial concept as the attitude of today's management.

In contrast to the two other centres selected for consideration in this chapter the Scanticon could be considered rather small scale. It should be remembered, however, that most meetings are usually for less than 100 people and last less than one full day so the need for the smaller scale facility is very important and even the classic large centres will recognise that their bread and butter business comes from the smaller, less glamorous and locally generated event. This is true too of the Acropolis Centre in Nice.

Key points

- ▲ *Its success is a result of finding out, and then supplying, customers' needs.*
- ▲ *The Scanticon concept was based on architects listening to organisers and delegates.*
- ▲ *It is a small-scale centre but marketed on the bases of quality and 'high definition'.*

Case study 7.2: Acropolis: Palais des Arts, du Tourism et des Congres. Palais des Expositions

Key features

- ▲ *Municipal award winning multi-purpose complex.*
- ▲ *Flexible design.*
- ▲ *Ambitious programming.*
- ▲ *Arts emphasis.*
- ▲ *Multi-lingual staff.*

Rationale for provision

'Award winning' has become a cliche these days but the Acropolis in Nice has probably won more awards than most large multi-purpose buildings. For a completely new facility which regularly holds major corporate events and international association meetings as well as opera and music seasons this is quite an achievement and again reflects the ability of some planners to think through in advance the purpose of their new structure.

It is unfortunate that the driving force behind the Acropolis has become discredited, for it was the vision and ability to achieve goals of M. Jaques Medecin, the then Mayor of Nice, that enabled that city to realise and benefit from this important structure. Indeed, it is the advent of the Acropolis that has enabled Nice to claim to be France's second most important city for business tourism.

In the mind of those from northern climes Nice and its association with the French Riviera conjures up the jollity of the second act of a twenties musical and the sunny pictures of Raoul Dufy. This happy perception works very much to Nice's advantage in attracting meetings of all sorts for there cannot be many who would not wish to go there.

Nice's other side is equally important but less visible; for whereas many of the cities and towns along the southern coast of France are very much tourist driven, Nice is still very much the working city it always was, and remains proud of its differences from its competitors in Cannes and Monaco.

Slightly inland from the coast was an area that had become somewhat run down and an urban regeneration project was considered. There were already some exhibition facilities in place so an extension of these to include conference facilities was a logical first step. After a lot of thought it was decided to build separately the Acropolis, dedicated to the Arts, Tourism, Congresses and Exhibitions and, to augment this with a brand new gallery of modern art.

Nice, the name, comes from Nike, the Greek word for victory, and it was to its Greek roots that the city turned when considering a new site for meetings. The name Acropolis or 'elevated part of a city' was selected and each of the various sections of the building bears a Greek name to reflect the original concept of the building and, in some senses, at least their use.

Its Technology

For the principal auditorium where conference messages are delivered we find the 'Apollon'. This has a seating capacity of 2,500 arranged in groupings in separate hexagons, differentiated by alternating colours and separated by low walls that reflect and diffuse the sound, the idea of the designer of the Berlin Philharmonic Hall, Professor L. Cremer.

When it was built in 1985, the design team concentrated on real, state of the art materials and aimed at the newest in technological equipment which would last.

The Apollon is one of only a few auditoria in France with 70mm projection facilities and its acoustical system is infinitely adaptable to suit the different type of performance and event using the technique of variable reverberation time.

The impressive stage is 1,200 square metres and incorporates a $380m^2$ mobile floor. At 31.5 metres deep it is one of the largest stages in Europe and has an orchestra pit for 120 musicians.

With a definite arts emphasis in the planning stages there has been ample provision for ballet rehearsal spaces and dressing rooms, showers and relaxation facilities. The overhead cranes and trap doors have also impressed the major international companies that have appeared there and enabled it to achieve the Grand Prix Lyrical Theatres awarded by the Association of Drama and Musical Critics.

Programming

With these excellent facilities, the Acropolis has established an international reputation for cultural events not only because of its flexible abilities and acoustic quality but also from the events that have been staged there, a real credit to the programmers.

But more than just another culture palace, the Acropolis has also achieved a reputation for economic dynamism. In its first seven years it played host to 1,800 events attracting more than a million people. As with most multi-purpose centres of this kind the majority of the events are regional. Nice can, however, boast that its primary centre's national and international events amount to 35 per cent of total bookings and account for over 70 per cent of the participants at professional events. The estimated delegate numbers exceed 66,000 per year (450,000 over the seven years) each person staying an average of 3.3 days and thereby injecting a much needed 220 million French Francs into the Nice economy each year.

The Acropolis is the lynch pin of the excellent marketing activity that the city has created. Under the name Nice Congress, the city is active in promotion all over the world, its personnel achieving high positions in the various industry associations and fully backed both financially and with the total encouragement of City Hall to go and attract the world to Nice. The research activity for congresses is very positive; so too is the relationship between the Convention Bureau, Acropolis and the local hotels and restaurants.

The building appeals to northern European companies for product launches and dealer meetings, whilst the international association market is also well represented in each year's conference calendar. The national market of French companies, associations and organisations has a regular habit of meeting there with a particular accent on the more local and regional activities and interests.

Consequently, the emphasis is very much on a multicultural facility and there is an extraordinary ability to maintain flexibility in the scheduling. Large conferences, booking as they do from two to five years out, usually are able to get the dates they require in the major auditoria.

A recent complication has been the complete closure for two years of Nice's Opera House for refurbishment but this was foreseen and a special purpose built rehearsal hall was created for their use so there would not be undue pressure on the Acropolis. Indeed the opera company moves in only on the day of the performance. This enables the halls to be kept at maximum stretch for the greatest commercial advantage.

Staffing

There are a total of 170 permanent staff running the Acropolis of which only four can really be said to be part of the full time marketing function.

Nice has gone the route of controlling the contracting side as far as possible within the building and has its own team to operate the audio visual, sound and other facilities as well as a team of contractors for the mounting and de-mounting of exhibitions. Fifty-five staff, therefore, make up the cadre of those organising the events and this includes the event managers and conference co-ordinators. Otherwise there is a small core of hostesses and receptionists which varies according to need and casual staff, as in most centres, play an important part for large events, some being engaged by the client (ie for registration and light porterage duties) and others engaged by the building for elements that affect the building's own performance.

The impressive nature of the truly multi-lingual staff both on the marketing side and on the event management level also has helped many a conference buyer to bring their event to this attractive and well sited venue which is the essence of the South of France with its unusual selection of colours, light and stylish approach to making the working side of a congress as pleasant as possible.

The current regeneration of the exhibition halls will bring additional activity to the complex and will, in turn, assist the city to maintain its strong position as one of France's major venues for international events.

Key points

- ▲ *The centre is a well planned complex linked to the process of urban regeneration.*
- ▲ *It is also part of Nice's attempt to become France's second most important city for tourism.*
- ▲ *It has established an international reputation through its combination of acoustics and programming.*
- ▲ *The multi-lingual staff enhance both marketing and operations.*

Case study 7.3: International Conference Centre, Birmingham

Key features

- ▲ *Local authority operated.*
- ▲ *Urban regeneration.*
- ▲ *'State of the art' technology.*
- ▲ *Flexible design.*

Rationale for provision

In contrast to Nice, few would claim Birmingham, in the heart of England, to be their favourite watering hole. However, the city has many years of success and achievement through its National Exhibition Centre situated just outside its boundaries. As this important facility has grown, and its portfolio of exhibitions increased, it has come to pose a considerable threat to the more traditional venues for trade shows in London and, in so doing, has lessened the Capital's grip on commercial and other meetings, conferences and related events.

As organisers of exhibitions increasingly rely on seminars and meetings to give prestige to their event and the increasing need for exhibitions to support a meeting financially, to increase delegates and to increase sponsorship, the City of Birmingham began to look to the advantages that would accrue if it, too, provided a world class meetings venue.

Once again this perceived need coincided with the need for an urban regeneration programme in a central area occupied by run down housing and warehousing. At the same time Birmingham's world renowned Symphony Orchestra was looking for new quarters, and the city's long established Repertory Theatre Company needed to upgrade its own theatre.

By bringing these needs into the planning, Birmingham created the opportunity to formulate a full, coherent proposal for the development of the artistic and commercial life of its inner city and thereby to create a multi-functional complex of buildings to appeal to the strong local civic pride and to attract international acclaim and patronage.

The city's ill famed Bull Ring project was one of the first attempts to re-model a city centre after the Second World War. Perhaps because it was one of the first such schemes and perhaps because of the institutional arrogance of the time, when ministries and urban planners held sway over a war battered public with few pressure groups, that the ill famed construction was built at all. Birmingham's City fathers were not to make the same mistake again. Sufficient, therefore, that before embarking on this latest grandiose project, they waited until others had made their conference mistakes before they themselves attempted to create a centre which would serve their environment, their people and their invisible income well.

By biding its time in this way, Birmingham has created a complex that suits it well and offers a varied, flexible and attractive venue to outsiders. A magnificent new open space has been created in the centre of the City and, with a clever integration of pedestrianised areas, the City Architect has created a welcoming environment for the individual or the group, which can arrive by coach, car, on foot or even along the re-generated canals for whatever experience draws them there.

The Facility Mix

The complex consists of the International Conference Centre itself, the brand new Symphony Hall, and the Birmingham Repertory Theatre. Add to this the new National Indoor Sports Arena with its ability to re-configure tracks and floors to accommodate many different sports and one has a very vital and exciting environment which, despite its varied functions, manages to weld together extremely well and there can be no doubt that the sum of the parts far exceeds that of the whole.

Particularly interesting is the way the City took advice from the established professionals in the conference field before coming to any conclusions as to space and layout. Spectrum Communications, the British consultants to the ICC in Berlin, were engaged to form the important link between architects and end users. Spectrum are very experienced consultants in this field and are also audio visual producers, event managers and conference professionals in their own right.

However, they did not just leave it to their own expertise and freely spoke to all the British and other professional conference organisers who were likely to be the new centre's clients. They took full account of the Guidelines for creating Conference Centres produced by IAPCO (the International Association of Professional Conference Organisers), and the guidelines for simultaneous interpretation produced by AIIC, the interpreters association, and the suggestions and requirements of other key conference organisations and their clients.

The result is a very flexible arrangement of spaces which enable to user to configure the building to their meeting's needs more readily than is usual, when the meeting so often has to be tailored to the building and its restrictions.

The main conference auditorium holds 1,500 and pride is taken in its sight lines and general level of comfort. Its stage is well suited to product presentations and is capable of taking a double decker bus through its street level doors. The latest technical equipment is available to all users here.

Symphony Hall is, of course, primarily for orchestral and concert use but can be taken at appropriate times by visiting meetings. This accommodates 2,200 and has a variable ceiling construction that can be configured for the appropriate sounds of speech, singing or orchestral playing.

A third hall of 3,000 square metres doubles as an exhibit area or a dining facility and again care has been taken to allow large vehicular access and high quality sound and video reproduction.

As with the other centres mentioned, there follow other smaller halls, rooms and spaces for the meeting organiser to use.

Commitment to quality

Birmingham's policy has been to look not only at the functionality of their centre and to put all their faith in that but to look at the time and effort required of staff so that not only the centre's client (ie the paying organiser of an event), but also the Client's clients are happy ALL the time they are in the building. To this end, the quality of the staff engaged has been very carefully considered. Their attitude is seen as the crucial element for the successful running of the building.

Barry Cleverdon the Chief Executive of the ICC says that everybody who enters his building has expectations and it is his brief that the staff do fulfil these expectations and that they are not fulfilled by accident or left to chance. This involves a huge amount of staff training on an ongoing basis.

He is ready to concede that Professional Conference Organisers have had a rough deal in the past at older venues so that very often they will approach a venue in an aggressive frame of mind. It is important that they can see from the beginning that the administration cares about their problems and wants to do all it can to make it a success. A client must never be made to feel they are at the mercy of the building and its staff.

Customer Care Programmes concentrate very much on the expectations of the delegates for the day ahead as they arrive in the building. These should be high and the staff are there to ensure they are not disappointed.

Scheduling is not a major problem at Birmingham since the City of Birmingham Symphony Orchestra has its own hall and its predetermined dates which are agreed three years ahead. However there are seven or eight conference or other events able to use the Symphony Hall each year. This is achieved without conflict as the priority lies with the music and entertainment programme and conference and related bookings are only put in sufficiently far out that they will not cause a problem or on days when there is nothing else planned for the Hall.

Number of staff is 355 and a further 330 casuals are called upon as necessary. Sales and marketing account for 30 to 35 of these and include the client liaison and co-ordination roles. Twelve are involved in planning and scheduling and the rest fall into various operational slots.

ICC Birmingham has perhaps one of the largest sales teams for conference work. The 10 sales staff have, as their regular task, the need to provide sufficient business to cover the operating costs of the building and to make a contribution to the debt charges of the capital cost of the building. So far this has proved to be a possibility.

The centre is administered by the National Exhibition Centre but is effectively City owned, run and funded and, since its opening in 1991, is making a very positive impact on the local infrastructure and economy. Opposite the complex, work is soon to begin on an additional leisure and entertainment complex on the Brindleyplace Waterfront, with cinemas and hotels, additional parking and offices. The purpose built Hyatt hotel, attached to the centre is already reporting good forward bookings.

Key points

- ▲ *The ICC represents Birmingham's plan to regenerate its inner city and boost its international reputation.*
- ▲ *The centre's design was based on extensive consultation with conference organisers and other experts and allows for many configurations to meet organisers' needs.*
- ▲ *It places much emphasis on sales and marketing.*

Conclusions

The impact of the Acropolis and Birmingham Centres has been enormous. Their areas have been cleaned up and brought to life again, attracting more businesses, restaurants and shops and a whole new focus. The Centres have been successful in increasing the invisible delegate spend in their respective cities, increasing outside respect and internal civic pride. In each case it can be said that there now exists the feeling that despite the difficulties of recent times there is now the possibility to look forward with some hope that through these new constructions people will be able to benefit from the promised upturns in the future.

The conference centres chosen for discussion in this chapter have been selected because of their success. It should be noted that for every really successful venue there are many that fall short of achieving what had been hoped of them in the beginning. This is nearly always because the brief given to planners, architects, designers and consultants was incomplete or not sufficiently developed and thought through in the first place. Local Authorities are frequently muddled in knowing what it is they wish to achieve and often lack the necessary unanimous drive and single mindedness of purpose. This is sometimes because of political rivalry, sometimes because of inefficiency.

Today, with all the examples available there is no necessity for the same mistakes to be made over and over. The conference industry is probably one of the most friendly and open of all despite a highly competitive climate. It is possible to enquire as to the merits and faults of buildings and their administrations and to receive very frank answers. Additionally there are many consultants willing and experienced in the creation and running of buildings; all this advice can be begun by a call to any large City Convention Bureau. Let us hope the new generation of conference centres will build on the successes such as those mentioned in this chapter.

8 Arts and entertainment facilities

Irene Waters

Introduction

Mention the arts and culture together and many people assume this means only the so-called elite arts, that is, grand opera, classical music, literature, painting and sculpture. In Britain these art forms have a minority appeal and receive public subsidy.

By contrast, the popular arts of pop music and cinema, for instance, attract mass audiences and can be commercially viable. Such distinctions are not universal, however, and even in Britain have become difficult to sustain over the last decade, as the collapse of cinema audiences in the early 1980s and the recent popular success of classical music and opera show.

If, however, we use the term *culture* in its widest sense to mean the whole way of life of an identifiable group of people, then all the arts are part of that culture. Used in this general sense, Europeans share common cultural heritage. Music, dance and mime and the visual arts transcend linguistic barriers and speak to us all. We do not need to be German to appreciate the music of Beethoven, Brahms or Schubert, nor Italian to gaze in awe at the works of Michelangelo, nor Dutch to enjoy the paintings of Vermeer and Rubens. Even Shakespeare, Strindberg, Ibsen and Goethe are appreciated in translation.

Nevertheless, Europe is divided into many nation states, some of which have a relatively short history of unification and others which are in the process of disintegration – mainly as a result of perceived cultural differences. Thus, on closer examination, we may detect many distinctive cultures at national, regional and local levels. The Scots, Welsh and Irish, for instance, Cornishmen/women, Scouses, Geordies, Bretons, Basques, Bavarians, et al are all intensely proud – and even aggressive – about their cultural identity. Ethnic minority groups or young people all have their own culture.

However, whereas cultural attitudes and norms of behaviour are a society's responsibility, the arts may represent different things to each individual: they are work for some and leisure for many and, as such, they must compete for time and money with other leisure activities. This has resulted in increasing pressure for high standards of provision and commercialisation.

Culture both reflects and influences attitudes, and diversity of culture is, arguably, the most important factor influencing the diversity of provision, funding and participation in arts activities in Europe. These topics provide convenient headings under which to examine some implications of this diversity for arts and cultural services managers. However, with the creation of the Single European Market on 1 January 1993, managers in EC countries will also have to deal with overall Community support and regulations. Whereas these are all general matters of organisation and policy they nevertheless set the parameters within which each manager must operate.

Provision

Underlying much of the resistance to the Maastricht Treaty (1992) is the fear of centralisation and a totalitarian state. This suggests a move towards emphasising European homogeneity at the expense of cultural diversity.

The present organisational structure of the arts in European countries results from historical factors and alternative solutions to common problems. It ranges from almost complete centralisation (eg France) to almost total devolution, as in Germany and Sweden. Between these two extremes lie systems such as those of Britain, the Netherlands and Denmark where plural administrations allow for some power to be retained centrally (though not necessarily all in one Ministry), funds may be distributed by quasi-non-governmental bodies with variable amounts of decision-making taking place at local level.

France's centralised system dates from 17th century royal patronage of the arts (Louis XIV, XV and XVI). The establishment of a Ministry for Culture in 1959 led to the development of an arts policy and attempts at decentralisation. Municipal involvement in the arts has a long tradition, with many cities having their own theatres, concert halls and museums.

Policy since 1959 has been directed towards increasing provision for the arts by the départements and regions. André Malraux, the first Minister for Culture, devised a scheme for a multi-arts centre (*maison de culture*) in each département. Fewer than 20 were actually built, however, and they were superceded from the late 1960s by more broadly-based *centres d'action culturelle*. A 10-year music plan was begun in 1968: each region was to have a conservatoire, a lyric theatre and a co-ordinator, though the effect of this on musical life is still somewhat muted. The communes are the largest contributors to the arts however, as successive governments preferred to spend on prestige projects in the capital, viz. the Centre Pompidou, Musée d'Orsay and the Opéra Bastille (see case study 8.1).

In Britain, too, facilities are concentrated in the capital and attempts to decentralise arts provision have also met with mixed results. In *The Glory of the Garden* (1981) the Arts Council proposed that one London orchestra should re-locate in the provinces to provide a better spread, but the players refused to move. However, Birmingham City Council succeeded in enticing the former Sadler's Wells Royal Ballet out of its London base in 1990 when it offered the refurbished Hippodrome Theatre, with studios and financial help for administration offices and support systems.

However, Sadler's Wells is mainly a touring company and this is a move from one major city to another, which does nothing to solve the problems of providing arts facilities in rural areas. Norway, aware of the dispersed nature of its small population, tackled this in the 1950s. Grants were given to build community centres, usable for many purposes, but which would receive the *riksintitutjoner* – state-funded and organised national travelling institutions for theatre, music, painting and sculpture, film and literature. This brought the arts to people, instead of expecting people to travel to central facilities.

In Britain it is largely left to the discretion of individual companies to tour small-scale productions to rural areas. Arts Centres, multi-purpose like the *maison de culture*, were intended for towns of 15,000–30,000 population. They were a development of the 1960s, an attempt to democratise culture, but providing for the arts in rural areas remains a problem (see case study 8.2).

Germany inherited a fairly even spread of facilities from the separate ducal states when these united in 1871. Apart from the Nazi period, when there was central control over all aspects of life, the separate states (*Länder*) have retained a leading role in arts provision, working with the *Gemeinden* (municipalities). The *Gemeinden* provide the largest share of public support for the arts. 'Municipal councillors, and their electors too, regard culture as an important element in their cities and overall prestige and so are ready to devote large sums to it.'[1] – often 6–8 per cent of their budget.

There is no central policy for the arts in Germany, and at Federal level the Minister for Culture is primarily responsible for issues involving foreign countries and general legislation on matters like copyright, tax laws, etc. The collapse of the Berlin Wall (1989) is causing problems for arts administrators as competition between the three opera houses and 32 theatres for audiences and public subsidy develops – though they would rather cancel productions than rebuild the Wall.

Obsessed as it seems to be with standardisation and centralisation, the EC might be expected to have problems co-ordinating such disparate systems. However, the Treaty of Rome (1957) contained no clause on cultural matters and, although a series of policy papers[2] have been issued, the Commission has regarded the arts and cultural affairs as peripheral to their main activities (ie economic, political and defence) until recently.

In 1988 the Council of Ministers approved the establishment of a Committee of the European Parliament in Cultural Affairs to evaluate proposals on cultural action by the Council of Ministers and the meetings of the European Ministers of Culture. A new clause was added to the Treaty of Rome in 1992 to formalise this cultural co-operation.

However, a number of pan-European arts projects had already developed in advance of this and others were planned.[3] The success of these reflects our common cultural heritage and reinforces M. Jean Monnet's comment that, with hindsight, he wished he had begun the process of European cohesion with culture.

Artists and performers have always crossed national boundaries as easily as their products. The introduction of the Single Market makes this movement even simpler, since it will no longer be allowable to discriminate between nationals of EC countries in terms of job availability or grant allocation.

Unfortunately the bureaucrats have produced regulations which, albeit well-intentioned, nevertheless appear ludicrous when applied to the arts and entertainment. For instance, the daytime practice and rehearsal, which dancers regard as normal, will use up permitted work hours, so they will be unable to perform in the evening; people who work in conditions where sound levels regularly exceed 90 decibels (as in symphony orchestras) must wear ear protection; anyone (including actors, singers and dancers) working on a stage with scenery in the 'flies' must wear a hard hat, and so on.

Funding

If such regulations drive arts administrators to distraction they may be encouraged by the prospect of additional finance from the Cultural Affairs Committee. Their report *Culture and the European City in the Year 2000* (published 1989) recommends that the Cultural Fund should have a budget of 1 per cent of the overall total spent by the Commission, ie a figure of around £3 billion at present prices. This money would be additional to funding from national sources – and would be especially welcome in Britain.

If public funding is a measure of the way culture and the arts are regarded, then in Britain their value must be among the lowest in Europe. Germany, France and the Netherlands, for example, each spend over twice as much per head on the arts as Britain, and Sweden nearly three times as much. As a percentage of total public expenditure the arts account for nearly twice as much in Germany and France as in Britain.

Countries differ, however, in what is grant-aided. In Sweden, theatre is heavily subsidised and there is free entry to half the national museums. The Dutch Pop Music Foundation has subsidised selected pop venues since 1984 to ensure fair rates of pay for performers and a high standard of programmes.

Both Sweden and the Netherlands are outstanding in their support for individual creative artists. As long ago as 1937 the principle of commissioning works of art for new public buildings was established in Sweden. The idea was taken up by the Netherlands in 1951, where 1·5 per cent of construction costs is permitted to be set aside for acquiring works of art. This 'PerCent for Art' scheme is now beginning to be more widely used. Artefacts are commissioned at the design stage so that they form an integral part of the architectural projects. The new British Library at St. Pancras, London, for instance, embraced the philosophy and work began on tapestries, sculptures and paintings – these have now all been cancelled as a cost-cutting measure.

In most continental countries film and the cinema receive public finance. Thus France now has a flourishing film industry; in Germany cinemas obtain grants for refurbishing, and in Norway most cinemas are state-owned. In Britain it took American blockbuster movies and the injection of American capital into building multiplex cinemas to revive the industry[4] (see case study 8.3).

Moving film from the responsibility of the Department of Trade and Industry to the newly established (April 1992) Department for the National Heritage is unlikely to help. When Arts Council grants rose, extra money was usually for a specific project or to rescue a major national company in distress, and the percentage of total government expenditure allocated to the arts continues to decline. In 1993/4 the Arts Council received 1·7 per cent less than it had been expecting under the three-year rolling programme (established in 1986/7 and abandoned from 1993/4). It is threatened with a further £5 million cut for 1994/5, and there is growing evidence of tighter ministerial control, even over artistic decisions. The much-envied 'arm's length principle' is being rapidly eroded.

Local authorities, under threat of central government capping and unrealistic standard spending assessments, have also been compelled to reduce expenditure (by 9·2 per cent in real terms in 1991/2). Though compulsory competitive tendering for the management of the arts facilities has been postponed it still threatens the role of local authorities. The system of parity funding also exacerbates the situation: Arts Council grants are related to the amount by which a local authority is prepared to subsidise an organisation. If a local authority is short of cash the effect is to double the grant cut, which may well result in closure.

The situation is further exacerbated by local management of schools, which may result in theatre, concert and museum trips being restricted if other activities are given priority. Paradoxically, this occurs at a time when the national curriculum is creating pressures on non-school-based resources such as public libraries, museums, theatre-in-education groups and peripatetic instrumental teachers.

However Britain is not alone in facing a recession and public expenditure cuts. Italy cut its 1993/4 arts budget by 6 per cent and in the Netherlands arts organisations were told to raise a greater proportion of their income themselves, a figure of 15 per cent being suggested. In Norway ticket revenues normally provide 7–20 per cent of an arts organisation's budget, but British theatres earn (ie excluding sponsorship) over half their income and orchestras over two-thirds.

This is in spite of returning a greater proportion of admission charges to the government in the form of VAT than any other European country. In Britain VAT is charged at 17·5 per cent on all admissions to arts and cultural events: elsewhere a two-tier system allows these to be rated at the lower level. In France, for example, VAT on cinema tickets is 5 per cent. Nevertheless books are zero-rated in Britain but not on the continent. Thus standardisation which imposed VAT on printed materials would effectively cut library book allowances as well as having repercussions on the book-buying public.

Increasing or introducing admission charges to make ends meet can be a false economy, as national museums and galleries have found. When voluntary donations were introduced at the Victoria and Albert Museum in 1985, attendances fell by about 40 per cent, and a compulsory charge at the Natural History Museum halved admissions after 1987. Leaving aside the vexed question of whether individuals should be expected to pay at the point of purchase to experience their cultural heritage (since there has always been a charge for special exhibitions and independent museums), the reduction in visitor numbers inevitably resulted in lower sales at museum shops and cafés.[5]

Nor is business sponsorship the solution as in a recession firms cut back on the amount available. Sponsorship forms a small part of arts organisation budgets in Britain and even less in continental countries.

Although the Conservative Government in Britain shows great reluctance to spend public money on arts and cultural activities, a survey commissioned by the Arts Council in the summer of 1991 found that the majority (69 per cent) of respondants were in favour of this.[6] Only two in 10 people (22 per cent) oppose public funding for the arts. Perhaps governments in continental countries are more in tune with their population in this respect?

Participation

If public funding represents official attitudes towards the arts and culture, participation reflects individual attitudes. The Arts Council survey found that a majority (54 per cent) of respondants claimed to be interested in the arts and eight out of ten (79 per cent) attended at least one type of arts or cultural event nowadays.

Although attendances at most arts events and venues in Britain rose during the 1980s there was little evidence that this represented a wider uptake. Household expediture on the arts and culture also rose (even allowing for inflation), which suggests rather that the same people were attending more frequently. In the early 1990s, however, new trends began to appear.

Luciano Pavarotti's rendering of *Nessun Dorma*, used as the 1990 World Cup theme, introduced opera to thousands who may scarcely have heard of Puccini let alone his opera *Turandot.* The record reached eleventh in the singles' charts and the *Three Tenors Concert* (Pavarotti, Domingo and Carreras) has become the best selling music video in the UK. Pavarotti's album (*The Essential Pavarotti*) outsold Madonna's at one point and he attracted an audience of 15,042 to an open-air concert in Hyde Park on a wet Tuesday evening (July 1991).

Opera has subsequently been performed at Earl's Court (*Tosca* 1991), Wembley Arena (*Turandot* 1991/2) and relayed from the Royal Opera House to Covent Garden piazza (*Tosca* 1992). The first two venues seat around 10,000, whereas the average attendance at the Royal Opera House (93/94 per cent capacity) is about 2,000.

Taking into account population differences, the audience for grand opera in Britain is roughly comparable to that in France and the Netherlands, though demand in Britain relative to attendance is, according to the Arts Council survey, particularly high. In Germany, however, about four times as many people attend opera performances.

Increasing accessibility on television has undoubtedly been one factor in achieving this demand: the average audience for a single Mozart opera is estimated at 8 million for example. But this alone would be insufficient – people must be motivated to switch on – and nor does it account for other changing tastes in music.

Sales of rock music recordings have declined since the 1960s and '70s, whereas classical music sales have grown by some 50 per cent since 1989. Nigel Kennedy's 1990 recording of Vivaldi's *Four Seasons* sold over 200,000 copies within 18 months and Henryk Gorecki's *Symphony No. 3* reached No.

3 in the early 1993 album charts, earning him a gold disc, a feat formerly only associated with pop stars.

By the end of 1990 the classics share of the music recording industry had reached 11 per cent, compared with 15 per cent in several other European countries. Thus Classic FM radio was launched in September 1992 with great optimism. This was not misplaced: by the end of the year it had an audience of 4·3 million a week. Many of these were new listeners to classical music as few had been drawn from Radio 3 and the 16–24 age group was double the projected number.

Nor was this increased interest in the arts confined to opera and classical music. Cinema audiences increased every year from 1984 (53 million, their lowest ever) to 103·6 million in 1992. Audiences for ballet and plays grew by 9 per cent and 6 per cent respectively between 1985 and 1990.[7]

All this suggests that, once the arts and cultural events are presented in an accessible way, people respond. Investment in buildings, equipment and the education and training of personnel are all important in making the arts available to everyone as the following three case studies illustrate.

The Opéra Bastille is an expensive, central government inspired and funded, major new building intended to improve access to an elite art form in the capital city. Queen's Hall arts centre occupies a converted building and serves an intensely rural area; it was locally inspired and is local authority funded. The MetroCentre cinema is a wholly commercial operation, an example of the American-style multiplex cinemas responsible for the upturn of attendances in the 1980s.

Case study 8.1: Opéra Bastille, Paris

Key features

- ▲ *Controversial, state funded opera house.*
- ▲ *National policy.*
- ▲ *Design faults.*
- ▲ *Programming and philosophy of use.*
- ▲ *Relationship between provision and politics.*

Origins

Controversy has surrounded this venue from its conception. In the early 1980s President Mitterand and his Minister for Culture, M. Jack Lang, envisaged a grandiose scheme to restore Paris as the cultural capital of the world. As part of this scheme the state funded three new buildings specifically to make the arts more accessible and popular: the Musée d'Orsay, the underground extension to the Louvre (the glass pyramid) and the Opéra Bastille. The latter was also seen as the culmination of the 1968 plan to develop musical excellence.

Planning authorities, many MPs and ordinary French citizens

opposed the building of more large institutions in Paris as this conflicted with the stated policy of decentralisation. The cynics had their worst fears confirmed when Lang told the objectors, 'Really the President is very keen on this new opera. It is part of his big, long-range vision on creative and popular access in this country. So you will have to vote for it.'[8] They did but was the project more about serving as a permanent memorial to the President (like the Centre Pompidou, named for a former president, Louis XIV's Comédie Française, etc) than about public access to the arts?

The building, subject of an architectural competition, had a restricted site – the former railway station – in the Place de la Bastille. It was scheduled to open on 14 July 1989, the 200th anniversary of the storming of the Bastille – hence its name.

It was planned to provide a 2,700-seat theatre with a system of six inter-changeable stages and a moving proscenium, a *salle modulable* (an adjustable space seating 1,500) and a 600 capacity recital amphitheatre in the basement. Building began in 1984, but two years later a change of government halted the work; selling part of the site and limiting building to a concert hall was seriously considered. But the project went ahead and the Socialists were returned to power in May 1988.

Design

At a cost of some £300,000,000 – more than double the annual Arts Council of Great Britain's grant at that time – the result is far from perfect. Acoustics are poor in the stalls and first balcony and many seats in the latter have a restricted view of the stage. From the second balcony singers up-stage appear small and remote. Steps are precipitous (due to the number of seats crammed onto a narrow site) and narrow.

Tom Sutcliffe, writing in *The Guardian* (17 July 1989) comments:

> 'The auditorium, with its prevailing colours of black and white, and just a few bits of wood-brown square trelliswork up the sides matching the backs of the uncomfortable seats, is cold, unwelcoming and devoid of atmosphere.'

In the recital amphitheatre the audience perches on stone steps. Sutcliffe considers it 'the first opera house in the world where the audience cannot go to sleep – however bad the performance.'[9] On the opening night the public were admitted only at basement level; the main doors remained closed because the crowd could not be handled in the foyer.

Politics and the programme

But the spirit of an opera house is more than its shell; it is its musical life. Behind all the enthusiasm of the first night here too lies a sorry saga. It was August 1987 before a musical and artistic director was appointed: Daniel Barenboim, who had been chief conductor of the Orchestre de Paris since 1975. With somewhat limited experience of conducting opera some doubted Barenboim's ability, but he had made a considerable contribution to Paris' musical life and understood French politics.

At about the same time a general director, a director of programming and various technical staff were also appointed, but no general administrator. There was no management structure and – arguably more serious – no budgetary guidelines.

The artistic staff planned the first season's productions and engaged singers, producers and conductors. Here too, controversy raged when details became public: was the programme too elitist and traditional or merely a cautious beginning, was the international jet-setting list of stars designed to establish a high profile or were French artistes and composers being slighted?

A year after his appointment Barenboim was suddenly confronted with President Mitterand's selection of Pierre Bergé as overall administrator of all three Paris opera houses. Although Bergé was known to be interested in music, and presented recitals by operatic stars, he was primarily a businessman, chairman of the Yves St. Laurent fashion house which he was reputed to have restored to profitability. If Barenboim's ability to direct an opera house could be questioned, so could Bergé's.

Different approaches led to clashes. Barenboim wanted to keep the first season's performances down to 40, rising to 160 in the third, arguing that a running-in period was necessary and that artistic standards should not be sacrificed. But Mitterand wanted 250. Bergé's businessman's attitude wanted the maximum cash returns for capital outlay. Then Mitterand's disapproval of the inaugural season's productions was conveyed to Barenboim.

In his determination to fulfil his brief to make the Opéra Bastille a modern, popular and cost-effective institution, Bergé sacked various management staff. One new general director lasted only three weeks, being replaced by relatively unknown René Gonzalez. Gonzalez had successfully run a small suburban *maison de culture* but allegedly knew little about opera. Barenboim refused Bergé's instruction to co-operate with him. Gonzalez then dismissed the highly respected technical director who, as a construction worker is reported to have put it, was 'the only man who knows how to turn the lights on in here.'[10] The president of the Bastille Association (a committee appointed to oversee the project) was also removed.

Barenboim refused the ultimatums of halving his salary, giving up his post as artistic director after two years, or remaining for four years but allowing Gonzalez to control the programme and choice of producers. He also refused to increase the number of performances, insisting on adequate rehearsal. Then Bargé discovered that, in the confusion of the general election, Barenboim's contract lacked proper signatures. He therefore declared the post of musical director vacant.

This prompted a world-wide storm of protest from musicians who retaliated by threatening to boycott the Opéra Bastille if Barenboim was not reinstated. Mitterand refrained from comment and Lang said that such decisions were M. Bergé's province. On 1 February 1989 Barenboim admitted defeat and left.

The first season's programme appeared to be in ruins. Amazingly the Opéra Bastille opened on schedule, though minus the *salle modulable* – a gala concert (with the new musical director Myung Whun Chung seated in the first balcony with the heads of state) on 13 July 1989 and a free concert the following evening. The full opera programme began on 17 March 1990 with Berlioz' *The Trojans*, not critically well-received.

By now the Opéra Bastille had its own general administrator: Georges-Francois Hirsch, who nevertheless still had to answer to Bergé. Hirsch reckoned, 'It will take three seasons to get to our cruising speed. Eventually I'm confident we'll achieve 250 performances per year with a different opera every night.'[11] But his troubles were not yet over. In November 1990 the theatre was closed for a week when the orchestra went on strike demanding a pay increase. The Prime Minister threatened to close the whole building for good unless management changes were made.

The Opéra Bastille's fundamental problems are political. It was set up by, and continually at the mercy of, politicians who do not know how to run an opera house – neither Mitterand nor Lang are even opera goers. With hindsight one can identify preventive measures which should have been taken, for example:

- appoint a chain of command, a full management structure and a budget at the outset
- establish that all members of the management team are compatible in outlook and in sympathy with the objectives
- delimit responsibilities; even when people do not see eye to eye over all details they can still work together satisfactorily if each is clear about his/her responsibilities and does not interfere with those of others. It is normal for the Artistic Director to make artistic decisions, for instance, and for these to be respected and not overruled.

The future

Opinions differ about Bergé's ability to manage. Tom Sutcliffe, writing in *The Guardian* (15 March 1990) suspects '. . . Mitterand's choice will prove extremely canny. Bergé is a hands-on director who claims he does delegate.' On the other hand, Peter Jonas (then managing director of English National Opera, a modern, popular institution which Bergé would like to emulate) considers Bergé showed a profound absence of the qualities necessary to run an opera house:

> 'Above all, you need the ability to balance conflicting demands, and an unfailing sense of diplomacy, in which M. Bergé has shown himself wanting. You can't get instant results in opera – it will take five years before you can expect the Bastille to work at full throttle.'[12]

In that case it is too early to comment further on the Opéra Bastille's performance.

Key points

- *The facility was part of the aim to make Paris the cultural centre of the world.*
- *It has been dogged by controversy and design problems since its beginnings.*
- *It has been greatly affected by the interference of political considerations in its mission and operations.*
- *It has suffered from a lack of continuity in its staffing.*
- *Its management approach, perhaps, should have been different from the outset.*

Case study 8.2: Queen's Hall, Hexham

Key features

- *Local authority arts centre.*
- *Converted building.*
- *Design constraints.*
- *Local arts policy.*
- *Outreach work.*
- *Programming.*

Origins

Hexham is a market town (population 10,500) in the Tyne Valley about 20 miles west of Newcastle. It is the administrative centre for Tynedale District Council, the most rural in Britain with a population of about 55,000 spread over some 880 square miles. The town centre is a designated conservation area with several historic buildings, the most notable being the 7th century Abbey, so there is considerable tourist trade during the summer.

The district has a long tradition of arts activities but lacked a permanent venue until Tynedale Arts Council took the initiative in persuading the District Council and Northumberland County Council to buy the dilapidated Queen's Hall for conversion to a range of arts activities.

The Queen's Hall had always been used for entertainment and the arts. Built in 1865–86 as the Town Hall and Corn Exchange on land leased from the Lord of the Manor, it occupied a prime position in the town centre opposite the Abbey grounds, and was a palatial building, resulting from an architectural competition. From its opening the Town Hall was used for balls, concerts, recitals, exhibitions and music hall. The Corn Exchange fell into disrepair as the agricultural market declined in the late 19th century.

In the 1920s Hexham Entertainments Company turned the Town Hall into a 650-seat cinema and the Corn Exchange became a 900-

capacity ballroom. After the Second World War attendances declined and the building once again deteriorated. In the 1960s the cinema became a bingo hall while the rest of the building housed a branch of the county library and the Registrar's office.

In the mid-1970s the County Council sought better premises for the library and the bingo hall closed. It then became apparent that a combined effort could not only save a handsome building from demolition but also provide a new library and a teachers' centre (both paid for by the County Council) plus substantial facilities for the arts. County and District Councils jointly funded the arts centre, with grants from the Arts Council of Great Britain, Northern Arts, the English Tourist Board, Department of the Environment, Hexham Town Council, various trusts and the Friends of the Queen's Hall. Capital costs of conversion came to £1,307,000 gross, about two-thirds of this being for the Arts Centre.

Mission

The Arts Centre thus opened in 1982 as a result of local initiative and is still funded and managed by the County and District Councils with voluntary help and a basic minimum of paid staff. The objectives are to provide for all people living in, and visiting, Tynedale and adjacent areas:

- a range of first class activities and events to foster and promote all forms of arts activities and appreciation of the arts at both professional and amateur levels
- to establish the building as a centre where people can come to work or train with professional artists and craftsmen and undertake their own creative work
- to respond to user needs and to support those in the locality already engaged in creative leisure activities
- to build a base for community arts activities
- to recognise and develop the educational potential of the centre
- to provide for all age groups
- to provide facilities for activities and events, chiefly cultural, but also social and commercial.

Design

Converted buildings are rarely ideal and, suitable though the Queen's Hall is in many respects, there are problems. The 406-seat auditorium, although long and narrow, has good acoustics and sight-lines (apart from a few seats in the balcony), but no audio loop. Stage depth, fly tower and lighting are also good, but there is no wing space on stage left and only six feet on stage right. Two small dressing rooms (one opening off the other) and toilets are in the basement two floors down. The bar area is small but double doors opening onto the library balcony relieves congestion.

The theatre has a projection box, so can also function as a cinema to complement – or compete with – a small commercial cinema in the town. Rehearsal space is available as well as an art gallery, studios and darkrooms. The teachers' centre scheme was abandoned and the spaces allocated for it have now become studios.

Consisting of three main blocks on seven different levels access to and across the building is difficult even for the able-bodied. Thus it is difficult, for instance, to entice theatre-goers to an exhibition in the art gallery two flights up. The director and administrator share an office at the top of the building, but the general office, reception and box office are on the ground floor. It is therefore difficult to streamline operations for maximum efficiency.

A licensed restaurant on the premises opens from 9am to 11pm. This is a franchise operation and the caterers are also responsible for the theatre bar – where they refuse to serve coffee during performance intervals. There are no facilities for selling confectionery and ice cream. However, the franchise is due for renewal in 1993 and, hopefully, terms will be re-negotiated.

Making the theatre space work at this ancillary level is one of Artistic Director Peter Cutchie's main concerns at present (he was appointed in 1992). He believes theatre should be a total experience from the point at which a customer picks up the telephone, or arrives at the box office to buy a ticket, to the moment of farewell from the staff; there should be a sense of occasion. This requires capital investment to refurbish and repaint frequently in order to generate a good atmosphere and pride in the building, plus the employment and training of additional staff. The emphasis must be on comfort and quality or people will go elsewhere. Unfortunately in these times of financial stringency and central government control of expenditure, local authorities lack the means however well disposed they may be towards the arts.

Queen's Hall has a management committee (Figure 8.1) reporting to the County and District Councils' recreation and amenities' committees.

Officers of the District Council oversee day-to-day financial matters and committee administration. Arts Centre staff are on the establishment of the County Council, with the Artistic Director being responsible to the County Librarian; thus library, arts and museum services throughout the county are co-ordinated (Figure 8.2).

Staffing

The Arts Centre is run by the director and five other permanent full-time staff, each with clearly defined duties: administrator; marketing officer; box office supervisor; senior technician; stage technician (ie assistant). In mid-1993 a temporary employee on a training scheme acted as receptionist/secretary and there was one part-time marketing/box office assistant. However, it was hoped to appoint two further box office/receptionists so that this could be open from 9am to about 5.30pm every day and continuously into the evening on performance days.

The permanent staff are the administrators and organisers; visiting professionals and amateurs supply the artistic input and volunteers fill ancillary posts. Weekly staff meetings are held, from which emerge

Chairman of Northumberland County Council Amenities Committee (ex officio)	1
Chairman of Tynedale District Council Recreation and Amenities Committee (ex officio)	1
Northumberland County Council	3
Tynedale District Council	3
Hexham Town Council	1
Tynedale Arts Council	1
Friends of Queen's Hall*	1
Queen's Hall Arts Centre consultative group†	1
Co-opted members	4
	16

Northern Arts sends one non-voting observer and appropriate council officers attend each of the minimum four statutory meetings per year.

* A group of about 350, an independent charity which supports the activities of the centre.
† The needs and views of the users of the Arts Centre are represented through this group.

Figure 8.1
Membership of Queen's Hall Art Centre Management Committee

'action points', staff taking turns to act as recorder. Although Cutchie discusses programming and operational matters, ultimately the responsibility – and therefore the final decision – is his alone.

Although all the staff have attended courses, training has been haphazard and mainly in-house. In 1993, however, a £2,000 training budget was identified; this will buy in expertise and enable staff to travel to other theatres and arts centres. With such a small staff some versatility is necessary: for instance, before the trainee appointment, all staff undertook reception duties and three (including the director) are trained for and take turns at the box office. A rota system requires all administrative staff to act as duty officer. The director makes a point of seeing every performance at least once, generally combining this with his turn as duty officer.

Another consequence of a small permanent staff is a reliance on volunteers. The Red Cross, for instance, attend all performances to provide the required first-aid service, and all ushers and attendants are volunteers. Cutchie believes, however, that they should receive the same training, make the same commitment and reach the same standards as paid staff. Shortly after his arrival he arranged a meeting to draw up a

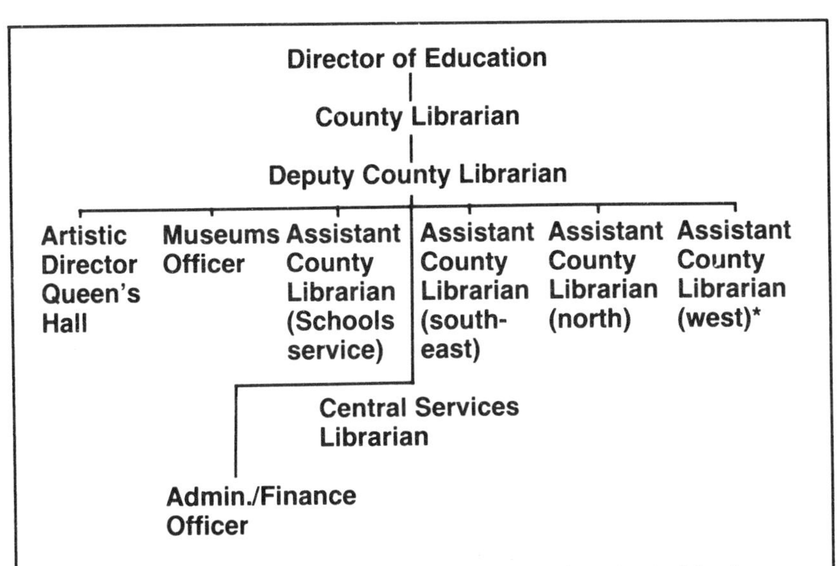

* An appointment made with the requirement that the holder have a particular interest in the arts since s/he is based at the Queen's Hall.

The County Council Amenities Committee is responsible for: libraries, museums and art galleries; public and local records; arts and entertainment. Responsibility for libraries, museums, arts and entertainment rests with the Director of Education and for county records with the County Secretary.

Figure 8.2
Northumberland County Library Management Structure

code of conduct/ground rules for ushers; these are now written down and reinforced at subsequent meetings. At present there is not a sufficiently large pool of ushers to provide a cloakroom facility – another aspect of the total quality experience which is receiving attention.

Cleaning, too, leaves much to be desired. Cleaners are contracted by the county council and unused to the different requirements of a theatre/ arts centre and, say a school or office. Two cleaners (one for the morning and one for evening) are supplied but the building is too large for one person to clean satisfactorily. Toilets are only cleaned twice a day and, furthermore, cleaners work Monday to Friday inclusive – whereas Saturday is generally the Queen's Hall's busiest day. However, this contract too is due for renewal in 1993 when, hopefully, terms will be re-negotiated.

The Arts Centre has been hampered by changes of Director. It developed well under Peter Kyle's management during its first five years, but in the next five there were two more directors (with interim periods when no one was at the helm) before Peter Cutchie took up the post. He hopes to settle it down. Besides re-negotiating contracts and appointing additional staff he aims to 'define the use of each space and then make it work for that. Any other use is a bonus'. He also sees outreach work as a priority.

Community arts

In 1986 the Manpower Services Commission (MSC) funded a team of 15 people to develop outreach work in Tynedale, but the project had limited success. The main problems were that the MSC had no experience of running arts schemes and it operated for one year only – far too short a period.

Since then there has been no on-going community arts work, though a full-time outreach worker was due to be appointed in mid-1993 and several one-off projects have produced results. The most outstanding piece of community arts is a tapestry, completed over a period of 18 months in 1984/5. The Arts Officer designed a 14 × 8 ft panel and ran workshops to teach the technique. Over 300 people (men, women and children) contributed to the weaving. The result, valued at around £2,000, hangs in the theatre bar.

Workshops have produced several other items for the Queen's Hall, a wooden screen with stained glass panels for the foyer, for example. Workshops generally link with exhibitions and/or performances, or with schools or specific groups. Thus each workshop is run by a visiting professional for a specific period of time. For example, the Jiving Lindy Hoppers (a jazz dance group – Queen's Hall has a good reputation for dance activities) worked with local schools for a week before their Saturday evening performance, and Marie Wright taught paper-making to anyone interested during her month-long exhibition in the gallery. From April 1993 six-session photography courses were offered on a continuous basis – a new departure.

Several amateur groups also use the Queen's Hall, including Hexham and District Operatic Society, Queen's Hall Theatre Club, Hexham and District Music Society, Northumberland Guitar Society, a Life Drawing Club, adult literacy groups and WEA classes. Besides studio and rehearsal space these groups – and local schools – put on shows (generally well-supported) for the paying public. This is another form of community arts.

The new outreach worker's task will be to raise awareness of the arts in remote communities, to stimulate arts activities where people are. It is hoped they will then be encouraged to visit Queen's Hall to enhance their work at either workshops, exhibitions or performances. Thus the job combines marketing and audience development. Initially funded for three years, it may be possible to extend this for a further three, by which time results should be visible.

Usage

This is the third different attempt to make the arts accessible to remote rural populations. For several years after opening, the Queen's Hall offered a transport subsidy to groups travelling from outlying areas of Tynedale, but take-up was low as too much effort was involved in assembling the group for the discount to be attractive. In the summer of 1991 Tynedale District Council provided a free minibus service to bring rural dwellers to a summer repertory season: only 14 people used it. The population is so widely scattered that the extra travelling time was not considered worth the free ride.

Further problems in Tynedale are the nature of the economic activity and the climate. Apart from those who commute to Tyneside, the majority of people work in agriculture or tourism. These activities leave little leisure time in summer, and, in winter, anticipation of severe weather – even if it does not materialise – makes people reluctant to undertake a long journey on poor roads.

Audiences have fluctuated over the years and according to the popularity of the activity/performance. In early 1993, for instance, some shows virtually sold out whereas others attracted fewer than 20. There are 20–30 known regulars, but many people from Hexham and to the east of the town go to Newcastle for arts and entertainment because it is equally convenient and has greater choice. On the other hand, Newcastle residents make the journey to Hexham for some events.

People are increasingly reluctant to book in advance. This may be due to limited box office hours or to the recession: folk now wait until the last moment before deciding what to spend money on. It could also be related to the Hexham area's tourism characteristic, as a one-night stop.

Marketing

A survey carried out by Arts Marketing in the summer of 1992 revealed that most people found out about events at the Queen's Hall from posters; this is highly unusual but understandable. Tourists are more likely to catch sight of a poster in a shop window or at their hotel or guesthouse than to read a brochure. The poster print was subsequently increased, although 17,000 brochures are still produced each quarter. Of these 4,000 are mailed out, 10,000 distributed to libraries, hotels, bed-and-breakfast houses, etc, and the rest available from the arts centre.

The performance programme, in keeping with the objectives of the institution, is varied, ranging through pop and rock music, classical, jazz and folk, poetry and prose readings, minority interest and local professional theatre groups to Compass Theatre and the English National Ballet, plus amateur events. Gallery exhibitions change monthly and usually have some local connection; both professional and amateur artists exhibit.

Prices vary according to the cost of the show and the audience potential, but are within most people's pockets in a typical A/B/C1 area. Most shows cost £4–6, though children's events may be as little as £1.50 while companies like English National Ballet command up to £12.50. Discounts are offered to students, the unemployed, holders of a Stage Pass (young person's theatre card) or Tynedale Arts and Leisure Card.

Friends of the Queen's Hall also qualify for a discount and party rates are available. Workshops and classes are about £5 per session and all exhibitions are free. Under-18s are admitted to everything at half-price, thus encouraging the audience of the future.

Conclusions

The Queen's Hall does not have an easy task. It is trying to provide the widest possible range of arts activities in what is probably the most difficult geographical environment in England. It has suffered from several changes of Director so it is scarcely surprising if local interest and enthusiasm wane in the face of this and tight hands on local government purse-strings.

Cutchie is aware of the need to re-build local support. During his first week in the post, when Michael Bentine was delayed en route, Cutchie himself went on stage and organised a discussion with the audience while they waited: 'What do you want from this arts centre?' he asked. 'It's your arts centre, so tell me what we should be doing.' Nine months later he admits he has not yet found all the answers. But he is working on it and, as the cinema has shown, audiences can be won back with attractive products and investment in comfort and customer service.

Key points

▲ *The centre is based on a long tradition of arts provision.*
▲ *It is very much a local initiative.*
▲ *It has a philosophy of use to reflect the wide spectrum of local need.*
▲ *The management approach is to optimise the use of the adapted facilities from the perspective of the 'total consumer experience'.*
▲ *It relies on a mix of dedicated paid staff and volunteers.*
▲ *The emphasis on community arts and outreach work has developed in recent years.*

Case study 8.3: MetroCentre Cinema, Gateshead

Key features

▲ *One of the largest cinema complexes in Europe.*
▲ *World's busiest 10 screen cinema.*
▲ *Clear product.*
▲ *Customer care.*
▲ *Standards.*
▲ *Training for flexibility and versatility.*

Origins

The Cinema opened in 1987 as part of the MetroCentre development. This comprises a mixed indoor shopping and leisure complex (the largest in Europe) with three miles of shopping malls, ten-pin bowling, laser shooting, Europe's only indoor theme park, restaurants, fast-food outlets and licensed bars as well as the cinema.

The project was devised in 1979 by property developer Sir John Hall to use 100 acres of derelict land on the south bank of the River Tyne. The first shops opened seven years later, with the rest of the development following over the next three years or so. The origins, rationale and objectives of the cinema are, therefore, inextricably bound up with those of the MetroCentre as a whole: to provide a top quality retail and commercial leisure facility for North East England.

Situated on the western outskirts of the Tyneside conurbation the MetroCentre is easily accessible, with some 1·5 million people within 30 minutes driving time. It has free parking for over 12,000 cars and more than 350 coaches. It is also well-served by public transport as shuttle buses operate every few minutes from both Newcastle city centre and Gateshead. Trains on the main Carlisle, Newcastle, Sunderland and Middlesbrough line use the special MetroCentre station. There is easy access for wheel chair users – some chairs are available on free loan for the duration of the visit.

The Cinema undoubtedly benefits from this location and the mix of leisure facilities. It has few competitors close by. In 1939 Newcastle had 41 cinemas; now there are only three in the city centre (a four-screen Odeon, a nine-screen Warner Bros. multiplex and a two-screen regional film theatre) and none in Gateshead. Other cinemas are over 15 miles distant. However, people often visit the MetroCentre for a day out and seeing a film forms part of that experience – as well as an opportunity to rest the weary feet. Some MetroCentre employees use the Cinema to fill in time between split shifts.

A corporate product

The cinema site was acquired by the American Multi-Cinema (AMC) Circuit during the initial stages of the development, but the Circuit was sold in 1988 and the name subsequently changed to United Cinemas International (UCI). Thanks to American initiative and capital the MetroCentre cinema is thus part of the third largest cinema circuit in Britain and the fifth largest in Europe. UCI operates in Spain, Germany and Portugal (besides other parts of the world) and is expanding wherever sites become available. The operational management of this cinema is therefore replicated in other countries, apart from minor modifications required by different legal systems.

Nevertheless the MetroCentre is undoubtedly UCI's flagship. It has been the busiest 10-screen cinema in the world for several years and regularly exceeds budget targets. Annual admissions in the year ending 31 December 1992 totalled 1·27 million. In the week ending 4 April 1991 it set a world record for weekly admissions (46,454).

Being part of a cinema circuit presents both opportunities and limitations to the Manager, Gerry Carey (appointed in 1988). There is the support from a large, prestigious organisation, but also constraints imposed by the structure of the industry.

For instance, the manager has little control over the product being offered to the public. Film producers decide what films to make and distributors hire them to cinemas. UCI has five film bookers, based in London, who see all films due for release, selecting those to be shown by the circuit and fixing the hire period for each cinema. However, a film which does well in Milton Keynes or Derby may crash in Gateshead and vice versa. This is where knowledge of the local audience and careful monitoring of admissions are important. The good manager suggests adjusting the length of run to either increase profits or minimise losses.

Marketing

Once film opening dates are known, marketing must be geared to these. Much publicity material and information about each film is produced centrally: all posters, for instance, are published by the film distributors, and in Britain the age range, to whom the film may be legally shown, is set by the British Board of Film Censors. UCI publish a monthly film guide (Take One, available in cinema foyers) to forthcoming attractions and items of interest to film goers.

Local publicity, however, is handled by the local management. Advertising boards at the MetroCentre car park entrance, by the cinema entrance and over the box office, list the week's films, including the certificates. Inside the foyer a board gives more detailed information. Every week 5,000 leaflets listing the films, starting times and admission prices are distributed; some of these are available at the box office and the MetroCentre general information desks, but other outlets (being continually increased) include libraries, hotels and community centres within the known catchment area. The listings service, in the local press and on radio, provides another reference point for titles, certification and starting times. Specific districts are targeted by newspaper advertising from time to time; these often include free or discount vouchers for concession stand purchases, thus enabling some monitoring of the penetration of the advertisement to be made. Additional publicity for particular films may warrant further media coverage, special previews and so on. Once a year cinema staff organise an exhibition, Magic of the Movies (see below), in one of the MetroCentre's squares.

There is no complacency, no attitude that 'everyone knows now that we are here', but a constant reminder to the public of the cinema's presence and attractions. That the cinema then provides a pleasurable experience is due to both management attitudes and the willingness of the company to invest rather than concentrate on short-term profits. Thus refurbishment takes place before it becomes obviously necessary. Litter bins, for instance, were replaced in early 1993 although they could have lasted another couple of years and carpets will be renewed even though, after five years and trampling by some six million pairs of feet, they do not appear shabby. Application for a capital sum and revenue funding for such purposes is made annually by each cinema manager.

Customer service

Customers thus receive a good impression, although of course, they may not analyse – or even be aware of – the contributing factors. A great deal of such behind-the-scenes customer care consists of attention to detail which the public would only notice if it were absent, viz.:

- staff are well-motivated and trained
- every film print is checked by a projectionist on receipt and any defective reels returned to the distributor for replacement
- notice boards, answerphone and newspaper listings are checked daily for clarity and accuracy
- ushers clean the auditorium after each show
- toilets are inspected and cleaned every 20 minutes
- all litter is removed on sight
- the floor in front of the concession stands is washed after each walk-in
- the entire premises is deep-cleaned every night
- food items for the concession stands are rejected if they are not up to standard or delivered at incorrect temperatures.

It is this attention to detail and the emphasis on customer service which are the key factors in the MetroCentre's superiority. Location, the size of the catchment area and its population, the relative lack of competition are all important but do not, of themselves, guarantee success. The distinguishing characteristic is, as Carey puts it, in '*living up to the promise*'. The UCI promise is displayed in the cinema foyer:

> . . . that when you visit one of our cinemas, our staff will be friendly, courteous and helpful. The foyers, corridors and auditoriums will be clean and tidy. The toilets will be clean and fully stocked. Refreshment areas will be clean and refreshments will be served hot or cold as intended. The film presentation will be of highest quality, with crystal clear pictures and top quality sound. If for any reason your visit is not up to our promise or your expectations please see one of our duty managers, and let us know your views. We value your impressions as much as we do your custom. Thank you.

Inevitably, in spite of all the care and attention, breakdowns occur occasionally and some customers complain. Complaints are often due to misunderstanding (eg the legally-enforced film certification) and staff are trained to deal with the matter expediently and with as little fuss as possible. If necessary, problems can be referred up through the supervisor, duty manager and even to the general manager. The aim is to defuse the situation and send the customer away feeling satisfied rather than disgruntled – a judicious use of complimentary tickets usually results in favourable word-of-mouth publicity.

Programme

The MetroCentre cinema functions solely as a place to show films. The box office opens at 12.30pm during the week, 10am Saturdays and Bank Holidays and 11.30am on Sundays. Performances start around 1.00pm on week days but earlier on Saturdays and holiday times. The last show begins around 10pm (11pm or later on Saturdays) and staff must remain until all customers have left and the cinema is clean and tidy. Other activities are thus not feasible.

Staffing

About 50 staff are employed, increased by 10–15 temporary personnel during the school summer holidays, the cinema's busiest period. All but 15 staff are full-time. The structure can be illustrated as shown in Figure 8.3.

General manager	1	Senior projectionist	1
Deputy manager	1	Assistant projectionist	1
Duty managers	4	Projectionists	2
Senior supervisors	4		
Supervisors	8		
Other staff	About 28		

Figure 8.3
MetroCentre cinema staff structure

Staff serve a three-month probationary period during which initial training takes place. This is done in-house and has both a practical side and the customer care aspect. The company has produced a training video and this is followed up with role-playing exercises. Although the comprehensive training manual is centrally produced, managers themselves (especially those like Carey who joined the company when it first began operating multiplexes in Britain) have supplied most of the ideas and material.

Everyone begins as an usher/cleaner and then moves on to gain experience on the concession stands. After that the more numerate may be given box office training; others help with public relations, scheduling or general operations work. In this way staff gain versatility as well as experience. The company has an examination system which offers opportunities for increasing responsibility and salary. Projectionists stand somewhat outside this system as their training is wholly technical and there are nationally recognised qualifications.

Training at management level involves attendance at UCI's Manchester headquarters, and some mobility is necessary in progressing up the career ladder. There is an identifiable structure and managers may work in other countries than the one in which they were trained, provided they are fluent in the language. Each duty manager has his/her responsibility: personnel; public relations and marketing; finance; training; the concession stands.

Every effort is made to involve all the staff and make them feel that their work and opinions are important, with the result that turnover is very low – some staff have been there since the cinema opened. A system of 'challenge groups' has been started recently to improve feedback from staff to management – it is the former who are continuously in contact with the public and this encourages observation and initiative. The annual Magic of the Movies exhibition relies entirely on staff ideas and effort. In 1992 some 900,000 people visited the MetroCentre during the week of the exhibition, almost all of them would at least have been aware of it even if they did study it carefully.

Having attracted the public's attention, the next task is to ensure a warm welcome and a good experience, thus encouraging further visits. As well as staff training, the building, its equipment and maintenance contribute to this.

Design

The MetroCentre cinema is fairly typical of multiplexes. The box office, with four paying points, occupies the centre of the frontage onto the mall. This is staffed continuously to handle personal advance booking; at slack times one person can handle this and the walk-in, but at busy times (eg the Saturday evening peak) all paying points operate at top speed.

Either side of the box office wide spaces allow easy access to the foyer. Ths is carpeted, well-lit, bright and cheerful. It is quite small for a 10-screen cinema, but congestion is minimised by allowing a five to ten minute gap between each film's starting time. The manager's office opens directly onto the foyer and closed circuit television provides him with constant control and instant availability.

At the rear of the foyer, carpet is replaced by tiled floors (for easier cleaning) in front of concession stands selling a range of soft drinks, confectionery, ice cream, hot dogs, popcorn and nacho chips, with a pick-and-mix sweet stand. Either side of this kiosk area a carpeted corridor leads to the auditoria. Thus only two to four attendants are required (depending on the busy-ness) to check tickets for all 10 auditoria. After the film, customers may be channelled through exits leading directly to the mall, bypassing the foyer and avoiding congestion there. The building is managed to produce maximum efficiency.

The auditoria range in size: two of 354 seats each, four of 225 seats each and four of 196 seats each. Additional wheel-chair spaces are available in each auditorium. Seats are wide, comfortable and have a convenient hole in one arm-rest for a soft drink carton; there is ample legroom and sufficient rake to ensure good visibility. Attendants check auditoria at frequent intervals during performances.

Different sized auditoria enable the film programme to be cost-effective. A film expected to be popular is scheduled to open in one of the largest auditoria – and a facility is available for showing one print on two screens simultaneously if required. Then, as demand falls, the film is transferred to smaller auditoria. This extends the run and, since the percentage of box office paid to the distributors declines with the length of run, profitability increases. *Ghost* (1990), for example, ran for six months at the MetroCentre, considerably longer than in the smaller cinemas. Thus the MetroCentre picked up trade from people who had missed the film at their local cinema and those who saw the film several times.

Profitability is also increased by shrewd scheduling: the most popular film starts first on each walk-in so that, when it is sold out, people who have queued are unlikely to turn away. They choose another film, generally returning later for their first choice, probably booking in advance. Because of this, Carey has been reluctant to introduce telephone advance booking: in his experience callers simply put down the phone if told that their first choice is unavailable. However, the service will be offered – after much careful staff training aimed at preventing this lost trade – in 1993 to coincide with the opening of an extra auditorium.

This will hold 500 and have its own concession stand. It will enable more than one popular film to be screened at the same time while still providing maximum choice, thus considerably increasing business while employing only four or five extra staff.

Customer feedback

Although commercial cinema has been criticised for being revenue oriented and only catering for the blockbuster audience, Carey is very aware that customer service involves more than this. UCI plan to carry out a coherent programme of audience research during 1993, but Carey's own less formal survey in 1991 – and on-going through customer comments – showed that the MetroCentre cinema's audience contained almost equal numbers of 19–25 year olds and over 35s, with only about one or two per cent of admissions from the over-60s. A core group of regulars has been identified, especially for the Saturday late shows which have a club-like atmosphere.

While operating schemes to retain this loyalty, there is also an awareness of the need to broaden the profile. Carey realised there were people who would not normally go near a multiplex cinema so, in 1992, he introduced a 'director's chair' feature: a Monday evening screening of a classic or cult film – with suggestions welcome. This was aimed at a more up-market audience, older customers and students, whom he hoped would return once they had tried the MetroCentre experience. It was also in competition with the regional film theatre. Even though audiences are sometimes small, the experiment seems to be working.

Pricing policy

In May 1993 a student rate was added to the pricing structure (Fig. 8.4). This was deliberately set at 50p below that of Warner Brothers, to entice Newcastle-based students across the river.

These prices are a function of the running costs of the cinema

Adults, matinee	£2·35
Adults, evening	£3·50
Children, senior citizens & students (all shows)	£2·00
All late shows	£2·50

Figure 8.4
MetroCentre cinema pricing structure 1993

combined with general parameters set by UCI and an eye on the local competition. They are kept as low as possible in deference to the low incomes of the North East. Criticism has been levelled at the high mark-up on kiosk goods, but this is defended on the grounds that these are optional (about 35 per cent of customers buy from them) and that, although the kiosks have a separate account, their profits help subsidise admission charges; thus the majority benefit.

Kiosk goods, in common with all cinemas, are offered partly to increase profits and partly to contribute to the overall experience of a 'good night out'. The sense of occasion comes from the welcoming atmosphere, comfort and total quality.

Key features

- ▲ *The cinema is part of a recent mixed development and benefits from its location.*
- ▲ *There are both benefits and constraints from being part of a large international organisation.*
- ▲ *Its marketing approach is very targeted.*
- ▲ *One of its characteristics is great attention to customer care and comfort.*
- ▲ *'Living up to the promise' is integral to its service delivery.*

Summary

These three case studies form interesting contrasts. The Opéra Bastille was politically inspired and its management controlled by politicians who do not understand the special requirements of an opera house. It is, perhaps a salutory warning of what can happen when there is too much ministerial hands-on approach to decision making – a trend which we can observe developing in Britain. The project has been beset by problems throughout its short history. Although money was lavished upon it, the result is, by all accounts, not particularly welcoming to either performers or the public.

Queen's Hall was a grass roots initiative, set up on a shoestring budget compared with that of the Opéra Bastille. As a building it has problems and is not particularly plush, but it is friendly and welcoming. Attendance is undoubtedly low at times, but people like the Queen's Hall and there would be an outcry if closure were hinted at. There are plenty of ideas for development but, as a local authority venue, a lack of investment.

The MetroCentre cinema illustrates what the commercial sector can achieve when it is willing to invest for long-term, rather than short-term, profits. It is spick-and-span, comfortable and welcoming. Though some people despise multiplexes, audiences flock to the MetroCentre. But there is an awareness that, to keep people coming to the box office, money and effort must be continually devoted to the maintenance of the high standards of the venue.

Notes and references

1 Ardagh, J. (1988) *Germany and the Germans*. Penguin.
2 Commission of the European Communities publications: *Community Action in the Cultural Sector* (1977); *Stronger Community Action in the Cultural Sector* (1982); *A Fresh Boost for Community Action in the Cultural Sector* (1987).
3 Arts projects already in existence (1993) include: European Youth Orchestra; Annual Cities of Culture scheme; MEDIA, a three-year rolling programme of projects for the film and television industries. Arts projects envisaged include: European Opera Academy; European Poetry House; European Centre for Contemporary Music; European Youth Theatre.
4 It is estimated that developing a multiplex cinema on a green field site requires over £6 million.
5 Further details may be found in the Committee of Education Science and the Arts Committee Report, 10 January 1990.
6 Research Surveys of Great Britain Ltd. *Omnibus Arts Survey*: Report of a survey on arts and cultural activities in Great Britain. Arts Council 1991.
7 Cinema statistics are taken from Cinema and Video Industry Research, the others are from the Arts Council Annual Report 1990/1.
8 Recounted by Augustin Girard, head of the research department of the Ministry of Culture, at an international conference held at the Arts Council of Great Britain in March 1987. Reported in *The Arts: Politics, Power and the Purse*.
9 *The Guardian* 14 July 1989.
10 Quoted in Christiansen, R. 'Opera Houses of the World: Opéra Bastille'. *Opera Now* No. 3, June 1989, p21.
11 Quoted in *The Guardian* 15 March 1990.
12 Quoted in Christiansen, op. cit. p20.

Further reading

Arts Council of Great Britain. (1991) *Report on a Survey on Arts and Cultural Activities in Great Britain* (two volumes of statistical tables accompany this).

Cummings, M.C. Jnr. and Katz, R.S. (1987) *The Patron State.* Oxford University Press.

Feist, A. and Hutchison, R. (1990) 'Funding the Arts in seven Western Countries'. *Cultural Trends No.* 5 Policy Studies Institute.

Mulder, P. (1990) *European Integration and the Cultural Sector* (a discussion document). Arts Council of Great Britain.

Stewart, R. (1987) *The Arts: Politics, Power and the Purse* (report of an international conference March 1987) Arts Council of Great Britain.